Confessions of an IT Scrum Master

Real Stories, Practical Tips, and Hard-Learned Lessons in Agile

Prabhakaran Anbazhagan

Apress®

Confessions of an IT Scrum Master: Real Stories, Practical Tips, and Hard-Learned Lessons in Agile

Prabhakaran Anbazhagan
Lake Barrington, IL, USA

ISBN-13 (pbk): 979-8-8688-2085-4   ISBN-13 (electronic): 979-8-8688-2086-1
https://doi.org/10.1007/979-8-8688-2086-1

Copyright © 2025 by Prabhakaran Anbazhagan

This work is subject to copyright. All rights are reserved by the Publisher, whether the whole or part of the material is concerned, specifically the rights of translation, reprinting, reuse of illustrations, recitation, broadcasting, reproduction on microfilms or in any other physical way, and transmission or information storage and retrieval, electronic adaptation, computer software, or by similar or dissimilar methodology now known or hereafter developed.

Trademarked names, logos, and images may appear in this book. Rather than use a trademark symbol with every occurrence of a trademarked name, logo, or image we use the names, logos, and images only in an editorial fashion and to the benefit of the trademark owner, with no intention of infringement of the trademark.

The use in this publication of trade names, trademarks, service marks, and similar terms, even if they are not identified as such, is not to be taken as an expression of opinion as to whether or not they are subject to proprietary rights.

While the advice and information in this book are believed to be true and accurate at the date of publication, neither the authors nor the editors nor the publisher can accept any legal responsibility for any errors or omissions that may be made. The publisher makes no warranty, express or implied, with respect to the material contained herein.

> Managing Director, Apress Media LLC: Welmoed Spahr
> Acquisitions Editor: Shivangi Ramachandran
> Project Manager: Jessica Vakili

Cover designed by eStudioCalamar

Distributed to the book trade worldwide by Springer Science+Business Media New York, 1 New York Plaza, New York, NY 10004. Phone 1-800-SPRINGER, fax (201) 348-4505, e-mail orders-ny@springer-sbm.com, or visit www.springeronline.com. Apress Media, LLC is a Delaware LLC and the sole member (owner) is Springer Science + Business Media Finance Inc (SSBM Finance Inc). SSBM Finance Inc is a **Delaware** corporation.

For information on translations, please e-mail booktranslations@springernature.com; for reprint, paperback, or audio rights, please e-mail bookpermissions@springernature.com.

Apress titles may be purchased in bulk for academic, corporate, or promotional use. eBook versions and licenses are also available for most titles. For more information, reference our Print and eBook Bulk Sales web page at http://www.apress.com/bulk-sales.

Any source code or other supplementary material referenced by the author in this book is available to readers on GitHub. For more detailed information, please visit https://www.apress.com/gp/services/source-code.

If disposing of this product, please recycle the paper

In loving memory of my dad, Anbazhagan; my beloved mom, Uma; my lovely wife, Girija; my wonderful kids, Venba and Inba—each of you is a source of love, patience, and strength throughout this journey.

Table of Contents

About the Author xv

Acknowledgments xvii

Introduction xix

Chapter 1: Confession #1: I Didn't Plan on Becoming a Scrum Master 1

The Unexpected Transition 2

A Team in Trouble 4

Agile Isn't Just for Code (But That's Where I Started) 6

Transitioning from Architect to Scrum Master 7

When Architecture Fought Agile 9

Winning Trust Without Code 11

The Project That Broke Me and Built Me 13

Confession Accepted 15

Chapter 2: Confession #2: Internal Conflict—The Architect vs. The Scrum Master 17

The Legacy of an Architect's Mindset 18

The Invisible Tug-of-War in My Head 20

The Anti-Pattern That Looked Like a Best Practice 21

When Stakeholders Go Silent 23

The Mindset Shift—From Blueprint to Feedback Loop 25

TABLE OF CONTENTS

    Minimum Viable Architecture—Myth or Method? 27

    The High-Stakes Feature That Forced Iteration 29

    Trusting the Team Over the Architecture 31

    Lessons That Only Conflict Can Teach 32

Chapter 3: Confession #3: When the Code Breaks, So Does the Team 35

    The Calm Before the Debt 36

    The Day the System Fought Back 38

    When Frustration Replaces Flow 40

    Scrum Master in the Middle 42

    The Retrospective That Changed Everything 43

    Debt As a Business Language 45

    Redefining Done and Changing Habits 47

    The Legacy Trap and Its Inheritors 49

    From Quick Fixes to Long-Term Fitness 50

    The Emotional Payoff 52

Chapter 4: Confession #4: Stakeholders Think Agile Is a Miracle Cure 55

    The Agile Sales Pitch vs. Reality 56

    First Signs of Trouble: "We Did Agile, But It Didn't Work" 58

    The Root of the Myth: Misunderstood Ownership and Effort 60

    Agile Theater: When Stakeholders Only Care About the Badge 61

    Educating Without Preaching: Playing the Long Game 63

    The Stakeholder 180: When Someone Finally Gets It 65

    Tough Love: Setting Boundaries on Agile Misuse 66

Lessons in Alignment: Recalibrating Stakeholder Expectations 68
The Cultural Layer: Agile As a Common Language.. 69
Final Reflection: Agile Isn't the Cure, It's the Commitment 71

Chapter 5: Confession #5: The Myth of Requirements (or Lack Thereof) 73

The Mirage of "No Requirements in Agile" 74
Requirements Were Treated like Afterthoughts... 76
The Sprint That Never Should Have Started.. 78
False Starts and Forced Assumptions.. 80
Discovery Sprints Aren't a Luxury.. 82
When Stakeholders Don't Know What They Want 84
Short-Termism: The Roadblock to Product Vision 86
Teaching the Value of Just Enough Planning 88
The Agile Compass: Navigating Without a Map, Not Without Direction 91
Final Reflection: Clarity Isn't a Constraint, It's a Catalyst................................... 92

Chapter 6: Confession #6: When Agile Meets Fixed Deadline.............95

The Calendar That Killed the Sprint 96
Reverse Engineering the Burndown... 98
Scope? Quality? Pick One 100
The Emotional Weight of Time... 101
Stakeholder Theater... 103
The Brave PO Who Said "No" 105
Negotiation at the Edge... 107
A Retrospective That Hurt and Healed 109
Replanning with Integrity... 110
Final Reflection: Running Isn't the Same As Finishing...................................... 113

TABLE OF CONTENTS

Chapter 7: Confession #7: Scaling Nightmares—Nexus, Chaos, and Customer Challenges 115

When Three Became Four 116
Frameworks Don't Scale People 118
A Planning Meeting or a Guessing Game? 120
The API That Broke the Sprint 122
The Split-Personality Product Owner 124
Behind Closed Doors: The Real Bottlenecks 126
Conway's Law Isn't a Suggestion 128
Trust Wasn't Lost; It Was Never the Goal 130
What Nexus Promised, and What We Denied It 131
What We Should Have Done Differently 134

Chapter 8: Confession #8: How I Learned Velocity Isn't Everything 137

When Velocity Became the Gospel 138
Chasing Points, Losing Purpose 139
The Hidden Cost of Fragmentation 141
Stakeholder Euphoria, Team Disquiet 143
Breaking the Spell (One Epic at a Time) 144
The Metrics We Weren't Measuring 146
Velocity As a Smell, not a Goal 147
New Metrics, New Mindsets 149
When Delivery Became Visible 150
Velocity Didn't Disappear, It Evolved 151

Chapter 9: Confession #9: Customer Feedback in IT—The Forgotten Metric 153

The Post-Go-Live Silence 154
Feedback by Proxy 155
The Feature Nobody Wanted 157
The Support Call That Changed Everything 158
Integrating Real Voices 159
From Defensiveness to Curiosity 161
Building Feedback Loops 162
Feedback As Product Strategy 164
When Feedback Sparked Innovation 165
Feedback Is the Fastest Way Forward 166

Chapter 10: Confession #10: Siloed Teams, Stalled Delivery 169

When Integration Became the Bottleneck 170
The Wall No One Saw—Dev vs. QA 171
A Release Held Together by a Workaround 173
UX in Orbit, Dev on the Ground 175
The Handshake That Never Came 177
The Teams Thread That Saved Us 179
From Siloes to Swarms 180
Sync Meetings That Weren't a Waste 182
The Map That Made It Clear 184
Agile Isn't Just Inside a Team, It's Between Them 185

Chapter 11: Confession #11: The Human Side of Scrum—People Skills that Make or Break Teams 187

The Developer Who Stayed Silent 188
The Comment Thread That Broke Trust 190

TABLE OF CONTENTS

Why Empathy Outperforms Efficiency 192
When Coaching Replaced Commanding 194
The Designer's Apology That Shifted a Sprint 195
Learning Nonviolent Communication in Retros 197
The Buddy System That Built Confidence 198
How Psychological Safety Sparked Innovation 200
Why People Quit Managers, Not Codebases 202
Soft Skills Are the Hardest to Scale 203

Chapter 12: Confession #12: Surviving Meetings That Should Have Been Emails 205

The Eleven-Hour Monday 206
Stand-Up or Stand-Still? 208
Sprint Planning Derailments 209
The Mirage of Alignment 211
Meetings Without a Pilot 213
Asynchronous Is Strength, Not Slack 214
Calendars As Cultural X-Rays 216
Decisions, Not Dialogues 217
Protecting Focus Time Together 219
Agile Isn't About Talking, It's About Moving 221

Chapter 13: Confession #13: The Costs of Cultural Blindness 223

The Star Performer Everyone Feared 224
When Microaggressions Become the Norm 226
The Silent Exit Nobody Saw Coming 228
Culture Debt: The Backlog We Never Logged 230
The Informal Escalations That Went Nowhere 232

Retrospectives As Therapy Sessions	233
The 1-on-1 That Changed My Role	235
Leadership Without Awareness, Leadership Without Trust	237
Burnout Is More Than Just Overtime	239
Culture Isn't Soft: It's the Hardest Structure to Build	240

Chapter 14: Confession #14: You Can't Hold Everyone Accountable All the Time 243

The Overburdened High Performer	244
Micromanagement Masquerading as Ownership	246
Retrospectives That Became Blame Sessions	248
Why Ownership ≠ Accountability	250
The Forgotten Middle Layer of Leadership	251
When Teams Lose Their Boundaries	253
The Power of Clear Agreements	255
Recognizing Accountability Instead of Punishing It	257
Shared Goals, Specific Drivers	259
Agile Without Accountability Is Just Theater	262

Chapter 15: Confession #15: When Teams Don't Play As One 265

The UI vs. Backend Standoff	266
Invisible Territories, Real Friction	268
The False Safety of Jira Tickets	269
When Ego Beats Empathy	271
Introducing the Concept of "We"	272
Stand-ups That Build Trust, Not Just Status	273
Shared Success Metrics	275
Team Wins That Weren't Code	276

TABLE OF CONTENTS

The First Real Cross-Disciplinary Demo 277

Agile Teams Are Built on Shared Wins 278

Chapter 16: Confession #16: Agile for Lean Tech Teams 281

Small Team, Big Dreams 282

Wearing All the Hats 284

Burnout in the Name of Velocity 286

Simplifying Without Cutting Corners 288

The Power of Direct Communication 290

Async Over Orchestration 291

Lean Doesn't Mean Undisciplined 293

Cross-Training Wasn't Optional 295

The Value of Saying No 297

Agile at Scale Begins When It's Small 298

Chapter 17: Confession #17: Execution vs. Process, The XP Influence 301

The XP Developer Who Changed Everything 302

Pair Programming That Actually Worked 303

Refactoring As a Lifestyle 304

Testing That Guided, Not Just Validated 306

Simplicity As a Survival Strategy 307

Continuous Integration As Muscle Memory 309

Stand-ups Became Tactical, Not Theatrical 310

Shared Code Ownership in Action 311

The Power of Tight Feedback Loops 312

Execution Over Ritual—The Confession 314

Chapter 18: Confession #18: When Agile Rules Bend (and Break) ...317

    The Day We Skipped a Retrospective 318

    Definition of Done…ish... 320

    The 3-Point Story That Became 30 321

    The Leadership Request That Broke WIP Limits... 322

    When Stand-ups Go Silent 324

    Process Adherence vs. Product Delivery 326

    Agile Framework ≠ Agile Thinking.. 327

    Breaking the Sprint to Fix the Problem 329

    Process Without Purpose Is Just Theater 330

    Agile Isn't Fragile, It's Flexible 331

Chapter 19: Confession #19: The Frameworks Are Coming, Don't Panic 335

    The Email That Launched a Thousand Trainings 336

    Scrum of Scrums or Just More Meetings 337

    Jira As a Jungle.. 339

    The Coach Conundrum.. 340

    Ceremony Creep... 341

    Framework vs. Flexibility 342

    Frameworks Don't Fix Culture 344

    When the Framework Helped... 345

    Tailoring Over Templating.. 347

    The Only Framework That Matters: Context... 348

Chapter 20: Confession #20: Is Agile Forgetting Its Roots? Learning from Toyota...351

    The Manifesto Rediscovered.. 353

    A Tale of Two Factories 354

TABLE OF CONTENTS

Respect for People 357

Stop the Line 358

Quality at the Source 359

Continuous Improvement, Really Continuous 361

Leadership Walks the Floor 363

Flow Over Resource Utilization 365

Learning from Masters, Not Manuals 367

Back to the Roots to Move Forward 369

Index **371**

About the Author

Prabhakaran Anbazhagan is an Agile leader, IT strategist, and enterprise architect with 20 years of experience in the technology industry. Having transitioned from senior developer and architect roles in product companies to Agile leadership positions in global IT services, he brings a unique perspective on what Agile truly means in high-pressure, delivery-focused environments. His work spans complex enterprise transformations, including award-winning Low-Code/No-Code and .NET implementations across North America. Prabhakaran is known for his sharp execution mindset, deep technical grounding, and honest reflections on the challenges Scrum Masters face.

Acknowledgments

Writing this book has been as much about reflection as it has been about words on a page, and I could never have done it alone.

In loving memory of my dad—your passion for work and eye for detail shaped the traits I carry as an architect. You were the first to believe in my positive way of thinking differently. The discipline and dedication you lived by became part of me, and they continue to guide my path.

To my mom—your quiet strength and unwavering support have been my foundation from the beginning. Every step of this journey rests on the values you instilled in me.

To Girija—thank you for your encouragement, patience, and for holding everything together while I poured countless hours into these chapters. You gave me the space to step away from family moments so I could write, and without that gift, this book would not exist.

To Venba and Inba—thank you for filling even the busiest days with laughter and reminding me that no deadline is more important than time with family. Your joy was the balance I needed when work and writing tried to take over.

To my colleagues and teams: My time in product companies and the service industry shaped me in unexpected ways. The product side taught me technical discipline and ownership, while the service side tested me with complexity, pace, and constant adaptation. Each came with wins and struggles, and together they shaped the confessions in this book. Your influence is invaluable.

ACKNOWLEDGMENTS

Finally, I would like to extend my gratitude to the Apress publication team. Thank you for believing in this project and allowing me to bring these confessions to life. Your guidance and trust have been invaluable throughout this journey.

This book exists because of you all. I hope the book has a significant impact and that it will be a testament to the power of community and support in achieving our goals.

Introduction

When I stepped into the Scrum Master role, I didn't plan it or expect to take on the role. I had one decade of experience in product-based companies and another decade in the service industry. In product companies, Agile felt almost second nature, something that empowered teams to innovate and adapt while still delivering value. But in the service industry, I got exposed to a different reality: client expectations, fixed deadlines, and contracts clashing with Agile's ideology. It forced me to see Agile in a new light, and it taught me that success had less to do with following the framework by the book and more to do with navigating people, pressure, and imperfect systems.

This book draws upon those lessons. It isn't another guide to running ceremonies or managing metrics. Instead, it's a candid account of Agile as it's lived: the breakdowns, the contradictions, and the insights that surfaced along the way. Think of it as a series of confessions, stories where things didn't go as planned, but where the learning turned out to be more valuable than the outcome itself.

Who might find this book helpful? If you are a Scrum Master who has experienced the disconnect between theory and practice, I've crafted this for you. If you're a product owner or team lead, the stories here will provide you with perspective on the challenges that arise when process meets people. Developers and architects may also see reflections of their own struggles, especially when navigating the blurry line between technical discipline and delivery pressure. And if you're simply curious about what really happens behind the glossy charts and Agile certifications, these confessions may offer a glimpse into the reality behind the roles.

INTRODUCTION

The organization of the book reflects that spirit. Each chapter is framed as a confession, beginning with a personal story and then widening into reflections that connect to broader Agile practice. The early chapters explore personal transitions, such as transitioning from architect to Scrum Master, or the painful realization that broken code can break more than just systems. The middle chapters delve into the realities of any organization: unrealistic deadlines, unmet requirements, lack of accountability, and scaling nightmares. Later, we will shift our focus toward culture, collaboration, and soft skills, which are equally crucial to technical challenges. The closing chapters return to fundamentals, revisiting the roots of Agile in Extreme Programming, Lean, and even Toyota's guiding principles.

What you'll find here isn't a set of prescriptive answers. Instead, you'll get stories, reflections, and patterns that might resonate with your own experience. I hope that these confessions provide you with language for the frustrations you may already feel, help you see familiar struggles in a new light, and remind you that the messiness of Agile is not a failure; it's the reality of working with people, systems, and constraints.

Agile focuses on delivering value rather than on rituals, charts, or creating an illusion of being busy. It is about providing value, respecting people, and learning continuously. This book is an invitation to hold onto that spirit, even when the pressure around you makes it most complicated to see.

Throughout this book, I've drawn from my own experiences across multiple projects and products. For confidentiality and professionalism, all scenarios have been generalized or anonymized. Any resemblance to specific clients, vendors, or systems is purely coincidental.

My goal in writing this book isn't to give answers but to share hard-earned insights from someone who has traveled this road. Whether you're transitioning into Agile from a technical role, implementing Agile in a service-oriented environment, or simply seeking motivation, let these confessions inspire you to view every challenge as a step toward mastering the art of Agile.

CHAPTER 1

Confession #1: I Didn't Plan on Becoming a Scrum Master

Life is what happens when you're busy making other plans.

—John Lennon

I didn't choose the Scrum Master role. It chose me at a time when I was fully anchored in the world of architecture, systems thinking, and hands-on delivery. For over a decade, I thrived in product companies where Agile came naturally. Code was king, and process was simply the engine behind it.

But everything changed when I entered the service industry. What began as observation about missed alignment with business priorities turned into an unexpected pivot. Leadership didn't act on my suggestion to restructure the team. Instead, they handed me the reins and said, "You fix it."

CHAPTER 1   CONFESSION #1: I DIDN'T PLAN ON BECOMING A SCRUM MASTER

That's how I found myself stepping into a role I never planned for, carrying a mindset that didn't fit, trying to lead a team that didn't trust me yet.

My technical background would be my greatest asset. It wasn't. It turned out to be my most significant learning curve.

This chapter is the story of that transition: of ego, humility, and adaptation. It's about learning to listen more than direct, to let go of clean code in favor of messy progress, and to embrace Agile not as a process, but as a way of leading through uncertainty. If you've ever found yourself struggling to shift roles, to earn trust, or to lead without a playbook, this one's for you.

The journey truly began when resistance met responsibility, and I was asked to lead from a space I never imagined stepping into.

The Unexpected Transition

I didn't plan on becoming a Scrum Master. I actively resisted it.

At the time, I was serving as a Lead Enterprise Architect, deeply involved in technical strategy, defining roadmaps, and driving design integrity across projects. I wasn't interested in ceremonies or backlogs; I was focused on architecture that worked and scaled.

There was this one team set up to handle foundational work that wasn't delivering: no business outcomes, no visibility, and certainly no stakeholder buy-in. I remember telling the leadership team bluntly: "This setup isn't working. We are overinvesting in workstreams with limited visibility, while other teams responsible for critical outcomes are experiencing increased strain." I even proposed dismantling the team and distributing their scope across other active teams to avoid waste.

But instead of accepting the analysis, the leadership team flipped the conversation.

They asked me to take over the team as their Scrum Master.

CHAPTER 1 CONFESSION #1: I DIDN'T PLAN ON BECOMING A SCRUM MASTER

To say I was stunned would be putting it mildly. I was frustrated. I had just spent weeks showing them why this team was misaligned, and now I was being asked to lead it in a role I didn't even want? It felt like being asked to pilot a plane I said shouldn't take off in the first place.

Their reasoning? They believed that putting someone technical at the helm would bring direction, clarity, and, more importantly, business value. They framed it as a move the customer would appreciate. I couldn't shake the feeling that they were passing the buck, handing me a problem child and hoping I could turn things around.

Reluctantly, I accepted.

But old habits die hard. To the team, I was still the architect, just one now scheduling stand-ups and retros. They didn't see the role shift. I had technical authority, sure, but not Agile credibility. Most saw me as a glorified meeting organizer. And truthfully, that's how I felt in those early days.

The first stand-ups were a disaster: an hour-long slog of updates, technical tangents, and scattered focus. I knew this had to change. I compressed it to 30 minutes, then down to 15. I made attendance optional on Fridays, offering asynchronous updates so no one had to skip a family moment to recite yesterday's tasks. That slight shift, respecting time and autonomy, built the first layer of trust.

Still, my architect mindset kept bleeding into the role. I obsessed over design quality. I couldn't stand the way some stories were half-baked or riddled with hidden tech debt. When the team cut corners to "make the sprint," I pushed back, sometimes too hard. I hadn't yet realized that "done" in Agile is different from "done" in design architecture. The servant-leader in me was buried beneath layers of structure and logic.

Looking back, that transition was more than a role shift; it was an identity clash. I had to unlearn, relearn, and then relearn again. The metrics didn't change overnight, but my perspective did.

CHAPTER 1 CONFESSION #1: I DIDN'T PLAN ON BECOMING A SCRUM MASTER

I didn't plan on becoming a Scrum Master. But maybe I needed that unexpected push, not to lead differently, but to see differently.

But taking the role was only the beginning; what I walked into next was a team that mirrored my own internal conflict.

A Team in Trouble

When I inherited the team, I wasn't stepping into a clean slate; I was stepping onto a fractured floor.

On paper, it was a balanced mix: Developers, QA, BAs, some onshore, some offshore, ranging from bright juniors to super seniors who would have seen it all. But beneath the surface, the team was split. A handful of individuals had found comfort in pushing deliverables from sprint to sprint without real accountability. They weren't lazy; they were drifting. And their inertia quietly dragged the rest of the team down.

The high performers? They were burning out. Delivering more, carrying dead weight, and yet going unrecognized. The leadership team, who entrusted me with this role, had not yet had the opportunity to recognize their contributions. It was one of my first internal battles: *How do I make the motivated ones feel seen when the system isn't built to reward them?*

The team had spent six months designing foundational models with the help of a domain Subject Matter Expert (SME). The work was meticulous, technically solid, but it never reached the real gatekeepers: the business SMEs. The validation never happened. Much of the output didn't align with business priorities at that stage. While positioned as groundwork for future use, it was clear that those enhancements were unlikely to materialize.

There was no big meeting. No postmortem. Everyone knew. One of the senior team members even said, "We're reserving it for future business enhancements" with a tone that made it clear: We all know that the future is never coming.

CHAPTER 1 CONFESSION #1: I DIDN'T PLAN ON BECOMING A SCRUM MASTER

Strangely, this wasn't a neglected team. The stakeholder who worked closely with the product owner joined nearly every Scrum ceremony. He gave timely feedback and even escalated issues when needed. But feedback isn't enough if the direction is misaligned from the start.

What I saw wasn't laziness, it was quiet surrender.

I had once called this team inefficient. I even suggest shutting them down. But as I watched them, I started to feel guilt creep in. Perhaps it wasn't their failure, but a failure in guidance, vision, or purpose.

The first signs of life didn't come from big gestures. They came from subtle changes, like giving the team room to breathe, creating space for asynchronous updates, and respecting their time instead of micromanaging it. That wasn't revolutionary, but it began to shift the tone. The team started seeing the ceremonies not as checkboxes, but as tools to protect their flow. We weren't perfect, but we were no longer aimless.

And then, something shifted.

We began taking on not only foundational technical work but also functional pieces that spanned across product teams. That's when the team started thinking differently. We weren't just coding; we were solving reusable problems that others would benefit from.

In our first proper retrospective under my watch, I looked around and said: "Everyone thought this was a joke, the commitment we made. But you turned the tables. You made the impossible possible".

And they had.

We began delivering sprint by sprint. We celebrated every small win. I made it a personal mission to make the next milestone happen, not just as a Scrum Master but as a voice behind the scenes, and give the team full credit every time.

That team wasn't broken.

They were waiting for someone to believe they could win again.

As the team started evolving, so did my understanding of Agile, and it pushed me to question everything I thought I knew about its purpose.

CHAPTER 1   CONFESSION #1: I DIDN'T PLAN ON BECOMING A SCRUM MASTER

Agile Isn't Just for Code (But That's Where I Started)

When I first encountered Agile, I saw it as a better way to manage code. It offered structure to chaos: sprints to break up work, user stories to organize tasks, and retros to improve the way we shipped features. In product companies, where software quality was the finish line, this mindset made perfect sense. Agile, to me, was a tool for developers. Nothing more.

For years, that belief worked. Our stories were technical. Sprint goals revolved around APIs and bug fixes. Every ceremony was focused on making the development process smoother. It worked because the goal was always to ship code. I never questioned that focus until it all stopped working.

The service industry exposed a different world. Our clients wanted Agile, but mainly as a ritual to get started. After the initial kickoff, shifting priorities and evolving requirements challenged our ability to maintain the delivery rhythm. Still, no one questioned it. We were moving fast, just not forward.

What frustrated me most was how easily we accepted dysfunction as the norm. Stories rolled over sprint after sprint. Delivery was reactive. The idea of user story readiness became something I had to fight for. And no one seemed to see how much we were hiding our waterfall thinking inside Agile wrappers. It looked like Agile in Jira, but in practice, we were wrapping old habits in new labels.

The turning point came when the business team dropped the illusion and admitted they weren't clear on what they wanted. It was a moment of raw honesty, and it gave us a new starting point. Instead of pushing for final answers, we began collaborating to shape just-enough clarity to move. Technical user stories were written with business deliverables in mind, not in isolation. That alone made a world of difference.

I set a rule: if a story wasn't clear, it wasn't eligible for the sprint. It was unpopular, and it caused tension at first, but it worked. Slowly, the backlog stopped being a graveyard of assumptions and started reflecting what we could deliver. Conversations replaced guesswork. Developers began asking the right questions, not just writing the correct code.

The energy shifted. The team began to feel like they were building something meaningful. They stopped viewing themselves as ticket-closing machines and started taking ownership of what they shipped. For the first time, it felt like we weren't just coding, we were delivering.

The client noticed the change too, though not immediately. One week, we had nothing to show; the next, we released features well ahead of schedule. At first, they were skeptical. It looked like we were gaming metrics. However, when real, working outcomes began to roll out quickly and visibly, their perception shifted. Doubt was replaced with trust.

Looking back, I realize how narrow my understanding of Agile used to be. I thought it was a developer's tool, a way to manage complexity. But real Agile is something else. It's not just about code; it's about people, ownership, alignment, and flow. It's about enabling a team to move with purpose and clarity, even in uncertainty.

Agile now means creating trust and shared ownership across the team, rather than using it as a cover for chaos. It's about delivering real value, not just staying busy.

Redefining Agile was one part of the equation, the harder shift came in redefining myself.

Transitioning from Architect to Scrum Master

I never wanted to become a manager. That was the one line I had drawn for years, and it's why I stayed in technical roles like architect, where I could influence outcomes without getting pulled into status tracking, people politics, or non-technical expectations.

CHAPTER 1   CONFESSION #1: I DIDN'T PLAN ON BECOMING A SCRUM MASTER

So, when leadership turned my feedback back on me, telling me, "If you see the gaps so clearly, take charge of the team," my first reaction was frustration. This wasn't what I asked for. I wanted the team either repurposed or reassigned. Instead, they handed me the reins.

But somewhere between that frustration and the first stand-up, it turned into a challenge I couldn't walk away from.

The role wasn't just unfamiliar, it felt like a step backward. As an architect, I had been a respected voice in system design, a go-to person for technical clarity. Now, I was suddenly running ceremonies, updating boards, and coaching a team that saw me more as a threat than a partner. Some feared I would make their lives harder. A few developers who had once leaned on me for help were happy to have me around. But the overall vibe? Skepticism.

And truthfully, I wasn't sure what I had signed up for either.

At first, I couldn't fully let go of my architect instincts. I still showed up in solutioning discussions and offered design feedback. It wasn't out of ego; it was a habit. More than once, I felt like I was wearing two hats: technical project manager by role label, Scrum Master in daily function.

The weight of delivery hit me differently. As an architect, my role had always been advisory. Now, I felt the full pressure of sprint outcomes, team morale, and stakeholder expectations. Every blocker felt personal. Every stretch goal felt like a bet I had made with someone else's energy.

In those first few weeks, I misunderstood the role. My technical background would make everything easier, and it did. I could understand team issues without hand-holding. Developers didn't need to overexplain problems; I understood. However, I also realized that the real power of a Scrum Master isn't in understanding the problem, but in helping the team move through it without governance becoming a cage.

That was the most significant shift. I let go of strict governance. I stopped asking the team to conform to a perfect process. Instead, I helped them build momentum. We took on stretch goals, not as pressure but as motivation. We learned how to carry unfinished stories in a way that created continuity, not waste. Some sprints burned a little extra. But the team saw results, and so did the leadership.

At first, there was pushback. The velocity spike looked suspicious. People thought we were gaming the numbers. But when they looked closer, they saw something better: a team that no longer avoided accountability, that delivered early more often than not, that no longer feared blockers or dependencies because they had figured out how to adapt on the go.

That's when I knew we had turned a corner.

What began as an unwanted assignment became the most transformative role I would ever take on. I didn't stop being technical, but I learned that leadership isn't about enforcing structure. It's about creating the right energy, trust, and space for teams to thrive.

And ironically, it wasn't architecture that helped me build that.

It was stepping out of it.

Still, old instincts don't fade easily, and the tension between structure and speed soon came to the surface.

When Architecture Fought Agile

There's a silent battle that plays out in every technically-minded Scrum Master: the fight between clean architecture and urgent delivery. I lived that fight sprint after sprint, especially in my early months, when I was still trying to lead with the mindset of an architect inside an Agile shell.

One of the clearest examples occurred during an integration we had to build with another customer's system within their broader ecosystem. Architecturally, I knew exactly how it should be done: clean contracts, reliable APIs, graceful fallbacks. But reality didn't care about architecture.

CHAPTER 1   CONFESSION #1: I DIDN'T PLAN ON BECOMING A SCRUM MASTER

The downstream system we integrated with had limited documentation and inconsistent availability, which complicated alignment. And each time their system went down, it reflected poorly on us.

We were starting to look like the bottleneck. That was a hard pill to swallow because technically, we weren't the problem. But perception matters. So, we made a tough decision: we created a stubbed simulation of the integration to allow dependent teams to progress while the external API matured. It wasn't elegant, but it unblocked progress.

That moment changed how I thought about trade-offs. I realized that my insistence on getting things "done right" was sometimes blocking us from getting things "done." Earlier, I would hold back on closing stories if I didn't feel the design met governance standards. I would push for refactoring, polishing, and alignment, even if the business didn't care. And that cost us.

It created friction too. The team kept going in circles, trying to meet expectations I hadn't even clearly expressed, expectations rooted in design ideals rather than delivery goals. At times, they were solving for my standards, not for the product.

Eventually, I had to step back and admit: the team wasn't failing. I was failing to adapt.

Letting go of governance wasn't easy. It had been a guiding principle in my career, my version of quality. But I didn't abandon it. I repackaged it. Instead of enforcing it up-front, I started capturing those improvements as backlog items or spike stories. I delegated ownership to the technical lead, not because I didn't care, but because I had to shift my focus.

As a Scrum Master, focusing more on flow mattered than focusing on form.

I began to prioritize delivery over perfection, approving stories despite design gaps, provided they delivered value, and we tracked them for future refinement. That cutting corners now felt like creating momentum. What once felt like lowering the bar now looked like building trust.

CHAPTER 1   CONFESSION #1: I DIDN'T PLAN ON BECOMING A SCRUM MASTER

I still believe in strong architecture. But I've learned something more valuable than governance.

In a Scrum Master role, the mantra is simple: Adapt to the business and enable the team. If that means mocking an integration instead of perfecting it, so be it. If that means shipping before it's pretty, so be it. Agile doesn't punish structure, but it does punish rigidity.

And no matter how clean the architecture, rigidity never ships.

Even as technical trade-offs became clearer, the deeper test was personal, earning trust in a role where code couldn't carry me.

Winning Trust Without Code

At first, it was clear the team didn't fully trust me. They didn't say it directly, but the resistance was there, in the way feedback landed with silence, in the polite head nods that didn't lead to the change. I wasn't just the Scrum Master. I was the architect who had been vocal about their inefficiencies, and now I was suddenly leading them. They had every reason to be skeptical.

Some voiced their concerns early on. One developer, during a casual chat, asked if I was going to make things even harder now that I was "officially in charge." That moment hit me. I realized trust wasn't going to come from ceremonies or JIRA workflows. It had to be earned: quietly, consistently, and without a title to lean on.

So, I started small.

I made Friday stand-ups optional. I told them they could send asynchronous updates and use the time for themselves or their families. It wasn't about making meetings shorter; it was about showing them that their time mattered, and so did their lives outside of work. They began to understand that I wasn't there to manage them; I was there to protect their time, unblock their work, and create space for them to breathe.

CHAPTER 1 CONFESSION #1: I DIDN'T PLAN ON BECOMING A SCRUM MASTER

I began following through on every blocker. No delays, no excuses. If someone raised a dependency or an issue. I chased it until it was resolved or escalated it without naming names. I absorbed the noise from leadership so the team could stay in the flow.

But the fundamental shift happened when I started spotlighting their wins.

Whenever a team member went beyond their commitment, I shared it with the customer. Not quietly, but in a visible email where their name stood out and their effort was the focus of the message. I brought the same recognition internally. I made it a point to use our rewards platform to celebrate small wins and reinforce the behaviors that made us stronger as a team. Not because the rewards were significant, but because they were symbolic. For many team members, it was the first time someone had acknowledged their extra effort in a tangible way.

That's when things changed.

The team started taking more initiative. They began owning stretch goals, not because I asked, but because they believed they could. Retrospective became honest. Risks were shared openly. Even the quieter members, the ones who had been coasting on the sidelines, started speaking up. And something else happened, something I didn't expect.

They began standing up for each other.

If someone is overloaded, someone else would step in. When a deliverable slipped, the blame didn't surface; instead, solutions did. We were no longer operating as individuals protecting our bandwidth. We were acting like a team.

Stakeholders noticed, even if they didn't say it in public. Appreciation often surfaced through informed channels rather than formal feedback loops, but it still resonated.

The same team that once viewed me with guarded distance was now delivering with cohesion and pride. They weren't just delivering faster; they were thinking bigger. They were no longer asking what they were told to do. They were asking what needed to be done.

And in those moments, I felt something profound but straightforward:

If I could earn that trust without pulling rank, without writing a line of code, just by showing up with consistency and care, then anyone could. All it takes is intent, focus, and the will to make it work.

That trust would soon be tested under pressure, in a project that demanded everything we had and more.

The Project That Broke Me and Built Me

There's a difference between a complex project and a defining one. This one was both.

I had made a bold promise. In just six months, we were set to deliver a complex feature, built entirely on the foundation laid in phase one. That code alone had taken over a year to develop. This wasn't a rebuild, but a continuation that required touching almost every layer of the existing system.

We had five teams on the ground. I led one. Each team operated like its own startup, with its own styles, vendors, tools, and philosophies. There was no shared execution rhythm or cultural alignment. We weren't scaling Agile; we were improvising it.

Pressure started from day one. Every conversation with stakeholders is loaded with urgency. The feature wasn't just high visibility; it was critical. It was the kind of initiative with significant business impact and high visibility across stakeholders.

And the closer we got, the heavier it felt.

The requirements weren't just vague; they were volatile. The scope kept expanding. Integrations broke. Testing revealed scenarios we haven't even considered. In one sprint, we uncovered a dependency that necessitated re-architecting part of the flow. Another sprint, two members nearly burned out. We were taking tasks like a war room, not a backlog.

CHAPTER 1 CONFESSION #1: I DIDN'T PLAN ON BECOMING A SCRUM MASTER

At one point, a stakeholder blew up during a review session. Too many gaps. Too many unknowns. I sat there taking the heat, not because we hadn't tried, but because effort doesn't always equal clarity. That day was one of the lowest moments. The team was exhausted. And truthfully, so was I.

But we didn't give up.

My goal was to push for a reset, but only in planning, while staying aligned. We regrouped with business leads. We clarified expectations, sliced stories tightly, and gave the QA team more forethought space to plan regression coverage. Every review became sharper. Every daily sync had more intent. Slowly, the fog started lifting.

We delivered.

Every major scenario was accounted for. We rebuilt what took a year, enhanced it, and shipped it in half the time. The work was solid. The impact was undeniable.

The delivery closed without fanfare or formal recognition. Just another checkbox clicked in someone's roadmap deck. But the absence of celebration didn't diminish the accomplishment.

That silence was more devastating to me than any all-nighter or escalation could ever be; our team members deserved so much better. The silence spoke volumes.

But it also built something in me I didn't expect.

I realized I didn't need applause to measure meaning. What mattered was what I saw in that team, people who stretched past their limits. Who solved problems they didn't create? Who didn't blame or break down, even when they had every reason to?

That project made me believe in people more than process. It taught me that nothing is impossible when a team believes in the goal. And, perhaps most unexpectedly, it made me realize that leadership wasn't what I thought it was.

I used to think I wasn't a people person. That's why I stayed in technical roles for so long.

CHAPTER 1   CONFESSION #1: I DIDN'T PLAN ON BECOMING A SCRUM MASTER

But somewhere in that storm, I learned how wrong I was.

What that project revealed about the team was powerful, but what it revealed about myself reshaped my leadership entirely.

Confession Accepted

I didn't plan on becoming a Scrum Master. I didn't want to lead a team. I didn't want to let go of architecture. I didn't like the responsibility of owning delivery timelines, unblocking teams, or decoding stakeholder feedback.

But I did all of it anyway.

Not because I was ready. But because the moment asked for it.

Looking back, I can see how much of my resistance was tied to identity, what I thought I was good at, what I thought leadership meant, and what I thought I couldn't do. I was wrong on all three counts. Yes, being an architect gave me systems thinking. But becoming a Scrum Master taught me people skills.

I learned to listen when I didn't have answers. To trust when I couldn't control. To move forward even when the metrics didn't tell a clear story. I learned to value progress over perfection, momentum over mastery.

Most of all, I learned that leadership isn't about having authority. It's about earning trust: one blocker, one decision, and one stand-up at a time.

There were no awards. No public credit. But I walked away with something more important: the belief that I could lead, not through hierarchy or expertise, but through consistency and intent.

Takeaway Confession   I didn't plan on becoming a Scrum Master. But I became a better leader because of it.

And that, I've learned, is how most of the best stories begin.

CHAPTER 2

Confession #2: Internal Conflict— The Architect vs. The Scrum Master

The test of a first-rate intelligence is the ability to hold two opposing ideas in mind at the same time and still retain the ability to function.

—F. Scott Fitzgerald

Transitioning from an architect to a Scrum Master wasn't just a title change; it was a challenge to my identity. For years, I believed that strong architecture was the backbone of successful delivery. I took pride in enforcing best practices, safeguarding long-term integrity, and designing systems meant to last. But stepping into the Scrum Master role forced me to see that what once made me effective could now hold my team back.

This chapter is not just about a career pivot; it's about letting go of deeply ingrained habits, embracing a new mindset, and learning that agility is more than just a process. It's a mindset rooted in trust, adaptability, and servant leadership: the kind where you lead by stepping back and helping others rise. The conflict between who I was and who I needed to become played out in team meetings, architectural decisions, and silent reflections.

Here, I share the struggles and breakthroughs that defined this shift: from enforcing structure to enabling ownership, from pushing standards to nurturing experimentation. Whether you are a technologist stepping into leadership or a leader wrestling with control, this confession may help you see that sometimes the most challenging part of Agile isn't the process: it's letting go of who you used to be.

To understand this transformation, we need to start with the mindset I brought into the role, the architect's lens that shaped how I viewed systems, teams, and success.

The Legacy of an Architect's Mindset

Before I became a Scrum Master, I wore the architect's badge with conviction and not just the title, but the mindset, the discipline, and the pride that came with it. Architecture wasn't just about design: it was foresight, responsibility, and resilience. I approached every system as if it were a living entity: carefully structured, loosely coupled, and built to withstand the test of time.

There were specific values I refused to compromise on. I was relentless about scalability. I designed systems to evolve, not just to work. Every design decision included considerations for go-live transitions and data migration scenarios that most people overlooked until the last minute. I enforced governance to ensure that teams didn't stray from architectural principles. These weren't just rules to me; they were safeguards for the future. In my mind, architecture wasn't about fast wins. It was about laying a foundation others could build on without fear.

CHAPTER 2 CONFESSION #2: INTERNAL CONFLICT—THE ARCHITECT VS. THE SCRUM MASTER

I took pride in being the person that passionate engineers could rely on. But I was also a tough nut to crack for anyone coasting through the job. I challenged people when they took shortcuts. I pushed back when timelines tried to bulldoze quality. And I was okay with being the "tough guy" in the room, because someone had to guard the long-term vision.

One of my proudest architectural moments came during a project that had already failed multiple times. When my team took over, we rebuilt the system from scratch. During the discovery sprint, I documented so many overlooked gaps that the client finally believed we could succeed where others failed. And we did. We delivered the complete solution within a substantial timeline, reflecting the complexity of the build. That win wasn't just delivery; it was validation of the architectural discipline I had honed over the years.

I was even praised on several occasions for slowing things down to protect the architectural vision. To me, that was a win. I believed that cutting corners, especially at the foundational level, was a debt that always came due.

Working with delivery teams was often a balancing act: sometimes mentoring, and clashing. I wasn't easy on them. I challenged every design shortcut. I questioned every deviation from the original plan. And in return, I often faced pushback, sometimes even friction. I considered it part of my responsibility to protect the quality bar, even when it caused tension.

Agile practices, back then, felt almost anarchic to me. The idea of shifting direction mid-sprint, while setting aside long-term planning in favor of quick iterations, felt misaligned with the principles I stood for. In truth, I maintained a structured approach within Agile, believing that strong governance was necessary to preserve long-term integrity. It frustrated me that teams lacked the ownership to see beyond the sprint, to plan for the bigger picture.

And so, when I eventually stepped into a Scrum Master role, those very instincts became barriers. Governance. Adherence. Zero tolerance for shortcuts. The same things that had once made me effective became the things I had to unlearn, or at least temper.

CHAPTER 2 CONFESSION #2: INTERNAL CONFLICT—THE ARCHITECT VS. THE SCRUM MASTER

But no mindset shift happens overnight. The real tension began not in principle, but in practice, when my architectural instincts met the realities of team delivery.

The Invisible Tug-of-War in My Head

When I first stepped into the Scrum Master role, I didn't recognize the internal conflict right away. I was still operating with the instincts that had served me well as an architect: meticulous planning, reusable design, long-term thinking. I believed these traits would be an asset to the team. But over time, I began to notice something unsettling: I was the one slowing us down.

My architect mindset didn't just accompany me; it led. I wasn't just facilitating the team; I was unintentionally directing it toward architectural precision, often at the cost of incremental delivery. I had already seen the impact of this in a previous project, the one with the unstable external API. Instead of mocking and progressing with client-facing features, I guided the team toward building a clean and reusable integration layer. The design was sound, but the foundation kept shifting. We ended up going in circles. At the time, I framed it as a technical discipline. But in hindsight, it was a symptom of the deeper struggle I was leading from a place of habit, not from the needs of the role I had taken on.

This duality began to show in the way I led. Sprint planning became difficult. My instinct was to look ahead, to account for dependencies and technical guardrails. But Agile demanded adaptability and just-in-time planning. I found it hard to let go of long-term vision. To address this, I proposed a compromise: we could take small, achievable steps with each sprint while capturing long-term considerations as technical debt, keeping them visible in the backlog, and reinforcing their importance in Nexus meetings. I even brought them up in Nexus meetings, reinforcing their importance without letting them derail short-term goals.

CHAPTER 2 CONFESSION #2: INTERNAL CONFLICT—THE ARCHITECT VS. THE SCRUM MASTER

The team saw my struggle, even if they didn't name it. Some probably thought I was too technical for the role. Others, I sensed, understood that I was wrestling with something complex. They gave me space, not in the sense of stepping away, but in giving me room to find my balance. It wasn't resistance. It felt more like respect.

There was, however, one moment that made the internal conflict unmistakable. We were still working through the same integration, and progress was stalling. In a team meeting, one of the developers finally voiced what everyone had been feeling. It wasn't criticism, it was honesty. And it hit me harder than I expected. It was the moment I realized the architecture wasn't the problem; my mindset was. I was clinging to an old identity in a role that required a new one.

That moment didn't fix everything, but it marked the beginning of a shift. I began to see the value in letting go: not of quality, but of control. And that changed the way I showed up for the team.

This internal conflict didn't just influence my thinking, it showed up in my actions. The way I led the team began to reflect a subtle but growing imbalance.

The Anti-Pattern That Looked Like a Best Practice

As an architect, I had always believed that sound systems were built from the ground up with foresight. The earlier you introduce sound patterns, the less likely you are to need to redo things later. So, when I moved into the Scrum Master role, I instinctively carried those habits with me.

One of the first things I did was to build a generic framework, even before we had clarity on all the use cases. I asked the team to create reusable components with extensibility in mind, which meant abstracting logic that had not yet been duplicated. At the same time, I pushed for organizing the system well, even in parts of the system that did not yet

CHAPTER 2   CONFESSION #2: INTERNAL CONFLICT—THE ARCHITECT VS. THE SCRUM MASTER

have objective complexity. Looking back, layering the system into data, business, and prematurely adding features created complexity that a simpler system could have avoided.

It did not stop there. I introduced static code analysis tools, enforced coding standards, and strongly encouraged writing unit tests, even for low-risk, short-lifecycle components. I also insisted on tightly controlled data model changes. If a developer needed to alter a field for a quick feature or fix, I redirected the conversation toward long-term schema planning.

All of this was the right thing to do. I was not trying to slow the team down. I was trying to protect them from future rework, technical debt, and hidden complexity that could come back to haunt us. Someone who could see the broader picture had the responsibility to guide the team in ways they could not yet know for themselves.

But reality told a different story.

Velocity started slipping. Sprint after sprint, the team delivered less than they had committed to. What looked like a simple story on paper, such as creating a new form or screen, ended up bloated with behind-the-scenes tasks: setting up support structures typically invisible to non-technical stakeholders. The problem was not just the extra work. These tasks were not being included in sprint estimates. The team was planning based on functionality, while I was enforcing invisible architecture alongside it.

Eventually, I noticed that team members were no longer bringing these tasks into planning at all. It wasn't that they did not care. These expectations had become burdens they did not know how to plan for. To fix it, I started explicitly including architectural tasks in story breakdowns, even if they were non-functional. That way, the work became visible, owned, and correctly estimated.

It took me some time to accept that not every best practice needs to be enforced up-front. Agile is less about avoiding all future rework and more about consciously choosing what to delay and defer. I learned that it is acceptable to defer structure, as long as you track it. So, I adapted. If something could not be addressed within the sprint, I captured it as technical debt. However, I did not just leave it there; I actively brought it back into planning discussions and flagged it during backlog grooming so that it would not be forgotten.

I still believe in quality. But quality is also a journey, not a starting point. The best architectural practices are those that evolve with the product, rather than those that are enforced too early, creating friction without immediate value.

It wasn't just the team that felt the weight of these decisions. Beyond the boundaries of our sprint board, stakeholders began to notice gaps between progress and perception.

When Stakeholders Go Silent

One of the most challenging moments in my transition to Scrum Master came not from within the team, but from the people outside it, the stakeholders. In the early sprints, we laid the foundation: integrations, component structures, and reusable frameworks. However, when it came time for sprint reviews, there was little to show that looked functional from a business perspective. The silence in those meetings said everything.

Stakeholders were not seeing progress. While the team was fully engaged in setting up long-term architecture, the business users were waiting for screens, reports, or features they could relate to. From their perspective, Agile was not delivering the promised incremental value. And while we know this groundwork was critical, explaining that to an impatient audience was not easy.

Eventually, some of the frustration surfaced. Stakeholders began questioning the usefulness of small stories and minor backend wins. They wondered how it would help the business. What they did not see was that the user stories themselves were still evolving. While the business

CHAPTER 2   CONFESSION #2: INTERNAL CONFLICT—THE ARCHITECT VS. THE SCRUM MASTER

was clarifying its needs, we were making incremental progress to avoid a complete standstill. These initial results weren't flashy, but they were essential for what followed.

The work was valuable, even if it was invisible. The integrations and architecture we were laying down would accelerate future delivery. But convincing others, especially non-technical stakeholders, took time. Fortunately, they saw the confidence I had in the path we were taking, and while they did not fully agree at first, they gave us the space to continue.

Still, that experience taught me something vital: visibility matters. So, I adapted.

We began presenting differently in sprint reviews. If APIs were complete, we showcased them through Postman. If the UI was not wired up yet, we mocked the data to demonstrate the flow. We found ways to make even backend progress feel tangible. At the same time, I explained how the foundational work we were doing would unlock speed in future sprints. It was not always accepted up-front, but over time, results made the argument for me.

I also began working more closely with the Product Owner to bring clarity to our upcoming scope. We introduced epic-level planning for forthcoming releases and identified technical or integration blockers before diving into user stories. This allowed the team to see the bigger picture and pivot when needed, ensuring fewer surprises mid-sprint and better alignment with long-term features.

Non-functional progress also became part of our delivery rhythm. Whether it was resolving technical debt, strengthening CI/CD pipelines, or addressing performance and security readiness, we surfaced that work and made it part of our plan. These were not stretch tasks. They were tracked and owned, usually by technical leads, so that we did not have to pause them for later.

The biggest challenge was reframing our sprint goals. I wanted to make them more business-oriented, but that did not sit well with everyone. Some felt it was outside the team's nature, especially since our focus had been primarily technical. But I stood my ground. I reminded them that other teams had built similar codebases with little regard for reuse or sustainability, and that business teams were not paying the price. If our team were to break that cycle, we had to enable reusability, shared learning, and functional alignment across vendors.

Stakeholders eventually came around. They saw how much faster we moved once the groundwork was done. They saw how future stories were completed more easily, reused across features, and required fewer rework cycles. But the fundamental shift came when we stopped expecting them to understand technical progress and started showing them how it was unlocking business value.

What began as a visibility problem soon became a process revelation. We needed to rethink how and when feedback was built into our flow.

The Mindset Shift—From Blueprint to Feedback Loop

For a long time, my instincts were anchored in planning. The more thorough the design up-front, the smoother the delivery will be. But Agile does not always work that way. And I did not fully understand that until the gaps started surfacing, right in the middle of what we thought was a stable progress. We began to notice recurring problems. Developers misunderstood the requirements, and the UX design overlooked platform behavior. Even after multiple reviews, business users gave new feedback during development that should have surfaced earlier. It was not negligence. It was just the reality that a polished Figma or prototype still could not simulate the experience of using the application. That realization marked a turning point.

We decided to shift the process.

Instead of waiting for polished builds, we created UI-only stories ahead of development sprints. These stories were small, fast to implement, and allowed the team to produce working screens using mocked data.

CHAPTER 2   CONFESSION #2: INTERNAL CONFLICT—THE ARCHITECT VS. THE SCRUM MASTER

As soon as the UI was ready, we demoed it, not just to check alignment but to spark a response. Business users reacted much more naturally to an in-application flow than to static mockups. Their feedback was more precise, more actionable, and surfaced sooner. This one change created a feedback loop that significantly improved our accuracy and confidence in subsequent development.

It was not just the practice that shifted. My mindset changed too.

The hardest thing for me to let go of was the idea that every change should be absorbed in the same sprint. Early on, I would force updates and adjustments on the fly. But I realized that not all change is meant to be absorbed immediately. Sometimes, the more courageous and responsible path is to acknowledge the shift, frame it as an opportunity, and move forward with proper planning in the next sprint. That mindset gave the team breathing room and allowed us to protect their velocity while still showing flexibility to stakeholders.

This new approach changed the dynamic between the team and the stakeholders. It was no longer about saying yes or no to change. It became a discussion about when and how. For stakeholders, the message was clear: their input mattered. We were not rejecting change. We were incorporating it at the right pace. For the team, it meant they were not constantly overwhelmed. Big-impact changes were tabled for upcoming releases, giving everyone more control and less chaos.

The result spoke for itself. Once we started building and reviewing UI ahead of development, feedback came earlier, changes were easier to incorporate, and confidence from the business grew noticeably. What had once been a reactive process became a proactive feedback loop, and it made all the difference.

On a personal level, this shift changed how I measured success. Before, success was about how closely the team adhered to architectural quality and sprint plans. Now, I measure success by how quickly we discover the unknowns and how effectively we act on feedback. The truth is, the pain the team was feeling early on was not even their fault. However, once we changed our approach, the pressure was relieved. The impact reversed. What once looked like a technical failure was a process failure, and we fixed it.

That is the essence of Agile. Not getting everything right the first time, but building a system that helps you discover what needs to change and gives you the courage to adapt.

The feedback loop mindset didn't stop with the UI, it began reshaping how I thought about architecture itself and the timing of decisions.

Minimum Viable Architecture—Myth or Method?

At first, the idea of "just enough architecture" felt irresponsible. Coming from a background where architecture was treated as the backbone of delivery, the concept of doing only the minimum up front seemed risky. After all, how could a system stand firm if its foundation was incomplete? But over time, I realized that the term was not about cutting corners. It was about building only what was necessary to deliver value while leaving room to evolve.

I began to shift my thinking.

We cannot create a one-size-fits-all approach for architecture. Timelines, cost, risk, and complexity all influence how much architecture a project needs up front. Trying to build a fully realized architecture from day one often leads to waste. What I learned was that an interim architecture can be a powerful strategy. It provides structure for short-term execution without locking the team into a rigid framework that may not suit future needs.

That was when I truly embraced the idea of agile architecture. Before incorporating every layer or abstraction, I started asking myself what the team needed right now to move forward without compromising long-term integrity. We implemented only the necessary components, such as basic

CHAPTER 2 CONFESSION #2: INTERNAL CONFLICT—THE ARCHITECT VS. THE SCRUM MASTER

layering, integration scaffolds, and core design standards, without over-engineering the system. The goal was to keep the architecture flexible and adaptable so that changes could be made easily as the system matured.

And it worked. In one project, we deliberately chose to delay advanced architectural features such as caching strategies, bulk data processing optimizations, and audit trail infrastructure. We marked them as technical debt and reviewed them at regular planning intervals. This gave us the ability to release faster and adapt more effectively to changing business needs while staying in control of the architectural evolution.

The team, rather than feeling constrained or anxious, felt empowered. They understood that we are not ignoring architecture. We are sequencing it. We gave the team freedom to build while keeping a close eye on what needed to be revisited. We tracked deferred decisions as technical debts, made them visible, and prioritized them alongside business features when the time was right.

The approach never backfired; it paid off better than we expected. The team delivered quickly without compromising the foundation, and we never had to go live with anything that violated our principles. We maintained architectural quality without blocking momentum.

The key difference I learned was this: cutting corners means deviating from architectural principles and hoping it will not matter. Deferring architecture means acknowledging that some decisions can wait, while tracking them carefully and ensuring they remain on the radar. One leads to erosion. The other supports adaptability.

I now see Minimum Viable Architecture not as a compromise but as a discipline in its own right. It requires judgment, transparency, and collaboration. It keeps the team agile and focused while still upholding the standards that matter. And more importantly, it aligns architecture with delivery, not the other way around.

One project in particular tested this thinking in the real world. It wasn't just theory anymore, it was a high-risk challenge that demanded experimentation and restraint.

The High-Stakes Feature That Forced Iteration

Sometimes the riskiest ideas are the ones that spark the most growth.

We were tasked with building a solution that allowed users to visually explore a floor layout, essentially a simplified map-based interface for indoor environments. The concept was to let users navigate through the layout and understand activity in different sections. It was a novel idea for its time, made more ambitious by the requirement to support touch, responsiveness, and cross-browser functionality.

HTML5 was still in its early stages, not yet widely adopted in production systems. Touch navigation in web applications was relatively unexplored. Yet HTML5 offered promise, particularly through the canvas element, which enabled interactive graphics across mobile, web, and desktop platforms. It felt bold, but potentially game-changing.

I knew from the beginning that we could not afford to build the entire product before validating one critical assumption: would the interaction model even work?

That is when I took the initiative to build a minimum viable product (MVP). I developed a prototype using HTML5 canvas that let users interact with a flat floor layout via touch gestures. The prototype responded to basic finger swipes and gestures, simulating directional movement within the layout. It would update the view in response, creating the feel of panning or zooming within the floor map. It was technically lightweight but conceptually ambitious.

CHAPTER 2   CONFESSION #2: INTERNAL CONFLICT—THE ARCHITECT VS. THE SCRUM MASTER

The MVP was never intended to be the final product. Its purpose was to answer one question: could we make this interaction feel natural and reliable across devices? Because if that part failed, the entire product vision would collapse with it.

When I shared the MVP with the team, the response surprised me. Everyone was impressed, but the most unexpected reaction came from the UI/UX team. They immediately saw the potential and were eager to collaborate. What started as a lone experiment suddenly gained creative momentum. The MVP became the foundation for reimagining the user experience from that point forward.

There were challenges. One particular challenge was achieving smooth transitions between different floors. We adjusted the approach by simplifying the design, jumping users directly to the next floor rather than simulating a continuous scroll. That compromise, while not as sleek as the original vision, still delivered the needed value and allowed the product to stay on track.

The MVP was eventually showcased at a major industry event. It was a huge success. Leadership recognized the innovation and backed it further, investing in new features and continuing to build on the direction the MVP had made possible.

On a personal level, this experience was transformative. I had built something that, at the time, was rarely seen in production apps. There was no documentation, no community support, just the draft HTML5 specification and my willingness to experiment. It gave me immense confidence that I could navigate ambiguity, invent where needed, and bring ideas to life with clarity and discipline.

If someone focused only on delivery speed had looked at this effort, they might have seen it as a detour. But in truth, this small, focused MVP saved the entire product. Without it, we could have gone months in the wrong direction. With it, we accelerated alignment, creativity, and execution. Once aligned, we completed the app in just two months, confident in the quality of what we were delivering.

The experience of letting the MVP lead opened the door to something deeper: trust. Not just in the process, but in the team's ability to choose wisely, even when I disagreed.

Trusting the Team Over the Architecture

As a former architect, it was instinctual for me to recommend structured, scalable frameworks like Entity Framework for data access. I had seen the consequences of brittle queries and knew the long-term benefits of abstraction and type safety. So, when a team proposed using flat SQL queries instead, my internal alarm bells went off.

It wasn't a proposal I would have ever supported in my architectural days. The risks were clear: tight coupling and security vulnerabilities. But something made me pause. Maybe it was the team's confidence. Or perhaps it was a subtle shift I would start embracing as a Scrum Master, the idea that learning doesn't always come from being told what's right. It often comes from trying, reflecting, and adapting.

So, I stepped back. I didn't override the decision; I watched.

I was alert, of course. I closely followed how they managed security. I quietly reviewed their SQL handling. But I didn't impose. And what I saw surprised me. The team was not only thoughtful in how they approached the implementation, but they were also fast. Performance improved in that module, and their solution worked without introducing the issues I feared.

Eventually, I suggested a micro-ORM framework, an alternative that preserved the performance of raw SQL while offering more structure and safety. The team was open to it, and together we transitioned to a more maintainable model that still aligned with their instincts.

That experience was a turning point. I realized my role was no longer to be the gatekeeper of what's "right." It was to help the team grow, make informed decisions, and own their path forward. Sometimes that meant staying silent. Sometimes it meant nudging with questions. But it always meant trusting them and believing that ownership, even with mistakes, leads to stronger, more resilient teams.

This shift didn't just empower the team. It changed me. I learned to coach, not control. To enable, not override. And in doing so, I became not just a better Scrum Master, but a better leader.

That shift in trust didn't come easy. It took inner conflict, trial, and reflection, lessons I couldn't have learned any other way.

Lessons That Only Conflict Can Teach

The hardest lessons don't come from failure. They come from seeing your greatest strengths, beliefs that once made you respected, start to become liabilities in a new role.

As an architect, I used to believe every system needed a structured foundation from day one. That mindset provided structure, predictability, and a sense of future readiness. However, when I stepped into the Scrum Master role, I realized that rigid layering up-front wasn't just unnecessary, but sometimes harmful. Teams struggled under the weight of abstractions that didn't serve immediate goals. Morale dipped, and worse, people hesitated to speak up. They knew I'd push for strict standards, even when those standards didn't match the sprint's purpose.

Letting go of that mindset wasn't easy. It wasn't easy. These weren't just practices to me: they shaped how I saw my role and what I stood for. But I saw the trade-off. By releasing control, I was creating space. And in that space, teams stepped up, owned their choices, and grew.

Over time, I developed a more situational approach. My rule of thumb became: enforce standards when they safeguard long-term impact without derailing short-term momentum. Otherwise, step back and let the team lead the way.

CHAPTER 2   CONFESSION #2: INTERNAL CONFLICT—THE ARCHITECT VS. THE SCRUM MASTER

This shift reshaped my definition of what makes a great Scrum Master. It's no longer about steering the ship alone. It's about enabling ownership, unblocking growth, and holding both delivery and technical health with equal respect.

Do I miss being an architect? Honestly, yes. I still sharpen those skills when I can. In many ways, I still consider this a temporary pivot: one that demands my full commitment, but not necessarily a permanent one. That said, this role has made me a better leader. I'm now more empathetic, especially to overburdened teams. I'm more open to experimentation, to letting go of premature perfection, and to trusting the process, even when it's messy.

If I could mentor someone making a similar transition, I wouldn't start with advice. I'd start with my story, because sometimes the only way to relate to this conflict is to live it or hear it from someone who has.

Takeaway Confession   What made me effective as an architect nearly broke me as a Scrum Master, until I learned that trust builds better systems than control.

CHAPTER 3

Confession #3: When the Code Breaks, So Does the Team

A chain is only as strong as its weakest link, and a team is only as strong as the trust it builds when things go wrong.

—Unknown

Technical debt is often seen as just messy code or postponed refactoring. In reality, it's something more profound. It silently eats into team morale, slows progress, and turns confident developers into cautious survivors.

And if you ignore it long enough, it stops being just a technical problem; it becomes a people problem. In this chapter, I would like to share a story about a greenfield project that nearly fell into its own legacy trap within months of its inception. We didn't inherit a mess. We created one. We moved fast, skipped steps, and told ourselves we'd fix it later. But later came quicker than expected.

What followed was more than just bug fixing. It was a test of trust, transparency, and resilience. We had to face hard truths. We had to slow down when everything around us said "speed up." And we had to do it without losing each other in the process.

This isn't a story about failure. It's about course correction. It's about what happens when a team chooses to roll up its sleeves instead of giving up. And it's a reminder that the real cost of technical debt isn't just broken code, it's a team slowly forgetting what progress feels like.

Acknowledging the deeper cost of technical debt was only the beginning; the real learning came from a project that started with promise, and slowly began to unravel.

The Calm Before the Debt

It all started like a dream assignment: a greenfield project with no legacy constraints, no brittle systems to unravel, and the freedom to build something from the ground up. For any developer, that's the golden opportunity. Our team had just been formed. A few of us had worked together before, but for the most part, we were a mix of seasoned and junior developers, all trying to gel while the clock was already ticking.

The energy in the early sprints was electric. You could feel the enthusiasm in every stand-up. There were whiteboards filled with diagrams, heated discussions about design patterns, everything you'd expect in the honeymoon phase of a new build.

But then came the timeline.

The official asks: Deliver a working product in six months.

On paper, it sounded tough but manageable. In practice, it meant feature cuts, fast decisions, and mounting pressure. Leadership was watching closely. There was significant visibility across the organization; this project was part of a larger transformative initiative, and it needed to make a splash. The message from the top was clear: "Show us progress, show it fast."

And so we did.

CHAPTER 3   CONFESSION #3: WHEN THE CODE BREAKS, SO DOES THE TEAM

We moved quickly: too quickly, if I'm being honest. The early demos were impressive. Stakeholders were happy. Product owners gave glowing feedback. That momentum gave us confidence, but it also started to blur the lines between smart trade-offs and risky shortcuts.

Code reviews? Skipped in the name of velocity.

Refactoring? Tabled until "sometime after MVP."

Test coverage? Just enough to get by.

I remember the moment clearly. A developer merged a chunk of fragile, high-risk code late in the sprint, and someone asked, "Should we at least review it once before pushing?" The response was half-laugh: "We'll fix it later." Everyone knew that later probably meant never. But nobody argued. The product demo was in two days, and we needed to show something that worked.

Looking back, it wasn't laziness or carelessness. It was a calculated compromise. We thought that as long as the core business processes ran smoothly, we could justify the chaos behind the scenes. And for a while, it looked like we were right. In just under three months, we had something usable. Real users were interacting with it. The business was thrilled.

"I've never witnessed a team operate at this speed!" one senior exec said. That kind of praise is hard to ignore, and harder to push back against.

So we celebrated. We demoed. We released.

But quietly, cracks had already started to form. Unit tests failed sporadically. New developers struggled to understand the codebase. Features that should've taken a day started dragging into multiple sprints. And still, we pressed on.

No one raised their hand to stop the train. Not because we didn't see the issues, but because we were all focused on not derailing the momentum. There was this unspoken hope that we could clean things up "just after this sprint." Then the next. Then the next.

In a retro, someone joked, "Are we shipping a prototype or a product?" It got a few laughs. But somebody said it out loud: we were already worried. We knew we had built something functional, but also fragile.

This was the calm before the storm. Everything looked fine on the surface. But underneath, we were accumulating problems faster than we were solving them. And the worst part? We knew it.

We just hoped we'd have enough time later to undo the shortcuts we were taking now.

Momentum carried us through the early sprints, but we soon reached the point where speed could no longer outrun consequences.

The Day the System Fought Back

It didn't happen with a crash. It didn't happen with a production outage. It wasn't a single bug that blew up the release.

The system just… slowed down.

Pages that once loaded in seconds now took double or more. Key flows became sluggish. Performance bottlenecks that had been brewing quietly under the surface started showing up everywhere, from non-prod environments to production itself. The energy that once fueled the team began to shift. Developers weren't shocked. They weren't surprised. They had seen it coming.

We all had.

The shortcuts we had taken were catching up to us. Best practices that were sidelined for the sake of speed, like efficient database queries, modular design, and async operations, were now screaming for attention. Our initial success had been built on momentum, but we hadn't laid the foundation for scale or stability. The cracks weren't theoretical anymore. They were visible, measurable, and unavoidable.

And still, no one panicked.

That's the thing about slow-burning technical debt: it doesn't cause an explosion. It causes erosion. A quiet frustration started to settle in. The team knew they had made trade-offs, and now they were living with the consequences. But the real challenge wasn't awareness. It was bandwidth.

CHAPTER 3   CONFESSION #3: WHEN THE CODE BREAKS, SO DOES THE TEAM

By the time these issues surfaced, the team had already moved on to the next set of features. Sprints were tightly packed with new commitments. Everyone was under pressure to keep delivering. And so, the broken pieces of earlier sprints were reluctantly patched in between sprint goals, usually as tech tasks or silent add-ons that never made it to the demo.

There was no dramatic confrontation. No finger-pointing. Just a shared recognition: "We said we'd fix it later. Later is here."

Leadership wasn't caught off guard either. They had seen the velocity we had demonstrated and the cost associated with it. Now, they were watching how we'd respond. The unspoken question from stakeholders was clear: "Can you clean up this mess without breaking your promise to us?" And to their credit, they didn't push back hard, but they didn't offer any room either. The next milestone was still expected. The next feature is still needed to ship.

At the time, I was still in the architect role, not yet the Scrum Master, and I could feel the tension pulling from both directions. I knew the architecture had flaws. I knew the team needed breathing room to fix what was slowing them down. But I also knew that breathing room wasn't coming anytime soon.

So, I defended the team.

Not by hiding the debt, but by helping frame it. I walked stakeholders through the trade-offs we had made and why they were necessary at the time. I worked with the team to identify areas we could gradually refactor without derailing current goals. We didn't call it "a pause." We called it "strategic course correction." It sounded more acceptable that way.

Looking back, that was the first time I saw how technical debt isn't just a development problem. It's an organizational rhythm issue. It affects prioritization, planning, morale, and trust. If it's not surfaced and addressed intentionally, it turns into background noise, just another pain point people get used to until they quietly burn out.

CHAPTER 3   CONFESSION #3: WHEN THE CODE BREAKS, SO DOES THE TEAM

The system hadn't crashed. But it was fighting back. And we were finally starting to listen.

The system didn't crash, but its resistance surfaced in ways that gradually wore down the team's spirit.

When Frustration Replaces Flow

At first, the team had moved fast and felt proud of it. But as time passed, the excitement started to fade. In its place, tension crept in. Developers who were once eager to push boundaries began showing signs of strain. Nobody said it outright, but you could feel the shift in how they approached the work.

They didn't avoid the messy parts of the codebase directly. Instead, it became an unspoken protocol to leave specific modules to a few careful hands. These were areas where one wrong change could ripple through the system and break everything. Giving everyone access to modify them freely felt risky, so we managed it quietly and cautiously. It was like walking across a frozen lake, hoping the ice would hold.

The anxiety of breaking something slowly replaced the fun of building.

The pride that developers once had in the product gave way to quiet frustration. Every new story felt heavier than it should. Every change came with hesitation. There wasn't a dramatic collapse. It was a slow erosion of enthusiasm.

Testers weren't spared either. The same feature that worked one day would break the next. Regression failures became a pattern. It felt like we were playing technical whack-a-mole: fix one issue, and another would appear. Eventually, we had to request additional time, nearly a week, to stabilize the system. Not to deliver anything new, but to make sure things wouldn't fall apart.

CHAPTER 3   CONFESSION #3: WHEN THE CODE BREAKS, SO DOES THE TEAM

Development didn't stop completely. Still, there were days when most of our engineering bandwidth was devoted to supporting QA. Developers weren't innovating. They were plugging holes. And everyone felt it. Nobody openly complained, but the fatigue was visible.

Retrospectives started to feel repetitive. The team was burnt out. Cameras were turned off. Updates got shorter. Participation began to dwindle. The problem wasn't a lack of progress. It was a lack of energy.

Velocity didn't plummet, but each sprint felt heavier. Even our wins started to feel less meaningful. Yes, we were delivering. But it didn't feel like we were building something we could be proud of.

I could see what was happening, and I saw it. The team was doing everything it could to stay on track, but they were carrying the weight of choices made in earlier sprints. It wasn't just a technical challenge. It was a mental one.

The spark for the break originated from the team, which recognized the need to stabilize the codebase. The Scrum Master coordinated the efforts to facilitate open communication regarding this idea. As an architect, I supported the decision by providing valuable data to reinforce our case. Leadership acknowledged the importance of the break to help the team recharge, and ultimately, the team recognized that this short pause could lead to improved long-term efficiency.

This solution will be explored through various perspectives in the following sections.

As fatigue settled in, it became clear that the burden wasn't just technical, it was organizational, and the Scrum Master stood at the center of it.

CHAPTER 3   CONFESSION #3: WHEN THE CODE BREAKS, SO DOES THE TEAM

Scrum Master in the Middle

The team was slowing down. Morale had dipped. Bugs were recurring. Everyone felt the drag, even if they couldn't always name its cause. In the middle of it all stood our Scrum Master: a capable facilitator, deeply engaged with the team, but not from a technical background.

They were empathetic. You could see that. They sensed the team was suffering, and they tried to help where they could. They arranged connections between developers and testers. They brought blockers to attention. However, they often couldn't grasp why things were taking so long. To them, a blocked test case was just another update in the stand-up.

What they couldn't always see was what lay behind: the fragile architecture, the patches built on top of patches, and the unspoken anxiety every time someone touched a volatile part of the codebase.

They tried pushing back when delivery pressure mounted. When stakeholders insisted on squeezing in another feature, they would ask, "Can we delay this?" But the features in question were mandatory. There was no wiggle room. We weren't in a position to strip them out or prolong the release. It wasn't just a matter of scope; it was a matter of business readiness. And so, the Scrum Master was left carrying a message that no one wanted to hear: "We can't slow down."

From where I stood, I could see both sides: leadership chasing milestones, and a team running out of steam. It wasn't surprising. We all knew the trade-offs we had made for speed. But now it was time for someone to acknowledge them.

The Scrum Master and I didn't clash about priorities. We both understood that without delivery, there was no go-live. But where we differed was in language. I found it hard to articulate architectural pain to someone without a technical lens. "Why can't we just fix the bug and move on?" was a reasonable question from their end. But to explain why that bug existed in the first place required walking through a maze of quick fixes, skipped reviews, and broken modularity. That's not a five-minute conversation.

CHAPTER 3   CONFESSION #3: WHEN THE CODE BREAKS, SO DOES THE TEAM

One moment stands out clearly. The testers were growing frustrated, raising defects daily that seemed to go nowhere. They were blocked. And it was exhausting everyone. So, a radical idea sparked from a retro: hit pause, just for a week. No happy path testing. No patching bugs. Instead, let the team focus on stabilizing the foundation and giving testers time to write test cases for upcoming sprints.

That pause changed everything. The Scrum Master helped broker the agreement, and I backed it with data and reasoning. Together, we negotiated a temporary truce. For the first time in weeks, the team wasn't in reaction mode. They were in rebuild mode. And they delivered.

That experience taught me something I would carry forward later in my career: you can't fix the engine while it's running. We're thankful that we're not heart surgeons. Sometimes, you need to take a side: slow down, realign, and let the team recover its rhythm.

At the time, I didn't feel the urge to step into the Scrum Master role. But that moment planted the seed. I saw firsthand how challenging it was to lead from the middle: to shield the team, manage upwards, and make trade-offs in real-time. And I saw what happens when a Scrum Master doesn't just run ceremonies, but advocates for recovery.

It was my first glimpse into what it meant to lead an Agile team.

The mounting tension eventually gave way to a moment of truth, one that surfaced during a retrospective that finally broke the silence.

The Retrospective That Changed Everything

It came after a particularly rough sprint. Bugs had piled up. Testers were frustrated. Developers were mentally checked out. Everything felt brittle. It wasn't chaos, but it wasn't control either. We were somewhere in between: a space where momentum existed, but stability didn't.

CHAPTER 3 CONFESSION #3: WHEN THE CODE BREAKS, SO DOES THE TEAM

The retrospective was already on the calendar. No one called it out of panic. But you could feel the tension as you walked in. Cameras stayed off. Voices were flat. The mood was cynical. People weren't hopeful. They were bracing.

The conversation started like most retrospectives: updates, surface-level blockers, small wins. But then someone said something that cut through the noise:

"We're just beating the bushes."

That broke the flow. For a second, no one responded. Then came the flood.

"We don't even know what's stable anymore."

"Every fix breaks something else."

"We patch the same issues over and over."

"It's not even testing, it's whack-a-mole."

The room cracked open. Blame flew first, mostly between developers and testers. Testers felt unsupported. Developers felt like they were in firefighting mode. Bugs were reported faster than they could be reproduced. It was emotional. Not explosive, but raw.

And then, after the wave passed, came the honesty.

No one wanted it to be this way. Everyone knew we had pushed hard to meet release timelines. Everyone had agreed to the trade-offs. But now, it was clear: we couldn't keep moving forward like this.

The turning point came not in a grand decision, but in a quiet shift of posture.

One developer said, "Let's just get to a stable mode, by any way possible." It wasn't a solution. It was a plea, a collective one.

We committed, right there, to doing whatever it took to stabilize. That didn't mean a full tech debt recovery sprint, and it didn't mean throwing the roadmap out the window. It just meant this: we were no longer pretending everything was fine.

The leadership team was informed, but the challenge was getting them to see the difference between a "defect fix" and a "tech debt cleanup." To them, both looked like the same thing. Bugs. Fix them. Move on. But we knew that wasn't the whole story. Some fixes were about symptoms. Others were about systems.

That retro didn't solve the problem, but it reset the room.

As the architect, I walked away with a new sense of urgency: not from leadership, but from within. I realized that while delivery was still king, sustainability had to have a seat at the table. Not just in design diagrams, but also in how we planned sprints, wrote code, and supported one another. I had a lot of work to do to enable that shift, even if it wasn't officially my job.

Looking back, that retro changed everything. It didn't give us a silver bullet, but it gave us honesty. And that was the first real step toward recovery.

That retrospective didn't fix the system, but it opened a door, one that allowed us to reframe our message in terms stakeholders could understand.

Debt As a Business Language

Stakeholders were frustrated. The product owners were under pressure. Bugs were popping up, old ones were resurfacing, and delivery timelines were under threat. From their perspective, things looked off-track, and they wanted to know why.

But when we brought up technical debt, it didn't land. At first, it seemed vague. To them, it was a black box. Something internal. Something that developers should "just handle." It wasn't that they didn't care, it's that they couldn't see it.

So, I started reframing it.

CHAPTER 3   CONFESSION #3: WHEN THE CODE BREAKS, SO DOES THE TEAM

Instead of talking about refactoring or modularity, I started showing them the trade-offs we had made to meet the first release. We hadn't taken shortcuts recklessly; we had made informed compromises to deliver business value on time. But now we were paying for it. Not in theory, but in real, trackable ways: reopened bugs, repeated failures in the same modules, increasing test cycles, and blocked testers chasing instability instead of writing new cases.

We showed dashboards that highlighted where the most defects were concentrated, and how many were resurfacing again and again. Instead of saying "we need to clean up tech debt," we said, "We need to stop testing this area until we fix the root cause. Otherwise, we'll keep wasting QA time and accumulating noise."

Those changed things.

One stakeholder finally said, "So you're telling me we're stuck in a loop, fixing the same thing while trying to build the next thing?"

Exactly.

It clicked for them. The idea that we couldn't test and fix in parallel, at least not effectively, made sense. And the bigger insight was this: it was better that this happened early in the second release than later, when the stakes would be even higher. No one wanted to be in the same place six months down the line.

The support began to show.

No one wanted to keep looking at defect dashboards swollen with red. No one wanted to report status without confidence. It was clear we had to pivot. While we didn't get an open invitation to pause entirely, we got the breathing room to reorganize and to be intentional about how we tackled the problems.

After that, the question "Can we fix it later?" stopped coming up. Everyone understood what "later" looked like. And no one wanted to go back there.

For me personally, that shift in communication was a turning point. I realized that as a technical leader, it's not enough to know the problem; you have to make others feel it. That doesn't mean dramatizing it. It means translating it.

When I eventually became a Scrum Master, I brought this lesson with me. I no longer talked about "clean code" or "best practices" unless they were tied to a delivery impact. And I never talked about technical debt without also talking about a plan: how long it would take, what it would unlock, and how it would reduce risk.

This experience taught me that technical alignment is not a negotiation; it's a shared language. And when that language is clear, teams and stakeholders move forward together.

Once the language around debt changed, so did the behaviors, and over time, those changes started to reshape how we defined quality.

Redefining Done and Changing Habits

We never officially rewrote our Definition of Done. There was no ceremony, no wiki update, and no formal agreement. But over time, the way we defined "done" changed anyway.

It started with small habits.

We began doing internal demos not just for stakeholders, but for ourselves. It provided developers with a space to view each other's work early, ask questions, and identify quality issues before they reached testing. Peer reviews, once skipped for speed, gradually made a comeback. And we created checklists not to add bureaucracy, but to remind ourselves of what had slipped through the cracks before.

These changes didn't happen overnight. They were phased in, quietly and gradually, sprint after sprint. But the impact was unmistakable. Morale improved. Code quality improved. And something more critical began to return: ownership.

CHAPTER 3   CONFESSION #3: WHEN THE CODE BREAKS, SO DOES THE TEAM

The team, once reactive and overextended, started getting ahead of problems. Once the system regained some stability, they began to raise red flags proactively. They weren't just completing tickets anymore: they were thinking critically about risk, maintainability, and impact. The mindset had shifted from "just get it working" to "let's make it solid."

One of the most effective habits we adopted was the idea of stability zones, areas in the codebase where we had seen repeated defects or volatility. We tracked them. We reviewed them during grooming. If work touched those zones, it triggered a higher level of scrutiny. It wasn't a blocker; it was a reminder to slow down and double-check.

This structure brought visible value. Product owners and leadership, who had once struggled to understand what we meant by "technical debt," now had visuals. Dashboards made the invisible visible. Ironically, the dashboard that sparked this shift wasn't part of any official deliverable. It was quietly built by someone in the leadership and shared informally. That small tool ended up being adopted across all Scrum teams. One of our senior leaders joked, "Funny how the dashboard, the one we didn't even budget for, became the one everyone depends on."

But behind the metrics and visualizations was something more profound: a culture change.

The most significant shift wasn't about test coverage or code comments. It was about restraint. The team learned to say, "Stop." If something was breaking repeatedly, we stopped testing it, stopped hacking around it, and called it what it was: a blocker. No more pushing through to say we were done. We prioritized fixing the root before moving forward.

This was where agility came to life: not in burndown charts or velocity graphs, but in our ability to adapt. We had pushed through a painful stretch, learned from it, and built guardrails to avoid falling into the same traps again.

Agility, I realized, isn't about how fast you go. It's about how you respond when things get hard, and how willing you are to slow down, reset, and get it right.

CHAPTER 3   CONFESSION #3: WHEN THE CODE BREAKS, SO DOES THE TEAM

Improving delivery habits wasn't just about short-term gains, it helped us recognize and avoid a long-term trap we were heading toward.

The Legacy Trap and Its Inheritors

This was a greenfield project, but there was a moment later in the delivery cycle when I realized something important. If we didn't take corrective action, we were at risk of turning this into a future legacy system.

It is easy to assume that legacy code only comes from outdated technology or decade-old decisions. But I have learned that legacy is not about the age of the code. It is about how it is built and maintained. A system that is rushed, poorly structured, and left without a recovery plan becomes a legacy the moment no one wants to work on it.

We were approaching that point.

If we failed to act, a future team would eventually be the one to face the consequences, whether it happened five years from now or ten. I had already been in that situation before, walking into projects where the original developers were no longer around. Every attempt to modernize felt like a painful and messy task. I knew exactly how it felt to inherit a system built on shortcuts.

I did not want that to happen again.

We began reviewing parts of the codebase that had been assembled quickly without a clear structure. Where there was no reusability, we added it. Where modularity was missing, we restructured. It was quiet, consistent refactoring that brought our system back into shape. This time, we were not just solving today's bugs. We were building something that could be maintained and extended in the future.

Eventually, new team members began joining. The difference was clear. They were able to onboard quickly, understand all the modules, and start contributing without being boxed into silos. We no longer needed workarounds to avoid fragile areas. There were no parts of the code where developers would say, "Let's not touch that." That silence spoke volumes.

We had avoided the trap.

I felt responsible not because I was the architect, but because I had experienced what happens when no one takes ownership. Whether we maintained the product or someone else did, we owed them a system that was clean, consistent, and understandable. As it turned out, we were the ones maintaining it later. And we were thankful we had put in the effort when it still mattered.

If I had to offer advice to another team moving fast, I wouldn't say never take shortcuts. Sometimes, business pressure makes them unavoidable. But I would say this: only take shortcuts when you have a specific plan to catch up afterward. Do not create debt unless you know exactly how and when you will repay it. Ownership is not about what you ship today; it is about what you leave behind.

Whether it is a ten-year-old monolith or a six-month-old microservice, the moment your team stops caring about structure and sustainability, legacy has already begun.

With a clear view of what could have gone wrong, we doubled down on sustainable practices that kept the system, and the team, healthy.

From Quick Fixes to Long-Term Fitness

After the chaos, the slowdown, and the recovery, we didn't go back to business as usual.

The lessons stuck.

What started as urgent cleanup work slowly evolved into a regular engineering discipline. Refactoring wasn't something we "fit in if we had time." It became routine. Tech debt was no longer a vague complaint in retrospectives. We tracked it clearly in Jira, alongside user stories. Every developer knew that addressing small cracks early was better than rebuilding foundations later.

CHAPTER 3   CONFESSION #3: WHEN THE CODE BREAKS, SO DOES THE TEAM

The best part? These practices weren't handed down from leadership. They were team-driven. The people who had lived through the burn were the ones who made sure we didn't end up there again.

In the months that followed, delivery improved. We regained momentum. Features were shipped on time. But more importantly, the defect counts dropped, and the mood lifted. Testers spent more time writing and validating new scenarios instead of retesting unstable flows. Conversations became collaborative again. Planning sessions focused on value, not survival.

Developers became more confident. The code was cleaner, the risk lower. Proactive cleanup became second nature. No one waited to be told to fix something: they saw a problem, and they owned it. Refactoring became a part of the job, not a side task.

As the architect, I made sure this discipline didn't slip. It became part of my governance approach. I made sure to call out any lapses, not to criticize, but to remind the team of the journey we had taken to get here. When the pressure ramped up again, I reminded the team that debt was never invisible for long.

And something interesting happened after I transitioned into the Scrum Master role. I found myself still looking for the same patterns. Not because I had to, but because I had learned that small red flags, if ignored, constantly grow. If anyone raised a concern, no matter how small, I ensured we created space to investigate it. Even if we couldn't fix it right away, we acknowledged it. That alone changed the team's attitude.

This shift didn't come from a single moment. It came from a series of recoveries, reflections, and slow changes. That's what long-term fitness looks like. Not just cleaner code, but a healthier, more aware team. A team that doesn't just move fast, but moves well.

These changes didn't just impact process, they transformed the team's mindset, paving the way for a quiet, but meaningful, recovery.

CHAPTER 3   CONFESSION #3: WHEN THE CODE BREAKS, SO DOES THE TEAM

The Emotional Payoff

The turnaround didn't come with a celebration. There was no confetti moment, no single release that changed everything. It showed up in quiet ways: like jokes returning to stand-ups, team members volunteering for complex stories, and a shared sense of "we've got this."

The team had emerged from the tunnel stronger. They weren't just functioning. They were confident. You could feel the shift. There was no more hesitation around problem areas. The fear of touching unstable code had disappeared. Instead, there was pride in having survived it, in having fixed it.

And there were signals. Small, but undeniable. The once-red dashboard modules had stayed green for weeks. Not a single defect. That alone felt like a trophy. The noise had died down: fewer firefighting, fewer escalations. The senior leadership team noticed. "It's been quiet," someone said. And in our world, that's the highest compliment.

I remember the moment it hit me. We had rolled up our sleeves, faced the real issues, and stayed with it instead of walking away or blaming each other. This was the moment when most teams broke. But we didn't. We lived through it and rebuilt something better.

As someone who had just begun stepping into leadership, this experience gave me one of my most important lessons: have empathy. No one wants to fail. If a team keeps missing the mark, the solution isn't pressure. It's understanding. Listen. Find the real pain points. Sometimes the problem is technical. Sometimes it's human. Often, it's both.

I hope readers, especially Scrum Masters, remember this: even when you step into a messy situation, there's always a way through if you choose to stay engaged. There's a saying in Tamil, "ithuvum kadanthu pogum." This too, shall pass.

CHAPTER 3   CONFESSION #3: WHEN THE CODE BREAKS, SO DOES THE TEAM

But it doesn't pass on its own. You have to engage. Ask questions. Pull people together. Work with the SMEs who can solve the core problem. Talk to your customer, your product owner, and your leadership team. Bridge the ground-level reality with the 10,000-foot view.

It's not glamorous work. But that's what makes it real.

As a Scrum Master, sometimes your most valuable role isn't to run the ceremonies. It's to connect the dots that no one else sees, and hold the team steady until the storm clears.

Takeaway Confession   Sometimes, the biggest fix isn't the code, it's in giving the team enough safety to say, "We are not okay," and the space to make it right.

CHAPTER 4

Confession #4: Stakeholders Think Agile Is a Miracle Cure

Agile isn't a magic wand; it's a compass. It points the way, but the journey still requires effort.

—Unknown

Agile often comes up as a promise in conversations. Stakeholders are told it will solve their delivery delays, improve transparency, and make teams more adaptable to change. On paper, it sounds like a perfect solution, an elegant fix for complicated problems.

But reality has a way of challenging the promise.

In practice, Agile only succeeds when everyone involved embraces not just its ceremonies but also its responsibilities. This includes stakeholders; however, in many organizations, they may not always be fully aligned with the Agile mindset that is essential for success. They expect flexibility without trade-offs, speed without structure, and adaptability without accountability.

CHAPTER 4   CONFESSION #4: STAKEHOLDERS THINK AGILE IS A MIRACLE CURE

This chapter explores the tension that occurs when Agile is misunderstood from the top down, turning it into more of a label than an authentic experience. Through valuable lessons learned, we will examine what happens when teams try to implement Agile only in name and what it takes to start closing that gap when stakeholders aren't aligned with the framework they have chosen.

That gap between expectation and execution often begins well before the first sprint, starting with how Agile is introduced, framed, and sold.

The Agile Sales Pitch vs. Reality

Agile will give us a quicker time to market.

Having a Scrum Coach in place will naturally help the team become a high-performing team.

This project will adhere to Agile principles from the outset.

These were not just phrases; they were assumptions baked into the customer governance model. But I later discovered that when Agile is treated as a marketing checkbox, the reality can be painfully different.

I wasn't a Scrum Master in the project, but I remember those kickoff meetings clearly. The customer leadership had already decided that the project would be Agile. They led the initiative, not out of a vision of transformation, but driven by a quiet sense of urgency to keep up with the times. Maybe a competitor had adopted Scrum. Perhaps someone convinced them that Agile could be the cure-all. Whatever the reason, the intention was to change. It was more about appearances.

Foundational changes in funding, roles, or governance didn't accompany the rollout. There was no shift in how accountability worked. No restructuring to empower product owners. No pause to ask whether the team understood Agile, or even had what they needed to make it work.

CHAPTER 4   CONFESSION #4: STAKEHOLDERS THINK AGILE IS A MIRACLE CURE

And yet, expectations were sky high.

Stakeholders assumed Agile would mean less planning, faster deliveries, and magical momentum. Ironically, they expected more documentation and more meetings, without giving teams any breathing room to figure things out.

I saw fancy slogans on PowerPoint decks: "Agile drives faster delivery" and "We will be more responsive to the market!" But none of those decks mentioned servant leadership, psychological safety, stakeholder commitment, or even the basic fact that teams need time to stabilize before delivering value consistently.

Worse, Scrum Coach was hired, but their authority wasn't absolute. Customers believed their very presence would fix everything, while stripping them of the power to drive meaningful change. As one stakeholder casually said, "Now that we have hired the Agile expert, let's sit back and see results." The irony? These "experts" could not even push back against the scope shifts mid-sprint without being overruled.

Looking back, it was clear we were doing Scrumfall; ceremonies on the surface, waterfall expectations underneath. And because there was no shared mindset or ownership model, Agile became a source of friction rather than a source of fluidity.

The most jarring part? There was no tolerance for learning. No space for growing pains. Teams were expected to deliver a Return on Investment (ROI) by the end of sprint one. If we miss a target, complaints come faster than retrospectives. In a world obsessed with velocity, no one paused to ask, "Are we building the right thing?"

The Agile pitch was sleek. The execution, sadly, was stuck in old-fashioned thinking.

While the pitch set high hopes, it didn't take long for cracks to show, especially when reality didn't live up to the promises.

CHAPTER 4   CONFESSION #4: STAKEHOLDERS THINK AGILE IS A MIRACLE CURE

First Signs of Trouble: "We Did Agile, But It Didn't Work"

It didn't take long before the first cracks appeared.

After just a few sprints, stakeholders began to grumble that something wasn't working. The word they used stung, not because it was untrue, but because it revealed just how deep the misunderstanding ran.

Agile seems slow. Let's change the approach.

That one word, slow, said more about the mismatch in expectations than any retro board could capture. From the outside, we were doing all the "right" Agile things: sprint planning, demos, retrospectives. But from the inside, it was clear the engine was misfiring. Agile wasn't the issue. It was the assumptions placed on it.

Stakeholders had expected something entirely different. Some believed that with Agile, requirements were optional, something the team could figure out "on the way." Others thought it meant they could make changes at any time, without consequences or rework. When reality didn't match the brochure, confidence quickly turned to criticism.

We thought you didn't require precise requirements.

Isn't Agile supposed to allow us to change things whenever we want?

"Why isn't it done yet?"

The frustration wasn't just loud; it landed hard. Some questioned whether Agile was the problem; others quietly doubted the team's ability to deliver. But doubt, when voiced too early, can crush the momentum before it even builds.

Behind the scenes, the real problem was obvious: everything was a priority. There was no sequencing, no agreed-upon roadmap. Every new idea became a must-have. And when the team missed or delayed even a single item, it wasn't treated as a learning opportunity; it was escalated.

CHAPTER 4 CONFESSION #4: STAKEHOLDERS THINK AGILE IS A MIRACLE CURE

One of the most invisible challenges we faced was the steep learning curve. It was built on a platform for which we had limited trained associates. Our teams required additional time to gain necessary expertise, but the customer's timeline did not allow for a transitional period. This resulted in immediate expectations and growing concerns on both sides.

The processes became paradoxical. Agile was being followed on paper, but the demands were pure waterfall: rigid timelines, fixed scope, and zero room for error. It was Agile in branding but Waterfall in soul.

The lowest point came after our first sprint demo. We had followed all the Agile steps. But when the working product was showcased, a stakeholder dropped a line that felt like a punch to the gut.

A college project would have been better.

That kind of remark doesn't just hurt, it derails. The team withdrew. Energy dipped. And while the ceremonies continued, the confidence behind them began to erode.

At that point, I confronted some of the stakeholders, not aggressively, but with clarity and conviction. I explained that Agile ceremonies alone wouldn't deliver results unless paired with clear priorities, stakeholder discipline, and realistic goals. I argued that blaming Agile was like blaming a treadmill for not running the marathon for you.

But I wasn't a Scrum Master then; I was the architect. My voice wasn't ignored because it lacked insight. It was ignored because it didn't fit the hierarchy. The decision to shift or adapt was never mine to make. Additionally, the project drifted forward, an Agile boat steered by a waterfall rudder.

However, the surface-level problems only hinted at a deeper issue, one rooted in the fundamental misunderstanding of ownership and effort.

CHAPTER 4   CONFESSION #4: STAKEHOLDERS THINK AGILE IS A MIRACLE CURE

The Root of the Myth: Misunderstood Ownership and Effort

Agile fails most quickly when it appears collaborative but functions like a control hierarchy. That's precisely what occurred here.

From the beginning, the customer had a product owner in place. On paper, it looked fine. They attended sprint planning, showed up for reviews, and participated in retrospectives. But presence isn't participation. And representation doesn't mean responsibility.

No one took proper responsibility for the backlog.

They were present, yes, but rarely engaged. Decisions were delayed or delegated. Discussions on priorities were infrequent and typically presented rather than refined collaboratively. Attending meetings was considered sufficient for involvement. At the same time, the responsibilities of ownership: clarifying trade-offs, advocating for priorities, and resolving conflicts, were often left to others.

> *Although it wasn't explicitly stated in every meeting, the underlying belief was apparent: delivery belongs to the vendor, and accountability stops there.*

Agile works best when the team has freedom to make decisions, adjust priorities, and collaborate on solving problems. But in this environment, that control was concentrated outside the team. Stakeholders weren't comfortable giving ownership to the people building the product. They feared letting go. Even when priorities shifted or requirements changed mid-sprint, the timeline remained fixed. Changes occurred, but expectations stayed rigid. It wasn't true Agile adaptability; it was controlled chaos.

Ironically, the team knew what to build. Priorities were set, but never wholly owned. That led to a different kind of dysfunction: developers working with a sense of futility. No matter how hard they pushed or how well they executed, they still faced last-minute changes, finger-pointing, and a lack of appreciation. The emotional toll manifested as frustration, followed by a state of passivity. You could sense it in how people stopped asking "why" and just delivered what was handed to them.

This wasn't about a skill shortage. It was about a lack of shared responsibility.

I focused on clarifying roles, especially regarding ownership and responsibility. I highlighted that Agile isn't a delivery playbook; it's a shared commitment. I explained that sprint planning should be a collaborative negotiation rather than a unilateral decision. It is essential to recognize that the responsibility for delivering value cannot rest solely with the vendor.

However, the response was somewhat lukewarm. There was a prevailing perspective that, having engaged our services, the expectation was for us to take full ownership of the delivery process.

That's the root of the myth: Agile is a delivery engine, not a collaborative mindset. A product owner can participate in the discussions, but managing risk is not solely their responsibility. That timelines stay sacred, but change is always welcome. The vendor leads the execution while the customer watches from a distance for support.

Until that myth is broken, Agile never begins.

Even with clear roles on paper, the day-to-day experience told a different story, where Agile looked the part but rarely behaved like it.

Agile Theater: When Stakeholders Only Care About the Badge

Agile has become the popular standard. Everyone wants the badge, "We're an Agile organization." But few are willing to embrace the behaviors that come with it.

CHAPTER 4   CONFESSION #4: STAKEHOLDERS THINK AGILE IS A MIRACLE CURE

From the outside, this project appeared to follow a textbook Agile setup. There were sprint planning meetings, backlog grooming sessions, daily stand-ups, reviews, and retrospectives. Stakeholders participated in key ceremonies. Dashboards were updated. Metrics were monitored.

But none of it mattered.

Stakeholders' presence often felt observational rather than collaborative. Decisions were seldom made in the room. Feedback was vague. At times, it felt like Agile Theater rather than real Agility.

Backlog grooming sessions became a performance. While stakeholders would establish the priorities, the team had limited ability to question or reorganize them. Rather than fostering a collaborative effort to prioritize, it became more of a unidirectional process. They claimed their hands were tied. So were ours.

The illusion of teamwork hid the truth: all authority, no responsibility.

The most significant waste of time? Endless meetings with no decisions. The right people were present, but approvals were delayed, and subsequent steps were postponed. Hours were spent on circular discussions. The team continued to attend these meetings, but internally, we were aware of their purpose.

> *Frontend rituals to fulfill governance, not backend actions to adapt and improve.*

Now and then, the truth slips out in phrases that reveal the real mindset.

> *Just tell us when it'll be done.*

> *We should finalize the scope soon.*

> *This feels too slow for Agile.*

And there it was, the performance falling apart.

We weren't genuinely using Agile for collaboration. Instead, we were using Agile terminology to justify non-Agile actions. Control wasn't shared. Trust wasn't established. Still, expectations remained sky high.

As the architect, I tried to speak up, not to challenge authority, but to point out the disconnect. I said outright, "What we're doing is anti-Agile." I intended it as a warning. But it was brushed aside. Roles weren't flexible enough to allow that kind of challenge. The Scrum Master couldn't push back. I wasn't supposed to lead the transformation. And so, nothing changed.

Meanwhile, the expense was steep.

Without genuine collaboration, we created a defect-prone product that continually advanced without adequate feedback loops. Quality declined. Morale dropped. Developers stopped suggesting improvements. Instead, they just focused on surviving sprint to sprint, delivering what customers wanted, even if it didn't make sense.

It became a system focused on compliance rather than communication.

Every day felt like we were delivering for appearance rather than results. Agile was the stage. The stakeholders were the audience. And the team? Just actors trying to keep the scene from falling apart.

Amid the disillusionment, I had a choice to make: argue louder or find quieter ways to influence change.

Educating Without Preaching: Playing the Long Game

In environments resistant to change, leadership often manifests quietly.

My official role was in architecture, encompassing structure, design, and scalability. But unofficially? I also managed damage control, acted as a translator, and served as a morale buffer. Agile has been misapplied, misunderstood, and mishandled, but I couldn't fix it through authority. All I had was influence and a stubborn sense of perseverance.

So, I took a different approach: modeling rather than preaching.

CHAPTER 4   CONFESSION #4: STAKEHOLDERS THINK AGILE IS A MIRACLE CURE

When Agile principles were warped into shortcuts for delivery or mere compliance routines, I didn't voice my concerns in the room. That approach was ineffective. The roles weren't designed to allow me to challenge openly, and when I spoke bluntly in earlier attempts, I was quickly shut down. My architect instincts aimed directly for the truth, but truth delivered without proper timing or trust often falls flat.

So, I have changed my approach.

Instead of addressing stakeholders publicly, I started clarifying things privately. I rephrased misunderstood ideas not during meetings but through side conversations, offline discussions, or visual cues in planning decks. I would explain, for example, why moving five stories into a sprint at the last minute disrupts estimation, morale, and flow, not through complaints but with logic.

I didn't always succeed in shifting mindsets, but that wasn't the point.

The actual transformation occurred within the team. Over time, I observed them taking ownership of the process. Even when stakeholders continued to demand more, the team began to push back with data, more realistic planning, and honest retrospectives. They began to see Agile not just as a series of meetings but as a rhythm for self-preservation and mental health.

Patience became the true mark of leadership.

I knew I wouldn't win every argument or even be allowed to have them. But I could demonstrate consistency. I could stay firm without raising my voice. Through that consistency, several improvements occurred: planning became more stable, hands-off methods were enhanced, and teams felt less reactive.

No stakeholder ever approached me and said, "You were right." But a few quietly began asking the right questions. And that was enough.

While most habits were slow to shift, sometimes it only takes one stakeholder to see things differently for momentum to build.

CHAPTER 4   CONFESSION #4: STAKEHOLDERS THINK AGILE IS A MIRACLE CURE

The Stakeholder 180: When Someone Finally Gets It

Not everyone remained in denial.

Most stakeholders clung tightly to their assumptions, treating Agile like a convenience store: drop in, pick what you want, and expect the team to sort out the rest. But one person didn't. Over time, something changed in them. And while it didn't happen overnight, it marked a turning point for them.

Let's refer to him as Arjun.

(Name changed for confidentiality.)

Initially, Arjun was like everyone else: attending ceremonies, meeting deadlines, nodding during demos. He didn't ask many questions and provided little feedback. However, he made decisions, and those decisions often came late, were reactive, or were closely tied to executive pressure.

Then something changed.

It wasn't a training session. It wasn't a major confrontation. It was a sprint demo.

During that sprint, the team worked hard to deliver a set of features with limited guidance. The output was functional but not intuitive. Arjun saw the result and, for the first time, didn't point fingers. He paused, leaned back, and asked a question we had never heard from him before:

Did we not discuss how this is supposed to behave?

A moment of silence. Then he continued.

Maybe I wasn't clear enough.

That one sentence opened the door. For the first time, Arjun wasn't blaming others: he was taking some responsibility himself. In the next few sprints, something important happened: he began attending grooming sessions prepared. He started asking about effort and trade-offs. He brought clarity, not just deadlines. And when scope creep returned, as it always does, he defended the team's boundaries instead of pushing past them.

It didn't make everything perfect, but it changed the room.

Now, when Arjun spoke, his words grounded the team. He became a voice of balance: someone who understood Agile wasn't about loading more work, but about delivering the right thing at the right time with shared responsibility.

It only takes one person to change the energy of a project. Arjun became that person.

> *Arjun didn't just take the shot for him; it connected. Because it did, the team finally gained an advocate who spoke their language at the table where it mattered.*

Encouragement helps, but every Agile journey also hits a moment where boundaries must be set to protect the team and the process.

Tough Love: Setting Boundaries on Agile Misuse

Sometimes, the most agile thing you can do is say no.

There comes a point in every dysfunctional Agile environment where diplomacy isn't enough: where allowing problems to persist silently causes more harm than confrontation ever could. That moment arrived for me when a dependent team's pressure nearly derailed ours.

It all started with a release deadline. A stakeholder from another team insisted aggressively that our team deliver specific features for an upcoming launch. The twist? Their team hadn't started development yet and wouldn't for another two or three sprints. Despite this, the urgency somehow landed on us, as though the delay was ours to fix.

No one doubted it.

CHAPTER 4   CONFESSION #4: STAKEHOLDERS THINK AGILE IS A MIRACLE CURE

Everyone just absorbed the pressure. My team felt concerned: working overtime to support a release that didn't need to be ready for weeks. The dependent team remained unchallenged, and the stakeholders continued to nod. That's when I decided to push back.

I presented the facts: our team's committed velocity, when the features are truly needed, the dependent team's actual start date, and why rushing now would only introduce risk without value.

"If their sprint isn't even starting for another three sprints," I finally asked, "what exactly are we rushing toward right now?"

It wasn't a challenge; it was a boundary. Not to push back, but to protect the team from unnecessary pressure.

The initial reaction was tense. The team in question didn't like the attention. But the logic was airtight. With my manager and Scrum Master backing me up, the case was undeniable. We weren't just defending our team; we were raising the right questions that no one else had taken the time to ask.

And something changed.

Stakeholders, who had previously followed the louder team without question, started asking their questions. The blind alignment began to diminish. Dependencies were examined more carefully. And for the first time, our team didn't feel like we were the only ones bearing the burden.

The moment of "no" became a turning point. Not because it won an argument, but because it rebalanced the equation.

Agile doesn't mean always saying yes. It means saying yes to the right things, at the right time, with the proper support. Sometimes, protecting your team is the most Agile act of all.

That moment of pushback didn't just reset expectations, it opened the door for new habits, better conversations, and deeper alignment.

CHAPTER 4   CONFESSION #4: STAKEHOLDERS THINK AGILE IS A MIRACLE CURE

Lessons in Alignment: Recalibrating Stakeholder Expectations

Change didn't happen overnight. It arrived in pieces: through habits, understanding, and subtle changes in dialogue.

After months of pressure and pushback, the team began taking ownership not only of the work but also of the narrative surrounding the work. And that changed everything.

One of the initial breakthroughs came from something deceptively simple: creating and sizing epic-level backlogs. We moved away from firefighting, sprint by sprint, and started thinking in terms of epics, breaking down work in ways that made effort and impact transparent to stakeholders. That became the foundation for something even more valuable: a forecastable roadmap.

Once we had sized epics, we could create a timeline. Sprint forecasting became feasible, although not perfect, and was achievable. And when stakeholders saw the flow rather than guessing it, expectations began to soften. What once felt like vague commitments started to feel like trackable conversations.

We also intentionally changed our communication methods.

We reduced the frequency of meetings, and when we did meet, we eliminated distractions; no more endless status updates. Instead, we concentrated on blockers and appreciations. What was slowing us down? What went well? The signal became clearer, and the noise faded away.

Just as importantly, we began setting boundaries, not just defensively, but transparently. If a request came in mid-sprint, we didn't mindlessly push back. We showed the trade-offs.

> *We can proceed with this, but that means we'll have to drop feature X.*
>
> *If you want Y sooner, we need to either delay Z or reassign it.*
>
> *This scope is feasible, but not within this timeline.*

CHAPTER 4   CONFESSION #4: STAKEHOLDERS THINK AGILE IS A MIRACLE CURE

This didn't eliminate conflict, but it reshaped it. Stakeholders began to view trade-offs as a collective decision, rather than just the team saying no.

And then, the shift occurred.

Questions have been changed.

They no longer focused on velocity; they focused on value.

Not "Why aren't we done yet?" but "What's the impact if we don't do this now?"

Not "Can you add this too?" but "What will this displace if we do?"

Empathy filled the room.

Stakeholders started to value the planning effort. They trusted the forecasts. They made room for blockers instead of pushing harder. And for the first time, it felt like we weren't just delivering to them, we were working with them.

> *Alignment doesn't come from perfection. It comes from being genuine, transparent, and willing to share the burden of tough decisions.*

Agile finally felt less like a process we were managing and more like a language we were communicating in together.

But alignment on process only goes so far if the culture underneath still speaks a different language.

The Cultural Layer: Agile As a Common Language

Agile only succeeds when it becomes a shared language: not just in vocabulary, but in how people think, lead, or relate to each other.

That wasn't the case for a long time in one project.

CHAPTER 4   CONFESSION #4: STAKEHOLDERS THINK AGILE IS A MIRACLE CURE

Everyone knows the terms: stand-ups, sprints, epics, velocity, but the underlying behavior still echoes the waterfall model. Plans were declared, not negotiated. Accountability was outsourced, not shared. Leaders gave directions, not feedback. And decisions were centralized, even though Agile was supposed to distribute them.

> *We were "doing Agile," but the culture remained command-and-control.*

The tension was evident, reaching a peak during a conflict between the Scrum Coach and several key stakeholders. The coach tried to shift the focus to team empowerment, iterative planning, and servant leadership, but it strongly clashed with current practices. Eventually, the coach left, and Agile went from a mandate to a memory.

But sometimes, culture doesn't change until the pain makes it unavoidable.

After that, the coach left, and we went through a tough release cycle. Misalignment, overpromising, and poor cross-team coordination led to a chaotic delivery process. It wasn't easy. However, it was strangely helpful.

Because after that storm, something opened up.

Stakeholders, some of whom resisted feedback for months, began asking more insightful questions. They appeared differently during sprint reviews. They stopped pushing scope mindlessly and started listening. Feedback, once dismissed as a delay, became part of the rhythm. Transparency, once avoided, was tolerated and then encouraged.

It wasn't a complete transformation. Ownership still lagged. Teams still needed reminders. But culturally, Agile stopped being just a show. It became the common language. People began thinking in terms of iterations and inquiring about trade-offs. Accepting that change has a cost. The ceremonies stayed, but now they had purpose.

> *That's when I realized, Agile doesn't succeed just by being implemented. It succeeds when it's truly absorbed.*

Not because everyone is trained or because a consultant provides a roadmap, but because the culture learns to ask different questions, value feedback, seek clarity, and trust the people closest to the work.

It took effort and setbacks, but gradually, we started to speak Agile, rather than just doing it.

It was only after these cultural undercurrents began to shift that the real lesson emerged, one that reframed how we saw Agile entirely.

Final Reflection: Agile Isn't the Cure, It's the Commitment

Agile doesn't fail because the framework is flawed. It fails when people treat it like a fix instead of a discipline, when it's expected to work like a cure rather than be practiced like a commitment.

Looking back, I now see that Agile wasn't our problem. It was our early warning system. From the very beginning, it revealed the truth about our delivery culture, truths we weren't ready to face. It exposed gaps we would have learned to ignore: unclear ownership, poor prioritization, and a deeply rooted habit of control without accountability. It reflected the disconnect between the language we used and the behaviors we normalized.

Agile didn't hide our dysfunction; it revealed it. It showed us that having sprint ceremonies on the calendar doesn't mean we're collaborating. That a product owner being present doesn't guarantee decisions are being made. That tracking velocity doesn't automatically mean we're delivering value. Agile was the mirror, and we didn't always like what we saw.

It would have been easy to dismiss it. Some did. I heard more than once that "Agile isn't working for this project." But the truth was more straightforward and more uncomfortable: Agile was working precisely as intended. It reflected the chaos, rather than causing it.

The change didn't come from switching tools or reading playbooks. It went from a slow, stubborn shift in how people started to show up. At first, it was just one or two who asked better questions, choosing to explain instead of escalating. Then, gradually, the conversations shifted, from status reports to blocker discussions, from control to trade-offs, from velocity obsession to real user value. It wasn't perfect. It was messy and frustrating at times. But it was real.

That's the part no one mentions when they pitch Agile as a solution. It's not a shortcut. It's a long, winding journey that only succeeds if you commit to sticking with it. Not just the teams, but also the stakeholders, sponsors, and leaders. Agile doesn't deliver results on its own. What it does is create space for people to collaborate, prioritize, and take ownership of the outcomes together.

What we learned: gradually, imperfectly, but significantly, is that Agile only starts to work when people stop trying to use it to fix their projects and instead start using it to face the truth about how they work. The moment we stopped waiting for Agile to save us and embraced the hard work of trust, alignment, and ownership was the moment things began to change.

Agile isn't the cure. It never was.

It's the commitment.

Takeaway Confession　If there's one confession I'll carry from this experience, it's that I once believed Agile would fix everything, until I realized Agile doesn't fix anything at all. What it does is uncover the hard truths we spend years avoiding. And in that moment of exposure, we either retreat to old habits or step up and commit. I've seen both happen. But the teams that thrive aren't the ones that follow Agile, they're the ones that own it, together.

CHAPTER 5

Confession #5: The Myth of Requirements (or Lack Thereof)

Good requirements are like a compass; they guide the project towards its destination while allowing for flexibility along the way.

—Unknown

There is a common misconception that Agile doesn't require requirements. We can start with a less focused approach to preparing requirements and catch up while building the application. However, the truth is that planning is crucial, and having clarity isn't just an extra; it's essential. I believed parts of this at one point, and many of my stakeholders thought it even more.

But reality hit differently.

CHAPTER 5   CONFESSION #5: THE MYTH OF REQUIREMENTS (OR LACK THEREOF)

Agile doesn't promise magic. It promises movement. And without direction, that movement turns into chaos. Teams that begin without any clarity aren't embracing Agile; they're improvising under pressure. And eventually, that pressure breaks something: the flow, the morale, the trust.

In this chapter, I reflect on the myth that Agile can thrive without requirements, exploring how it played out in real projects, what went wrong, and what we ultimately learned. These stories aren't about tools or templates. They're about people caught in a process they didn't fully understand, and how we found our way back to sanity through better conversations, thoughtful discovery, and just enough planning to stay grounded.

Because Agile doesn't work without requirements.

It works when requirements are allowed to evolve, within a framework that keeps everyone facing the same direction.

The stage was set for misunderstanding, and it didn't take long before that misunderstanding became a recurring theme in our Agile journey.

The Mirage of "No Requirements in Agile"

"Agile doesn't need requirements. Let's start building something; we'll refine it later."

- It's a tempting shortcut, but it often leads to long-term detours, rework, and regret. Agile welcomes change, but that doesn't mean it thrives in chaos.

I've heard this so many times I can't count. Usually, it's said with a confident smile, as if Agile is some magic trick that allows you to start coding without understanding what the business actually needs. One customer even kicked off the engagement with a breezy "We haven't documented any requirements, and we don't plan to."

CHAPTER 5   CONFESSION #5: THE MYTH OF REQUIREMENTS (OR LACK THEREOF)

When I joined that project, I wasn't the Scrum Master, but I still remember the phrase echoing in my mind like a warning signal in disguise. The team was actively engaged in development, but there was a need for greater clarity. There was a common misconception that Agile meant speed over shared understanding. Many stories lacked the completeness needed for smooth execution, and formal validation was often bypassed. Every sprint started with energy but ended with work that felt more stitched together.

As someone with an architecture background, I was trained to expect some level of basic planning, at least for business stories. I'm all for lightweight technical stories because developers know the domain, but expecting developers to infer business intent without foundational context? That's how team end up rewriting features instead of delivering value.

In the early days of that project, tensions surfaced quickly. Delivery timelines were questioned, even as the team was tasked with both building the solution and shaping the requirements simultaneously. It felt like we were laying the foundation while still sketching the blueprint. Every sprint brought its share of surprises, because clarity was always a step behind execution.

We weren't just lacking direction; we didn't have the space to pause and think. The team, eager to show progress in demos, often had to move forward with partial clarity. The focus subtly shifted toward delivering visible output over ensuring we were solving the right problems. And when issues emerged, the response was less about how we captured stories and more about why the team didn't interpret them as intended.

That's the common misconception: the idea that Agile can succeed without requirements. In reality, Agile works with evolving requirements, not none. There's a difference. If you want to change the flavor of a dish mid-sprint, sure, we can add some spice. But changing the main ingredient while it's already in the oven? That's a recipe for trouble.

CHAPTER 5   CONFESSION #5: THE MYTH OF REQUIREMENTS (OR LACK THEREOF)

To this day, I explain it like this: evolving requirements are welcome, but they shouldn't derail the committed goals of a sprint. If the story isn't ready, admit it. Groom the backlog. Avoid placing unrefined ideas into the sprint, which ends up transferring ambiguity into the team's court. Agile isn't a shortcut for chaos; it's a compass that helps us navigate it.

If I could re-educate stakeholders on one thing, it would be this: "Prioritize only well-shaped user stories. If something isn't ready, it's better to acknowledge it than to force it forward. The backlog is a staging area, not an emergency room."

Agile doesn't remove the need for clarity. It simply allows clarity to develop without halting momentum. The sooner teams and clients understand this, the fewer broken sprints we'll need to recover from.

These early signs of misalignment weren't isolated, they reflected a larger pattern of how requirements were undervalued across the effort.

Requirements Were Treated like Afterthoughts

If you aren't clear on what your business needs, don't rush the team into guessing. Agile isn't a shortcut to avoid clarity; it's a guide that supports progress as clarity emerges.

It was a modernization project: a fresh product, a newly formed team, and an ambitious vision. On paper, it looked like a clean slate. But what landed on our desk wasn't a roadmap; it was a blank canvas with a fast-approaching deadline.

Designs were still evolving. The user stories were often incomplete, vague, or placeholders at best. The team was asked to begin "foundation work": setting up core structures, page flows, and basic wiring; yet, none of it was grounded in confirmed business processes. Still, the momentum was hard to stop. "Let's make progress," we were told. "We will refine things along the way."

CHAPTER 5 CONFESSION #5: THE MYTH OF REQUIREMENTS (OR LACK THEREOF)

And so, we began. Slowly. Hesitantly. Unsure if the direction we were heading was even relevant.

As the lead enterprise architect, I wasn't the one leading Scrum ceremonies, but I was closely engaged with the development team. I could sense the discomfort in our stand-ups as developers struggled to piece together purpose from fragments.

BAs didn't have signed-off requirements because, frankly, there was no formal process to indicate readiness or sign-off within the user story lifecycle. The only gate we had was a casual review that happened just before grooming, and by then, it was often too late to fix foundational gaps.

The business process was still changing. The product owners were working through open questions with the client. Meanwhile, the client's consultant, supporting the client, provided us with "business" requirements. But we later discovered that those inputs didn't fully align with how the customer's business operated in practice.

It all fell apart during the first demo. Two sprints in, we showed what we had built to a panel of business users. Their reaction wasn't just disappointment; it was disbelief.

This is not how our business operates.

Where did these flows even come from?

You obviously don't understand what we need.

The room went silent, then defensiveness arose. The product owners were stunned, and the client stakeholders scrambled for explanations. Everyone was shocked, except the team. We could feel it coming closer little by little, and eventually, we had to confront it head-on.

That demo damaged something, not in the code, but in morale. The team had tried, guessed, and built with heart. But now their work was dismissed as irrelevant. It felt like betrayal. They weren't angry; they were disengaged. And that's worse.

CHAPTER 5   CONFESSION #5: THE MYTH OF REQUIREMENTS (OR LACK THEREOF)

We made it to the initial go-live, even if just barely. We delivered something, but we all understood it was a fragile foundation. The real turning point came later. That's when the planning session became real. That's when stakeholders realized that ambiguity carries a price, and Agile gives us room to adapt, but it doesn't eliminate the need for clarity.

Looking back, here is the lesson I keep with me, and I share it every chance I get:

If the business is still forming, don't rush the team into making assumptions. Agile works best when clarity develops over time, but it still needs a starting point. That's not iteration; that's risk without guardrails. Taking a moment to align early could cost far less than circling back for rework later.

That project made me rethink what Agile discovery truly means. It's not about driving in the dark. It starts with something meaningful, then evolves responsibly.

But it wasn't just about unclear inputs, it was about decisions made despite that uncertainty, which led to one of the most pivotal missteps in our delivery.

The Sprint That Never Should Have Started

If you're not prepared, speak up. Transparency builds alignment, while unspoken gaps quietly derail even the best efforts.

It was one of those moments when everything inside me said, "Don't do this," but the sprint started anyway.

There was uncertainty surrounding the scope for the next phase, and the backlog had not yet reached a ready state. Yet the momentum to "keep the team moving" was strong from all sides. Leadership and stakeholders alike hoped to avoid delays. So we moved ahead, even without the clarity we needed.

CHAPTER 5 CONFESSION #5: THE MYTH OF REQUIREMENTS (OR LACK THEREOF)

The team's reaction was almost critical, if not for the frustration.

Are we going to do this? With what?

They weren't joking around. They were confused, unsure what to build, and looking to me, as their Scrum Master, for answers I didn't have.

And honestly? I had already warned them. I had told the stakeholders, the leads, everyone who would listen: "We are not ready. Starting a sprint without a groomed backlog turns Agile into ritual, not progress."

But the decision had already been made. So, I let it unfold. Sometimes the only way to reveal structural gaps is to let the system show its own imbalance.

As expected, the sprint fell apart. The stories we selected were full of unknowns. There was no clear understanding of the business process, which made every delivery attempt feel like guesswork. And by the time the missing inputs started coming in, it was too late. The rework needed would have been as much as starting over.

So, we missed the sprint. And through that failure, we finally gained the chance to reset.

We paused development and temporarily moved the team to support another group with prepared work. Meanwhile, we initiated an interim discovery phase: conducting discovery, aligning on scope, and validating business flow to set the next phase for success.

The sprint demo? It told the story clearly, but confusion had replaced clarity. But no one blamed the team. I had already given the stakeholders a clear heads-up. "If we go forward with this sprint, it's likely to break down before it delivers anything meaningful." And if the only goal is to keep the team occupied, it's wiser to redirect them across other deliverables and bring them back once we are truly ready. That way we burn stories, not just time.

There was hesitation at first. But after the results, there was no resistance to change. They understood.

CHAPTER 5   CONFESSION #5: THE MYTH OF REQUIREMENTS (OR LACK THEREOF)

The team emerged from the sprint quiet, but not disheartened. There is a particular kind of silence that follows effort, not defeat. When people know the outcome was beyond their control, they need someone to voice it.

What we learned that day shaped our Agile practice in the future. Every sprint now begins with a straightforward check-in.

Are we really prepared to commit?

If not, we pause and have the tough conversations early. Clarity upfront is better than cleanup later.

Agile doesn't reward activity; it rewards clarity. Pushing forward without real readiness often costs far more than taking a short pause to prepare.

That sprint taught us the cost of starting without readiness, but we weren't done learning. Another integration effort soon revealed a different kind of risk: quiet assumptions.

False Starts and Forced Assumptions

When answers are missing, assumptions fill in the gaps. And if those assumptions are wrong, everything built on them is also flawed.

It was a crucial integration, a cornerstone of the new system we were updating. Everything relied on it. Yet, everything about it was unclear.

There was no clear documentation, no defined data contract, no test environment that mimicked production, and worst of all, no reachable team on the other side. We weren't integrating with a black box; we were navigating an invisible system with no active feedback.

We tried. We reached out. But the responses were minimal, slow, and vague. The communication was always reactive, not proactive. When we asked a question about a specific constraint, the response only addressed that constraint. It was like climbing stairs, step by step, with difficulty.

CHAPTER 5   CONFESSION #5: THE MYTH OF REQUIREMENTS (OR LACK THEREOF)

The business logic? Unknown. The validations? Undocumented. The actual integration team remained largely unavailable throughout, making it difficult to gain early insights.

So, we made assumptions.

First, we guessed what validations they might be doing. Then, when that failed, we made more assumptions:

We assumed minor rounding would be acceptable, as no precision rules were clearly specified.

Since we did not receive any constraints, we assumed that they would perform data type validation.

We made a wild guess about what is optional and what is mandatory.

There was immense pressure to deliver. The existing integration was being sunset. This wasn't just a nice-to-have modernization; it was a kill switch for the old path, and we were racing against it.

The business clearly stated:

We have to go live with the new one. Just get it done.

So, we did. The team moved forward, constrained by time and limited clarity. It felt like a high-stakes sprint with no room for exploration or iteration. Guardrails were minimal, and validation was sparse; we hoped that what we delivered would align with expectations.

I wasn't the Scrum Master in this case; I was the architect. I played the intermediary role, communicating between our team and the customer's SMEs, trying to understand what the system expected. Even the client-side leadership occasionally discovered unexpected behavior from their own system.

They said, we wish we could give you more clarity.

But we aren't even sure what that team's reasoning is.

CHAPTER 5   CONFESSION #5: THE MYTH OF REQUIREMENTS (OR LACK THEREOF)

It felt like navigating uncertainty on a ticking clock.

After much struggle, countless cups of coffee, and sleepless nights, we finally achieved our goal. When we reached the milestone, the process left the team fatigued and unsure about the stability of the integration.

What I took away from that experience was sobering:

When clarity isn't possible, creativity becomes your only defense.

Assumptions are unavoidable in Agile. However, unless they are tracked, validated, and managed, they can turn into liabilities.

Now, whenever I see a team rushing into an assumption or a heavy sprint, I don't just ask, "Are we clear?" I say:

> *Let's list every assumption we're making right now. Say it out loud, then ask: 'How will we know if this causes problems later?"*

Because nothing is more dangerous than a silent guess included in a production release.

After firefighting through uncertainty, the need for upstream clarity became impossible to ignore, prompting a shift in how we approached preparation.

Discovery Sprints Aren't a Luxury

Discovery isn't wasted time; it's anticipation of future success.

After several setbacks, we realized something needed to change. We had been moving too quickly with too little clarity, rushing into loosely defined requirements, chasing deadlines, and fixing problems we could have avoided. Eventually, the pressure to "just keep going" shifted to a more realistic approach: recognizing that slowing down might actually help us go further.

CHAPTER 5 CONFESSION #5: THE MYTH OF REQUIREMENTS (OR LACK THEREOF)

We chose to begin a discovery sprint, even though we didn't officially call it that at first. There was no formal pause or major announcement. It started quietly during a transition between two large development efforts, when a brief period of breathing room allowed us to consider our next steps more thoughtfully.

We focused on what truly matters: understanding the business needs, honestly assessing what our platform and team can deliver, and checking how prepared our integration points are for upcoming changes. These weren't just formal meetings; they were practical, engaging sessions centered on what's feasible, aligned, and well-planned.

We conducted backlog refinement with a genuine purpose this time. Wireframes were discussed with business users before being presented to the team. Data flows and integration behaviors were clarified from the beginning. And for once, the stories that entered the backlog were not just placeholders; they were decisions.

Some stakeholders initially pushed back. A non-development sprint appeared to slow momentum. However, many still felt the effects of our past mistakes. They remembered the confusion, rework, and late pivots. Although this pause was uneasy, it felt necessary.

Not the entire team was involved; some remained finishing previous tasks. However, those who attended the discovery sessions felt something different: a sense of clarity. A much-needed feeling of relief after weeks of scrambling. Instead of entering the next sprint, guessing what success should look like, we began with a shared purpose.

No one needed to say, "We should have done this earlier." The value spoke for itself, through sharper stand-ups, more connected demos to business value, and a team carrying a quiet confidence we hadn't seen in weeks.

Now, when someone says that discovery is a waste of time or just "extra process," I try to ground the conversation.

CHAPTER 5   CONFESSION #5: THE MYTH OF REQUIREMENTS (OR LACK THEREOF)

Be mindful, as you may be approaching a crucial turning point; Agile thrives on flexibility and collaboration, but that doesn't mean structure is the enemy. Sometimes, adopting a more phased or sequential approach during discovery can help reduce ambiguity and align expectations early. Its not about abandoning Agile; its about choosing the right level of structure to support meaningful iteration later.

Yet not all gaps stemmed from process; sometimes, they came from stakeholders still discovering their own evolving needs.

When Stakeholders Don't Know What They Want

We can fix technical problems anytime. But if we don't surface business clarity early, we're building with blindfolds.

There was a time when we not only discovered requirements late, but also found understanding late. It was a large-scale project aimed at digitizing what had historically been a very manual, spreadsheet-driven business process. And in the beginning, even the stakeholders were still exploring what a digital solution might look like.

It wasn't about politics or misalignment. It was simply that the clarity of vision was still forming, something many transformation projects encounter.

Early on, conversations often circled around familiar Excel tables rather than application wireframes. During UX sessions, feedback tended to be explorative rather than directive. We built based on the initial tasks, but it wasn't until the demo that the true business needs and reactions started to surface.

CHAPTER 5 CONFESSION #5: THE MYTH OF REQUIREMENTS (OR LACK THEREOF)

And they weren't minor adjustments. After the demo, we often found ourselves rewriting user flows entirely. Even worse, during User Acceptance Testing (UAT), steps away from production, we encountered new stakeholders whose perspectives triggered additional changes.

The warning signs were there. One group would join during UX reviews, another for the demo, and yet another during UAT. Each wave introduced new gaps. Features that once seemed complete suddenly open to reinterpretation. The application kept changing, not because we built it incorrectly, but because we had not established a shared understanding.

As the architect, I worked closely with the Scrum Master to keep the team steady, but it was a challenge. Frustration was evident in stand-ups, review sessions, and even casual Teams chats. Yet, we understood the context. The business teams weren't intentionally creating churn; they were learning alongside us. This project was as much a discovery of their process as it was a delivery of software.

The turning point came after our first challenging release. That's when we adopted a new rhythm: business workshops before UX. These weren't long sessions filled with jargon. They were simple, visual, and designed for storytelling. We would whiteboard processes, mock user journeys, and walk through real business use cases, before even thinking about screens or stories.

And it worked.

Suddenly, the same stakeholders who had been previously confused were now leading the sessions with clarity. They were pouring out process flows, edge cases, validations, and "what-if" scenarios that would've never surfaced during UAT. These workshops became the heartbeat of every release cycle, transforming everything.

By the time we reached the third release, we no longer feared demos. Business feedback was sharper, more relevant, and aligned across teams. There were fewer surprises in UAT, and delivery felt less like damage control and more like a well-executed process.

CHAPTER 5   CONFESSION #5: THE MYTH OF REQUIREMENTS (OR LACK THEREOF)

That experience changed how I approach stakeholder engagement forever.

Now, I tell every new Scrum Master and Product Owner the same thing:

> *Don't delay your focus on business validation until UAT. Get key business users in the room early. Solve the business flows first, and the tech can follow.*
>
> *Because if you wait until the end to make sure the business is on board, you're not Agile. You're just doing Waterfall with daily standups.*

While the alignment eventually improved, a different challenge emerged, one that traded ambiguity for acceleration, often without room to think ahead.

Short-Termism: The Roadblock to Product Vision

> *Agile isn't about speed. It's about value. And if you confuse the two, your delivery will outpace your direction.*

There's a new trend quietly taking over Agile programs, one that appears productive on the surface but slowly erodes the product vision from within: short-termism. And I've seen it take root more times than I can count.

It often starts innocently. A customer, fresh off their first release, finally sees something working. After years of slow progress, the velocity of Agile feels like a breakthrough. Momentum builds, enthusiasm grows.

> *Can we go live every quarter?*
>
> *Can we push releases every two months?*
>
> *Isn't that what mature Agile teams do?*

CHAPTER 5 CONFESSION #5: THE MYTH OF REQUIREMENTS (OR LACK THEREOF)

For a product company with years of embedded Agile culture. But in the service industry, where many customers are still learning Agile while doing it, that same pace can become a liability.

I recall a customer who had never gone live in under two years. But once they tasted an MVP, they wanted multiple releases per quarter. The motivation wasn't funding or compliance; it was Agile culture. They'd heard that fast releases were the mark of a "modern" team. And from that point on, cadence took priority over clarity.

The result? Execution became an afterthought. The release itself, its checklist, its ceremonies, and its overhead became the real product. Teams were caught in constant delivery mode, bouncing between UAT, bug fixes, deployment prep, and the next sprint kickoff without a moment to reflect or refine.

Parallel development became the norm. The team was planning, scoping, and designing two or sometimes three releases simultaneously. Discovery overlapped with UX. UAT overlapped with development. And somehow, it was all meant to run smoothly, relying on the same people, velocity, and stakeholders.

It didn't.

Our team was working tirelessly, often burning the midnight oil, which started to take a toll on our work quality. The speed picked up, not because of increased efficiency, but due to the immense pressure we faced. Although our stakeholders initially were full of excitement, they started to experience stress. The product's trajectory frequently changed, not because of a new vision, but because there wasn't enough time for careful consideration. In conclusion, I recognized the urgent need to advocate for a more balanced strategy to ensure success!

I plotted out the reality: the overlapping release cycles, the resource constraints, the business logic debt we were accumulating sprint by sprint. I showed them that while it was technically possible to run multiple

CHAPTER 5   CONFESSION #5: THE MYTH OF REQUIREMENTS (OR LACK THEREOF)

releases in parallel, the real bottlenecks weren't the developers; they were the stakeholders. You cannot scale UX design, business validations, and integration testing indefinitely. Execution needed breathing room.

I asked for a strategic planning window, a pause to step back and realign.

While there was alignment in place, execution kept slipping. One more deadline. Another urgent release. A sprint deemed too critical to delay. By the fourth or fifth release, each one was more complex and taxing than the last; the need for change became undeniable.

Eventually, we made the shift gradually. We adjusted the rhythm and started discovery earlier. We also reduced the number of active parallel initiatives. And at last, we began to build for impact, not just delivery.

What I learned through this experience is something I now share with every client, every team:

Short-term delivery should always be a strategy, not a default.

You cannot pursue it unthinkingly, especially if stakeholder engagement, requirement stability, and vision alignment are still evolving.

Now, when a customer wants to go "Agile at breakneck speed," I don't talk about sprints. I talk about readiness. Because

> *Speed without focus doesn't take you further; it just breaks you faster.*

To balance that pressure for speed, we had to revisit how we planned, not by adding process, but by right-sizing it.

Teaching the Value of Just Enough Planning

You're not running a factory of AI bots. You're leading real people, plan like it.

CHAPTER 5   CONFESSION #5: THE MYTH OF REQUIREMENTS (OR LACK THEREOF)

There was a time when we treated planning like a checkbox. Before each release, we designated the same buffer periods: before UX, before development, and before UAT, as if every release were the same. It didn't matter if the upcoming change was a minor tweak or a major module launch. We used the same cookie-cutter planning structure every time.

It made us feel organized. But it didn't make us efficient.

Eventually, the cracks started to show. We were planning for execution instead of planning on top of execution. The "buffer" we had proudly built into our schedule became a blank template we pasted over every milestone.

What triggered the change wasn't some major catastrophe. It was the slow burn of a struggling team. The team was showing signs of fatigue with each release. Even short releases, meant to be lightweight, were draining. We were stacking delivery expectations without ever questioning: Do we need this much structure for every cycle?

After four or five rapid releases, we took a step back.

Instead of defaulting to blanket processes, we started sizing the business complexity, the effort involved, and the integration dependencies, and then planned the release schedule accordingly. At any given time, we limited execution to two concurrent release efforts. Everything else: UX, discovery, and story grooming could proceed in the pipeline. But the development team? They had breathing room.

This shift changed everything.

The developers were relieved. No more mental ping-pong between overlapping releases. With better focus came better ownership. They started treating their features like product engineers, not ticket-pushers. Stories weren't just "next up" items; they were theirs to own from idea to delivery.

Stakeholders noticed the difference, too. They weren't just seeing faster delivery; they were seeing cleaner delivery. Fewer late-stage surprises. More alignment. They welcomed the new model, even if it meant abandoning the illusion of perfectly fixed release cycles. Some releases were shorter. Some took longer. But all of them were clearer.

89

And that was the trade-off: consistency in clarity, not uniformity in timeline.

What made it work wasn't a new tool or framework; it was common sense.

We didn't change how the teams executed. We stopped pretending that all work needed the same overhead. And more importantly, we acknowledged the truth we had been ignoring: teams aren't machines, and context switching comes with a cost.

These days, when people ask me how to balance planning, I keep it simple:

> *Use what works for your team. Don't force a planning model because it looks Agile on paper. If you notice constant rework due to unclear flows, try designing the UI a sprint earlier. If multiple teams are burning out due to parallel streams, stagger your development. Planning isn't about control, it's about clarity.*

And when I see clients trying to run five parallel releases, I remind them:

> *There's no universal formula that can scale delivery across teams like automation. We're working with humans, not AI bots. Respect the context-switch tax. Respect the lead time humans need to work with purpose.*

"Just enough" planning isn't a compromise. It's a discipline. And it takes wisdom to know when to stop planning, and start building.

That led us to embrace a subtler shift, focusing less on mapping every move, and more on setting direction with confidence, even in uncertainty.

CHAPTER 5   CONFESSION #5: THE MYTH OF REQUIREMENTS (OR LACK THEREOF)

The Agile Compass: Navigating Without a Map, Not Without Direction

In Agile, you don't need to see the whole trail; you need to know which way is uphill.

There's a difference between being lost and being uncertain.

Early in my journey, if a project didn't have complete requirements, I saw red flags everywhere. No detailed roadmap? No full UX? No 20-page BRD? That felt like a setup for failure.

However, Agile changed that lens, though not overnight, but rather project by project. We had to deliver something, even if we didn't have everything. And the secret wasn't brute force; it was learning how to guide without controlling.

Most of our projects didn't start with complete answers. You've seen that in earlier stories: unclear scope, pivoting business needs, assumptions that unraveled mid-sprint. But over time, we learned to trade control for clarity. We didn't need to map every turn; we just needed a compass.

Sometimes, that compass was a shared goal. Sometimes, it was a well-articulated user persona. Often, it was simply a matter of having a clear understanding of what not to build. One step at a time was okay, as long as we could see that one step. That shift changed everything.

With even partial direction, the team engaged differently. The team wasn't building blindly anymore; it was moving with purpose. And it showed in the way they asked questions, took ownership, and solved problems. The panic faded. Autonomy emerged.

There were moments when someone would still say, "We'll figure it out as we go." But unlike the chaos we saw in earlier projects, this time it worked, because we had enough guidance to keep us from drifting. We weren't free-falling. We were navigating.

CHAPTER 5   CONFESSION #5: THE MYTH OF REQUIREMENTS (OR LACK THEREOF)

Stakeholders noticed the change too. It felt unfamiliar to them, especially those used to seeing everything modeled, signed off, and locked in. However, as they saw results and their feedback shaped the following steps, they became part of the compass. Alignment replaced resistance. Collaboration replaced checklist approvals.

For me, that was the most significant shift as a leader. I stopped being the one who pushed a roadmap and started becoming the one who clarified direction. Agile has genuinely opened my eyes to the essence of leadership, not just having a flawless plan, but embracing adaptability in the face of change.

The Agile compass embodies a collaborative understanding that steers our choices when documentation falls short. Although it may not detail every step, it reliably directs us toward delivering meaningful value.

So, when a team asks, "We don't have full requirements, can we still start?"

I now respond:

If you know what success should feel like, even if you don't know exactly how it looks, you've already got your compass.

That's all Agile is.
Not map-driven. Not milestone-obsessed.
Just clear enough to move with confidence, not chaos.

These stories, layered across projects and roles, all pointed to the same realization: clarity isn't about control, it's about purpose.

Final Reflection: Clarity Isn't a Constraint, It's a Catalyst

Agile doesn't remove the need for direction; it removes the illusion that everything must be known upfront.

CHAPTER 5 CONFESSION #5: THE MYTH OF REQUIREMENTS (OR LACK THEREOF)

If there's one thing I've learned about requirements in Agile, it's that clarity is not a luxury; it's a compass. Agile isn't about speed. It's not about skipping requirements. And it's certainly not about charging forward without a map. It's about knowing where you're headed, even if you don't see every step of the journey.

The most significant shift for me was letting go of the false binary: that we either need complete requirements or none at all. The truth lies in the middle. We need just enough to get started, and just enough discipline to learn as we move forward.

Looking back at earlier projects, with missed demos, reworked features, and growing team fatigue, it became clear the problem wasn't in the process, but in how we approached it, as if momentum could substitute for clarity. At first, it was easy to believe that "going Agile" meant we could find clarity through building alone, hoping that starting would guide us. To improve, we should emphasize clear goals and effective communication, ensuring that everyone understands the project's direction from the outset.

And while that belief may give stakeholders the illusion of progress, it's the teams who bear the cost, the developers who build without context. The Scrum Masters are trapped between expectations and ambiguity. The architects find themselves weaving together assumptions instead of real solutions.

To every Scrum Master facing vague stories and stakeholder pressure, I say this: take a stand. Don't let the backlog turn into a wish list. If stories aren't ready, stabilize. Take a sprint, maybe two, to regain clarity. But don't normalize the chaos. Anything beyond that, and you're no longer running a sprint; you're running in circles.

Clarity isn't about piles of documentation; it's about shared purpose. A team that knows why they're building, even if the how is still emerging. It means resisting the urge to appear productive through blind decisions, because even the busiest teams can build the wrong product.

CHAPTER 5   CONFESSION #5: THE MYTH OF REQUIREMENTS (OR LACK THEREOF)

So, when a client says, "We're Agile now, we don't need to plan," I don't push back. I reframe the conversation. Agile doesn't eliminate planning; it elevates adaptable planning to a necessity. It's not about locking down certainty. It's about preparing well enough to pivot when the moment comes.

Don't start a project without requirements. You wouldn't start an engine without fuel. You need something, just enough, to move forward. If the discovery phase doesn't uncover enough to guide the first step, it may be worth pausing to align before moving forward. Fill the tank before you hit the road.

Takeaway Confession   Clarity is not the enemy of agility, it's what makes it possible. When pressure mounts to "jump straight into development," your job as a Scrum Master isn't to demand certainty; it's to protect direction. Whether it means carving out discovery time, aligning on business value, or helping stakeholders prioritize what truly matters and what can wait, you're not there to follow process for the sake of process. You're there to be the compass. Agile doesn't need a map, but it always needs a reason to move.

CHAPTER 6

Confession #6: When Agile Meets Fixed Deadline

We must not confuse the urgency of the deadline with the importance of work.

—Unknown

There's a moment early in almost every project when someone asks:

"So, what's the date?"

It doesn't matter that we've chosen Agile. It doesn't matter that we've agreed to iterative delivery, evolving scope, or timeboxed sprints. There's always a date. A demo. A go-live. A board meeting. A promise.

And suddenly, everything that Agile stood for: discovery, collaboration, adaptability, feels like it's being squeezed into a Gantt chart someone swore they would never build again.

I have seen it too many times. The roadmap becomes a finish line. The backlog becomes a checklist. And velocity? That can be misused.

CHAPTER 6   CONFESSION #6: WHEN AGILE MEETS FIXED DEADLINE

This chapter isn't about blaming deadlines. It's about understanding what happens when deadlines, especially immovable ones, collide with Agile values. It's about the trade-offs we make, the pressure we absorb, the burnout we risk, and the decisions we justify in the name of "making it."

And it's about what happens when we stop pretending everything is under control, when we say what no one wants to hear:

This plan won't work, not in this form.

Deadlines, even when presented flexibly, often shape the story before it begins. Ours was no different, set in motion before the team had even formed.

The Calendar That Killed the Sprint

We'll keep it flexible, but ideally, we want to go live in three to six months.

That was the opening statement I heard when I joined the project, just before the discovery phase even began. No UX, no reference applications, no baseline roadmap. An ambitious timeline was shared with the business, although it is still early in the planning stage. And while the word "flexible" was used, it quickly became clear: this date was only flexible in language, not in practice.

We didn't even have a whole team when we kicked off. The team, composed of UX professionals, a business analyst, and several developers, approached the project with enthusiasm. However, they showed a concerning lack of urgency in establishing a delivery strategy. While the team brought new energy to the kickoff, I found myself balancing both architectural responsibilities and a healthy skepticism, especially given the uncertainties.

What unsettled me most wasn't just the lack of clear scope or the nascent team structure: it was that I, as the architect, was being asked to steer through a brand-new platform with a steep learning curve, while the train was already racing down a fixed track toward a launch date no one fully understood.

CHAPTER 6   CONFESSION #6: WHEN AGILE MEETS FIXED DEADLINE

Sprint planning began, sort of.

There was no long-term roadmap, no epic breakdowns, and no milestone map aligned with working software. We began with a few technical user stories, including UI setup, domain modeling, and basic security scaffolding; however, the core business features were not yet visible. The team didn't seem bothered. At that point, no one was alarmed. The excitement of a new beginning still energized them.

I voiced my concerns.

I asked why we weren't mapping out epics or aligning with a business value stream. I pushed for upstream refinement and long-term planning. But without a Scrum Coach in place and a Scrum Master who was more focused on making sure stories were being "burned," I became the odd one out.

The team hadn't yet aligned around the importance of planning toward meaningful business delivery milestones.

Weeks passed. Sprints ticked by.

Although the team consistently delivered story points sprint after sprint, stakeholders soon realized that they were not receiving any tangible business deliverables. This prompted them to question whether they could maintain the timeline.

The team retrofitted backlogs to include more features. Teams started working backward from the timeline, compressing features into shorter time frames and skipping key validations. The backdating began, business expectations were reinterpreted, and development was rushed. Everyone moved faster, but with less clarity. The first visible sign of stress was not in the code but in the faces during daily stand-ups.

I could see it: fatigue, disengagement, burnout. We were no longer constructing with clarity; we were attempting to keep pace.

Despite the stress, the team successfully delivered the goods. We met the deadline. Leadership proudly celebrated achieving the record delivery timeline, even though the hidden costs weren't immediately apparent. We skipped taking the time to stabilize and reflect properly, but kept moving forward with determination. We jumped into the next release, two months out, on the same trajectory, without questioning the model we had just survived.

Externally, it appeared to be a success. Internally, we felt we were pushing beyond what was sustainable.

The rush to meet the date brought more than exhaustion, it created patterns. And some of those patterns began to change how we worked and what we valued.

Reverse Engineering the Burndown

At first glance, everything seems to be going well; outsiders might think the team is performing exceptionally. The reports are very promising, with good velocity and burndown charts.

But behind the numbers, something else was happening.

We were slicing stories thinner and thinner, not to improve focus or deliver incremental value, but to avoid spillovers. Whenever a story became complex, we would quietly break it down mid-sprint into subtasks or replace it with a "spike" to justify the effort. The original story would be set aside quietly, and new ones would take its place in the next sprint. It wasn't intentional misinterpretation; it was an unconscious form of avoidance, shaped by pace and pressure.

There was no shared Definition of Done. We were running too fast for that kind of discipline. What passed for "done" was often just "coded and pushed." Testing was occasionally deprioritized, and documentation and code reviews were often abbreviated due to time constraints.

I wasn't the Scrum Master for this project; I joined as the architect. However, I could see a concerning trend developing with each sprint. While the project initially appeared to be a model for other teams, the reality was that they were building small features without a proper plan in place. This approach was unlikely to lead to a successful closure.

CHAPTER 6   CONFESSION #6: WHEN AGILE MEETS FIXED DEADLINE

Everyone acted in good faith, but the metrics gradually began to reflect momentum more than meaning. The system incentivized showing progress, so the team took the necessary steps to maintain the metrics. We gradually started to pay more attention to burndown as the leading indicator, even though it didn't always show the true value for the business.

When I raised concerns, I felt like I was speaking a different language. I questioned why we weren't tying stories back to epics and why no one was asking how close we were to achieving meaningful business outcomes. But I was alone in that conversation. Leadership was still learning Agile, and the team was euphoric with their apparent momentum. After all, they were burning story points sprint after sprint. It felt good. It looked good.

But it wasn't good.

A few sprints in, the disconnect became harder to ignore. Business stakeholders began asking where the real functionality was. While we made good progress, the product was still evolving toward the level of business impact we envisioned. We had sprint reviews, but they focused more on demonstrating progress than on highlighting value. No one openly addressed the issue or accused anyone of manipulating the board. However, at some point, we lost sight of our goal. The focus naturally shifted toward increasing throughput, but it was done without tying it to clear business results.

The reports showcased the team's delivery but did not highlight the business value. Although there was no intention to deceive, we acknowledge that we might have missed the larger aim: Agile is not just about monitoring points; it is essentially about nurturing a sense of purpose.

In our rush to deliver quickly and keep pace, we failed to ask the essential question: Are we providing anything valuable to the business team?

If I were to do it again, I'd start by accepting that the first few sprints of any new project are a learning curve, not a race. I would push for epic-level burndown tracking to anchor teams in absolute value. And I would be the first to say that a flat line is better than a beautiful lie.

Because sometimes, the most Agile thing a team can do is admit they're not there yet, and recalibrate before the numbers start telling a story no one can believe.

Metrics can blur the gaps they were meant to highlight. But occasionally, it's the product itself that reveals what we missed.

Scope? Quality? Pick One

The feature wasn't complex on the surface. However, once it reached production, it failed subtly, yet meaningfully. Unexpected behavior occurred when a feature interacted with existing records, something we hadn't anticipated during design or testing.

The issue did not require an urgent hotfix or emergency deployment, as we had a built-in configuration that allowed us to suppress the problem without needing any additional deployment. With a single adjustment, the feature was disabled for existing records, while leaving new ones unaffected. The surgical team achieved this workaround by making a straightforward configuration change.

It was a smart technical move. But behind it was a humbling realization: this edge case had slipped through every layer, from requirements to validation. It wasn't just a gap in the code; it reflected a shared assumption we haven't yet challenged.

We have decided to suppress the feature openly. We didn't sweep it under the rug, nor did we resort to quick fixes. Everything was discussed openly, and the path forward was a collective decision. And then, we sat down for one of the most honest post-mortems we'd had in months.

There wasn't much finger-pointing, just acknowledgment. Quiet reflection. And, for me, a realization that even the cleanest-looking delivery can carry invisible risk when no one asks, "What happens to the data we already have?"

From that day forward, legacy data became part of our acceptance mindset. Every new story or flow was cross-checked not just for future behavior, but for how it coexisted with everything that came before. We changed how we wrote scenarios.

That moment reminded us that data readiness is crucial for long-term stability and vital for preventing issues like this in future releases.

If I faced the same decision again, I wouldn't hesitate to act. Suppressing the feature was the right decision, not to avoid responsibility, but to buy time to do things properly. We didn't ship a broken product. We hit pause, adapted, and resumed with clarity.

What stuck with me most wasn't the error; it was how we recovered from it. Everyone missed it. Everyone owned it. And that shared responsibility is what turned a mistake into momentum.

Fixing a feature is one kind of challenge; sustaining a team through mounting delivery pressure is another. The strain wasn't just in our systems, it was showing in us.

The Emotional Weight of Time

Every critical delivery project can impact an individual's health. We might find ourselves stretching our limits and working beyond our capabilities, but eventually, our bodies will react. There will come a day when our bodies demand rest, and that's when we'll notice team members skipping stand-up meetings, falling ill, turning off their cameras, and becoming quieter day by day.

The team stretched beyond reason during a sprint cycle that looked normal from the outside. Every feature felt like an epic disguised as a user story. Stories came in broad, vague, and barely refined; they were just placeholders for work that was already underway, with no proper acceptance criteria and no breathing room for discussion. Developers were writing code without clarity, testers were validating in ambiguity, and business analysts were racing against a blurry vision, often two sprints behind where they needed to be.

We were trying to deliver two parallel releases. The backlog hadn't been shaped; the prep phase had been rushed. While one release captured the leadership's full attention, the other, quietly delayed by the team, became the perceived reason for the holdup.

After a long stretch of hard work, the team pulled off a milestone. It wasn't easy. It took nights, weekends, and every ounce of focus the team could muster. We expected a simple celebration or at least a recognition. Instead, the conversation shifted, understandably, to emerging priorities. Looking back, it's clear that the team's expectations for acknowledgment didn't match what leadership was focused on.

That moment visibly drained one of our strongest contributors.

A developer who had held it together for weeks finally hit the wall. The challenges of pressure and the feeling of being unappreciated can be tough, causing us to feel overwhelmed. I noticed this emotional strain in my colleagues, and it was hard to miss. I, too, experienced burnout as an architect, navigating the pressure in my own way.

Our current approach may not be as sustainable as we envisioned. Teams sometimes focus predominantly on the agile process during retrospectives, which can lead to neglecting more overarching concerns. When leaders do not fully consider the perspectives of their team members, it can create feelings of frustration within the team. This may result in a hesitancy to voice similar concerns in the future. Acknowledging this pattern is essential, as it significantly influences our team's morale and willingness to engage openly.

In hindsight, I don't hold the individuals responsible; instead, I have the system we entered accountable. We were attempting to run an Agile project without adhering to the principles of Agile development. No preparation. No discovery runway. No time for analysis. Business analysts were slogging to feed one release, and here we were expecting them to support two in parallel. We kept promising "faster to market," but in hindsight, we were using Agile more as a shield than a strategy.

If I had to do it again, I would call it out sooner. I will insist that we only start when we have truly begun: this means completing the prep, organizing the backlog, and ensuring the team is emotionally and mentally ready. Two months isn't a delivery plan, it's a bet. And when that bet fails, it's the team that pays.

We often talk about scope and quality in Agile. However, we rarely discuss morale. Energy. Spirit. That's the real fuel. And once it's gone, no chart, no burnup, no roadmap can bring it back.

Internal stress tells one part of the story. External expectations, from those watching the play unfold, add an entirely new layer.

Stakeholder Theater

The stakeholders believed we were practicing Agile, at least on the surface, but beneath the surface, old habits still influenced daily routines. In reality, our execution is hindered by the need for Agile ceremonies and the additional hours spent preparing daily reports. As a result, the team has less time to focus on actual execution.

What struck me the most wasn't the misunderstanding; it was the certainty. Stakeholders believed they were practicing Agile because the team delivered in sprints and there was a Jira board to track progress. But under the hood, the expectations hadn't changed at all. Fixed scope. Fixed deadlines. No space for surprises. And there was no absolute trust that the team could own the delivery.

That's the part no one tells you about Agile adoption: it's not just about training teams. It's about untraining stakeholders who still believe control equals progress.

CHAPTER 6   CONFESSION #6: WHEN AGILE MEETS FIXED DEADLINE

The command-and-control mindset didn't disappear; it evolved to suit the new format. One week, the team was praised for delivering a sprint on time. The next, we were asked to squeeze in a last-minute feature. Priorities often shifted, not based on evolving customer needs but on internal changes revealed during the review meeting. Sometimes, these pivots happened without warning. Occasionally, even mid-sprint.

The team felt it.

The team took genuine pride in what they built, solutions we were truly excited to demo. However, the impact didn't meet our expectations. Sometimes, our work was misunderstood, downplayed, or overshadowed by other urgent escalations. Gradually, the enthusiasm began to fade. When efforts aren't recognized or acknowledged, even passion can start to feel like routine.

The worst part? The reporting overhead.

Stakeholders requested daily reports: PowerPoint decks, Excel trackers, and RAG statuses that weren't directly aligned to Agile delivery practices. These were habits carried over from a waterfall past, adapted to preserve a sense of visibility and oversight. We spent considerable time formatting dashboards and summarizing progress that was already captured in Agile tools, time that we could have used to improve the product. I tried to change this.

When I eventually stepped in as Scrum Master for the team, I didn't resist the reporting. I reframed it. I extracted insights from the Agile dashboards, including velocity, cumulative flow, and dependency trackers, and presented them in a format that looked familiar but required no effort from the team. It wasn't about resistance. It was about shielding the team. I absorbed the pressure so the team could stay focused.

One stakeholder noticed. They appreciated the view, not just of progress, but of risk and inter-team coordination. They became a supporting voice behind the scenes, one of the few who started asking better questions during reviews instead of demanding more slides.

The performance of agility continued: part effective, part habitual.

Some stakeholders preferred visibility approaches rooted in traditional governance models. We learned to navigate it: to shield the team, to interpret expectations, to deliver what mattered without bending until we broke.

I have come to accept that not everyone is ready or willing to change. Some still view authority structures as more effective than collaborative models. That's their reality. As a leader, my job isn't to convert every stakeholder; it's to protect the space where agility can survive.

In the service industry, textbook Agile often remains aspirational. But dignity in delivery? That's still within reach. You meet them halfway. You translate what they need into what the team can afford to give. You absorb the friction. Not because it's easy, but because sustaining balance requires it.

Amid the swirl of shifting priorities and unspoken tension, one moment of clarity stood out, not from escalation, but from restraint.

The Brave PO Who Said "No"

It started with a familiar pattern, scope creep disguised as "just a little more." The sprint had already begun. The backlog was whole. But stakeholders, energized by business urgency and pressure to deliver beyond expectations, began asking for more.

We were heading straight into overcommitment. Again.

And then something unexpected happened.

Our Product Owner, let's refer to him as Jason (Name changed for confidentiality), said no.

Not in anger. Not defensively. But with clarity. Jason didn't just push back; he redirected. He walked the business through the backlog, acknowledged the requests, and calmly showed what was already committed. He didn't challenge their vision; he challenged their timing.

CHAPTER 6   CONFESSION #6: WHEN AGILE MEETS FIXED DEADLINE

What made his "no" resonate wasn't resistance; it was reasoning. Jason asked, "What can the business live without for now? What can be delivered differently? What's essential versus aspirational?"

After that conversation, not only did he reject the new requests, but he also removed a few existing stories from the sprint. Not to cut corners, but to give the team breathing room. He understood the complexity of what we would be committing to. He knew we couldn't keep quality intact without narrowing our focus. And he knew that pushing more into the sprint would mean trading long-term stability for short-term optics.

The response? Respect.

Stakeholders did not push back because the business aligned with their interests. And once that alignment was in place, the rest followed. The focus was solely on the features that were critical to the business, rather than the good-to-have features or stakeholders' aspirations.

We didn't lose anything, except perhaps the illusion that overdelivering is always the answer. What we gained was clarity. Focus. And, quietly, a bit of relief.

That moment changed something.

We realized that courage in Agile leadership doesn't always come from the loudest person in the room. It doesn't always come from the org chart. It comes from someone who sees the whole board: team health, business pressure, and user experience, and decides that protecting quality isn't negotiable.

Jason didn't ask permission. He just did the right thing.

And in doing so, he set a new tone. Stakeholders still attempted to expand the scope later, but they now knew there was a voice at the table that wouldn't automatically agree. A voice that could navigate with confidence, not just compliance.

What I took away from that moment was this: change can come from the quietest seat in the room. Sometimes, the person who is only partially involved in IT becomes the one who protects it best. And next time, I won't wait for a title to expect leadership.

Because every time someone chooses sustainability over speed, clarity over chaos, and team health over the illusion of urgency, they've already said yes to what matters most.

That brave "no" gave us breathing room. But as we approached the following delivery line, we found ourselves negotiating in real time once again.

Negotiation at the Edge

We were in the final stretch of a release when the unexpected hit: not a showstopper bug, a last-minute test scenario. Unplanned but valid.

It came from a tester who decided to go beyond the planned test cases. A small one, but in a production environment, small is never small. The problem arose not from someone catching the bug, but from the timing of when they saw it.

The decision room came alive. A virtual war room (a common IT term for an urgent coordination meeting) of key stakeholders gathered, balancing risk, release timelines, and system stability. There was no time to fix it cleanly, without disrupting everything else in the process. And so, the question emerged: Can the business live with a workaround?

After some serious back-and-forth, we decided to go for something practical. We provided a workaround that the business can live with, and we will address it in the upcoming release, which is scheduled for two months. While everyone seemed to be on the same page publicly, some unspoken frustrations began to surface beneath the alignment.

In Agile, we welcome emergent thinking. We value initiative. But initiative without timing becomes friction. When delivery and validation came from different teams, collaboration challenges intensified.

What should have been a shared win, we caught this before it went into production, and soon shifted from celebration to uneasy questions about roles and responsibilities. There were concerns about whether testers had broadened their scope, and whether developers should have anticipated such edge cases. And the spirit of a Scrum team, the very idea of one team, one outcome, strained under differing interpretations of responsibility.

The team successfully executed the release, marking a positive achievement. While there was an overall sense of relief, it is important to consider the concerns some team members expressed.

In the days that followed, the catch went quietly without any fanfare. Nonetheless, this experience imparted an important lesson: when trust is scarce and teams function more autonomously, even a well-thought-out choice can lead to a lingering feeling of disconnect.

Agile thrives on shared ownership and struggles to realize its full potential within vendor silos. When delivery and validation come from different teams, instead of cross-functional teams, you risk creating transactional delivery pipelines. And in those pipelines, timing becomes a source of tension, and collaboration becomes a source of conflict.

If I were to lead that negotiation again, I would handle the issue the same way, but I would frame it differently. I would acknowledge the tester's sharp thinking as a win. I would guide the team to view the discovery not as a mistake, but as proof that our team is working effectively. And I would make sure everyone understood: catching something late is not ideal, but seeing it together is still a success.

Because at the edge of delivery, it's not just the product that gets tested. It's the team.

Not all lessons surface during delivery. Some of the most transformative moments arrive when the sprint is over, and people finally speak their truth.

CHAPTER 6   CONFESSION #6: WHEN AGILE MEETS FIXED DEADLINE

A Retrospective That Hurt and Healed

The new delivery plan was taking a toll on our team. We all understood what we are committing to, but not the full weight of it. Those of us inside the storm knew something more profound was off; we couldn't name it.

That retrospective began like any other. Virtual faces, polite nods, the usual checklist: what went well, what didn't, action items. But under the surface, something was cracking. People were tired, tired of changes arriving out of nowhere, tired of building based on assumptions, tired of doing their best only to be told it wasn't enough.

Then someone finally said it.

"Why do we keep getting new requirements every time a different user starts testing? Did we even talk to all the people who use this system?"

It hit like a thunderclap. Not because it was confrontational, but because it was true. We hadn't failed in delivery; we had failed in discovery. The business users who had lived with the old system for years each held pieces of the puzzle, but that knowledge was scattered, siloed, and never fully shared. And in our rush to modernize, we'd assumed alignment where there was none. We were building a future version of a system without fully understanding its present.

One by one, voices joined in. Not to blame, but to illuminate. We realized that we'd been working in a partial vacuum, talking to a subset of available users, instead of pushing harder to reach the ones who held the real operational insights. It wasn't neglect; it was unawareness. We simply didn't realize they were part of the picture.

By the end of the meeting, something shifted.

The team agreed: no more surprises. From that point on, we would involve everyone, even if they seemed peripheral. Leaders promised to bring their functional teams into the fold. Analysts changed their engagement patterns. Conversations widened. Understanding deepened.

It wasn't a retro filled with blame or metrics. It was one filled with honesty, with healing. The kind that doesn't just change stories, it changes behaviors.

In the retrospectives that followed, there was no shame, only honesty. The mood improved. Teams began questioning assumptions sooner, validating with more people, and discovering edge cases before they became blockers. We didn't just pivot, we matured.

It's easy to celebrate the retros that yield quick wins. But this one gave us something rarer: self-retrospection. We had defaulted to using the most accessible voices, not necessarily the most essential ones.

And sometimes, real change starts not with a process, but with a question brave enough to surface the truth.

The emotions shared in that retrospective weren't just vented, they were acted upon. And what followed was a decision to rebuild the plan, not just the product.

Replanning with Integrity

The retrospective didn't just clear the air; it cleared the path forward. After the emotional unpacking, we couldn't go back to "business as usual." Something had to change.

The project we selected was known to carry significant risk because of its technical complexity, which had remained untouched for years despite internal awareness. Still, on paper, our plan looked achievable. It wasn't a flaw in our code; it was a flaw in what we assumed we knew.

We thought we had covered enough ground with the business users. The few we reached gave us what we believed was sufficient insight. For the rest, we assumed we could fill in the gaps along the way, but those gaps turned out to be much wider than expected. The retrospective made that painfully clear.

We knew the delivery was a calculated risk, one we had already acknowledged earlier due to its historical complexity. But at that time, our plan still felt achievable on paper. The main challenge was the involvement of business users. With limited discussions, we assumed that we had addressed most of the necessary information. For those we couldn't reach in time, we could clarify the details during the course of delivery. Unfortunately, we were mistaken in this approach.

We took on the task of modernizing an experience that business users had relied on for years. On the surface, they agreed to the change. But once implementation began, concerns began to emerge.

They weren't looking for new screens or altered flows. Their comfort lay in the muscle memory built over years, and change threatened that familiarity.

To make things even harder, we found that users scattered their requirements across different silos and were unavailable for alignment during the development process. Some stakeholders became intermittently available. Others offered partial feedback. Gaps in understanding grew more visible as development progressed.

The plan no longer made sense.

I was the architect at the time, closely working with the team. And it became clear: to them, to us, and eventually to the leadership that what we would scope wasn't feasible; not because of poor intent, but because the assumptions during early estimation didn't hold true. The user behavior we expected did not appear. What we thought would be simple turned out to be entangled with organizational dynamics, sensitive, and high-stakes.

We didn't wait for production to expose the gaps. We recalibrated.

There was no need to fight for alignment. Everyone involved—business, IT, and project managers recognized that the path forward had shifted. We extended the timeline. We increased the scope to account for rework. We slowed down, not because we wanted to, but because it was the only way forward that still honored quality and user experience.

CHAPTER 6 CONFESSION #6: WHEN AGILE MEETS FIXED DEADLINE

It wasn't easy.

Initially, confidence took a hit. Up until then, our team had a reputation for meeting every timeline. That streak broke here. There were whispers questioning whether we were ready for high-complexity deliveries.

But here's the thing, our focus wasn't on legacy, it was on integrity. We were trying to do the right thing.

And once we named the problem, owned the timeline shift, and brought everyone back to reality, something surprising happened: trust began to rebuild. Quietly. Slowly. But firmly.

We adjusted. We delivered. We went live successfully.

That moment taught me something I'll never forget: early honesty might hurt, but late denial destroys. If we had pretended we could push through, we would've risked releasing an unstable product and exhausting the team. Instead, we stayed transparent, faced the music, and found a better rhythm.

In retrospection, I wish we had raised concerns even earlier. We underestimated the resistance we didn't anticipate from users we hadn't yet engaged. And that resistance, fed by siloed knowledge, came at the worst time, just when we needed clarity.

Now, when I lead teams or advise on delivery planning, I hold this line: If we don't have enough runway for proper discovery, we shouldn't launch. The basic checks are in place to ensure that we do not encounter engine failure midway.

Sometimes, integrity doesn't mean keeping promises. It means having the courage to remake them, before the team absorbs the cost.

Slowing down to regain alignment wasn't failure, it was clarity. And that clarity reshaped everything that followed.

Final Reflection: Running Isn't the Same As Finishing

We often say Agile gives us speed, but speed toward what? This chapter has been about the collision between intention and reality, planning and pressure, and agility and immobility. It started with the illusion of velocity, the beautiful burndown charts, the full sprints, the teams "doing Agile." But beneath that surface was a different story: stress, shortcuts, suppressed features, performative behaviors, and decision-making under pressure.

What became painfully clear is that execution is not the same as momentum. Just because we're delivering something doesn't mean we're providing the right thing, or doing it in a way that sustains the team. Every section in this chapter pointed back to a central truth: if the foundation isn't solid, if planning is thin, if alignment is superficial, if quality is compromised, Agile won't prevent failure; it'll only get you there faster.

Yet in the middle of that chaos, there were also signs of courage and integrity. A Product Owner brave enough to say "no." A team retrospective that turned pain into alignment. A moment where someone caught an issue at the 11th hour: not to delay delivery, but to protect quality. These weren't process wins. They were people who won.

As a leader, whether you're a Scrum Master, an architect, or part of the business, it's easy to chase timelines. But staying silent to preserve a deadline can cost more than taking a moment to realign. Recovery is possible, but only if we pause, listen, and make changes when it hurts the most to do so.

CHAPTER 6   CONFESSION #6: WHEN AGILE MEETS FIXED DEADLINE

Agile is not a shield against pressure; it's a mirror to it. And what we do with what we see is what defines us.

Takeaway Confession   I used to believe that if the board looked clean and the sprints were complete, we were doing fine. However, I have come to realize that metrics cannot tell us what we are delivering to the business. Deadlines can be rigid, but ignoring morale comes at a cost. Agile alone isn't the key to success, but it holds us together, which can take us toward success. Sometimes, we should be bold enough to say, "This plan needs a pivot, let's adjust and succeed together."

CHAPTER 7

Confession #7: Scaling Nightmares—Nexus, Chaos, and Customer Challenges

Scaling isn't just adding more teams, it's multiplying the chances of misalignment.

—Unknown

When I learned that we were introducing a new framework in a challenging multi-team environment, I felt excited to understand it. I was curious to discover how it would address real-world problems that Agile could not.

This chapter isn't a critique of Nexus as a framework. It's a confession of what happens when the spirit of Nexus is lost in the race to deliver. We had all the proper ceremonies, some of the right people, and absolutely none of the patience. Integration became a checkbox. Scrum of Scrums became more about updates than integration planning. Product Owners often leaned into team-level priorities, unintentionally diluting the shared vision Nexus requires.

The worst part is that it was incompetence that caused the chaos, not conflicting ambitions. All teams aimed for success, but in doing so, they inadvertently undermined each other. We delivered code and features but lacked confidence and stability. While it looked like we were scaling, we weren't necessarily progressing in alignment.

This chapter dives into the reality behind the buzzword. From broken APIs to confused POs, missed dependencies to a fractured backlog, you will see how our best intentions turned into our biggest blockers, and how Nexus, had we respected it, could have been our lifeline.

Let's unpack the mess, one integration at a time.

When Three Became Four

We didn't scale because we wanted to. We scaled because we had to.

The customer needed more. More features, more functionality, and most of all, more speed. As the scope expanded and the timelines grew tighter, the team anticipated the decision to increase capacity without any debate.

The adoption of the first release necessitated the addition of new features to the product. Customers requested a scale-up to meet increasing expectations, which marked the beginning of scaling up the team.

With several delivery partners involved, the decision to distribute responsibilities across multiple functional teams initially seemed the most practical approach.

And on paper, it was. We divided the teams by functionality. Each would own a distinct slice of the product. But as anyone who's scaled Agile in the real world knows, the lines between "functional areas" rarely stay neat for long. Almost immediately, the cracks began to show.

CHAPTER 7 CONFESSION #7: SCALING NIGHTMARES—NEXUS, CHAOS, AND CUSTOMER CHALLENGES

We were operating with cross-functional teams, but without clearly established integration patterns or dependency ownership. Developers on one team frequently encountered roadblocks caused by stories that others had built or failed to make. Delayed integrations weren't the exception; they became the rhythm of our sprint cycle. Although nobody was truly at fault, everyone felt the weight of blame. Tension built. Communication frayed. Morale dipped. With multiple vendors involved, accountability became fragmented, and communication challenges grew. Some people focused narrowly on their scope, unintentionally deflecting broader integration issues. However, the actual problem wasn't the quantity of teams. It was the absence of a framework to support them.

I encountered a similar scenario before, where we effectively used Nexus to coordinate Agile delivery across multiple teams. Nexus had offered a structured way to align teams, surface dependencies early, and hold the right conversations at the right time. So, when things began to spiral out of control, I proposed that we apply the same approach here.

At first, it looked like we were on track. We stood up a Nexus Integration Team. We set up cross-team forums. We had decision-makers in the room. But then something shifted, and not in a good way. Urgent requests and short-term firefighting hijacked the very meetings meant to foster alignment and a shared vision. Business stakeholders prioritized immediate concerns during the forum. IT leads used it to report individual progress. The conversations became reactive rather than integrative. The original purpose of Nexus, which was to resolve complex, multi-team dependencies, got drowned out in the noise.

I spoke up. I said we were misusing the Nexus forum, that we were defeating its purpose. Instead of support, my concerns were met with silence and eventually sidelined. The participants viewed the meeting as an opportunity to air their grievances, rather than resolve them. The focus shifted away from process improvement toward short-term issue resolution.

CHAPTER 7 CONFESSION #7: SCALING NIGHTMARES—NEXUS, CHAOS, AND CUSTOMER CHALLENGES

In hindsight, I wish I had done more than speak up. I wish I had drawn a line and said, "We don't scale like this. Not without the right scaffolding. Not without discipline." I wish I had paused everything until we had set up the proper foundation: not during implementation, not when the pressure was already unbearable.

But we didn't pause. We pushed forward. And that's when things started to unravel.

We had chosen a framework, but what we hadn't yet grasped was that structure alone couldn't fix the human gaps it exposed.

Frameworks Don't Scale People

We adopted Nexus with excitement, not skepticism. It was new. It was structured. It felt like a system we could hold on to as the delivery scope expanded and deadlines drew closer. I had first seen it in action during an earlier engagement. A strategist named Tony had introduced it to me, and it changed how I viewed the problem of cross-team dysfunction. It was the first time I saw a framework that addressed not just delivery cadence but inter-team accountability, shared dependencies, and the gaps that fall between organizational cracks in the service industry.

When the opportunity arose to reapply to Nexus, I was hopeful.

The idea energized leadership. The concept of a Nexus Integration Team (NIT), coordinated refinements, and stakeholder visibility sounded exactly like what we needed. No one pushed to rush it. We had the time to set it up properly. For the first few weeks, it worked. People showed up. The right conversations began to surface. The team mapped the technical dependencies, which eased the pressure to align across vendors.

But then, one production issue hijacked a Nexus sync. And that changed everything.

CHAPTER 7 CONFESSION #7: SCALING NIGHTMARES—NEXUS, CHAOS, AND CUSTOMER CHALLENGES

A well-meaning but urgent stakeholder opened the forum to address a pressing issue. Once they did, others followed suit. Nexus became a triage zone for daily fire drills. Instead of using the presence of key decision-makers to resolve long-term cross-team problems, we used it to triage the day's pressing issues. And just like that, Nexus lost its original intent.

The meeting became a formality. A ritual. Something people attended, but no longer believed in.

Some teams still tried. Others began to retreat into their backlogs, pushing delivery pressure onto others. I had to step in more than once when a team attempted to misuse Nexus to force another into expedited delivery. "What's the urgency here?" I'd ask. "Can we take a moment to align on business priority before escalating?" That often helped diffuse tension in the moment, but underneath, the erosion of trust had already begun.

Cross-team refinement? It stopped. Without anyone taking ownership of the interdependencies, the team only discovered issues after they blocked a sprint. We weren't preventing problems. We were reacting to them. No one came prepared with dependency insights anymore. The NIT aimed to coordinate among various teams, but over time, it turned into just another status room. Less meaningful integration, more formality.

For a short time, the Nexus sessions were on track, mainly due to guidance from someone experienced in facilitation. They understood the nuance. They made space for tough conversations. When facilitation shifted to someone less familiar with the framework's intent, the direction began to drift. Within a couple of weeks, the team bent the framework instead of following it.

And I? I lost my voice in that room. I wasn't the coach. I wasn't the owner. I was a Scrum Master trying to maintain the spirit of Nexus, despite lacking the authority to prevent its misuse. I raised my concerns. No one acted on them. Eventually, I stepped back. I only joined those meetings when asked.

CHAPTER 7   CONFESSION #7: SCALING NIGHTMARES—NEXUS, CHAOS, AND CUSTOMER CHALLENGES

Looking back, I realize what was missing. Not structure. Not process. But belief. Belief in the framework's purpose. Belief that people needed to change how they interacted, not just change where they interacted.

If I had one message to leave with that team, or any team attempting to scale, it's this:

Frameworks don't scale people. People scale people.

You can't retrofit collaboration with rituals. You can't fix organizational behavior with a calendar invite. And you certainly can't transform a team dynamic by introducing a new acronym amid a crisis.

Ensure that you use the framework for its intended purpose. Don't bend it to your convenience. Because once you do, the framework becomes an illusion of control, and chaos has a way of slipping through the cracks.

Even with every role in place, the execution faltered where clarity should've led the way—especially when it came to planning.

A Planning Meeting or a Guessing Game?

You could feel the tension in the room before the Sprint Planning even began.

We were already navigating a high-takes delivery, tight timelines, evolving business rules, and complex cross-team dependencies that left much open to interpretation. Yet we began the sprint with complete focus, trying to turn noise into deliverables. They set the date, and the expectation loomed, leaving no possibility for turning back. Whether we were ready or not, the clock was ticking.

The teams held separate Sprint Planning sessions, as Nexus recommends joint planning only if dependencies are extreme. While Nexus was still within my influence, I fought to maintain sanity. When another team requested an integration that wouldn't be necessary for a couple of months and still needed finalization, I confidently expressed my thoughts on their request to clarify and prioritize the matter. They hadn't even started their discovery sprint. I asked: "Can we revisit this when we are closer to implementation readiness?"

But resistance only worked for so long.

Our planning sessions became dominated by confusion as we struggled to determine what we were building and when we needed it. We would get vague requests: "Start the integration." "Prepare the payload." The team had not yet defined the backend workflows, and the consuming logic remained unclear, while the APIs still existed only in mock form. We provided mock APIs and clarified that production readiness would depend on aligned prioritization and finalized requirements.

The bigger issue wasn't technical feasibility. It was the lack of a Definition of Ready. In most cases, requirements didn't even exist. There was no business logic to validate, nor were there any acceptance criteria to test against. Our teams were sprinting on assumptions: testing the waters, seeing what broke, and adjusting later. While the ceremonies remained, the underlying alignment and clarity were often missing, resulting in confusion that undermined the intended goal.

The Product Owners' structure posed its own challenge; each team had a different PO, and alignment between them was inconsistent. While they were engaged in their sprint planning ceremonies, their alignment across teams was loose at best. In some cases, developer preferences strongly influence the backlog, occasionally steering it away from broader business priorities. There were moments when the backlog reflected team perspectives more than end-to-end business alignment.

And yes, stories were forced into sprints. The deadline was fixed, after all. "We've got to move some needle," they'd say. So we did, though not always with clarity on the proper business direction.

Teams' confidence during these sessions was understandably low. They moved forward with limited direction, enough to take action, but not enough to be confident they were heading in the right direction. A clear sense of completion often felt out of reach. Sprint 1 revealed significant gaps in story completeness, with many items reaching only partial implementation by the end. We were aware of it, but under the circumstances, there were few viable alternatives.

In one instance, a feature critical to the business, so crucial that its absence would disrupt operational workflows, had to be delivered within a six-month time frame. Yet, the first sprint kicked off with assumptions, half-defined user stories, and placeholder data structures. Instead of shaping the solution from clear requirements, we were navigating a high degree of ambiguity under tight constraints.

Retrospectively, we should've started discovery months earlier. We needed stakeholder inputs, structured backlog refinement, and alignment across all product areas. But planning wasn't proactive. It was reactive. In the absence of a stable plan, forward momentum, however fragmented, was often interpreted as progress.

Planning started to feel more like an exercise in perceived control, with Jira tickets masking significant unknowns.

What we needed wasn't more process; it was more honesty.

That planning ambiguity soon translated into delivery confusion, and one particular API change made those cracks impossible to ignore.

The API That Broke the Sprint

As is often the case, the sprint disruption started with good intentions, but lacked complete information.

We aimed to standardize a crucial functionality that we previously distributed across the system. The idea was to consolidate logic and expose it as a clean, reusable API. Several teams had expressed a dependency on this capability, and one team, in particular, had flagged it early. So we prioritized it. We developed the integration based on the expressed needs of one team, ensuring it was stable and ready for use ahead of their planned timeline.

CHAPTER 7 CONFESSION #7: SCALING NIGHTMARES—NEXUS, CHAOS, AND CUSTOMER CHALLENGES

But we missed something.

Another team encountered a blocker mid-sprint due to an uncommunicated dependency. The team planned to implement a similar integration, but the backlog did not reflect that intention. Instead, had logged dependencies on a different API, one that ultimately wasn't part of their implementation plan. By the time the mix-up came to light, their sprint had started, and the integration they needed hadn't been developed, as it hadn't been flagged during refinement.

I remember the moment it landed in our lap. One of the teams raised a blocker, noting that the required API wasn't available as expected. I checked the records. The story hadn't been selected during planning, reportedly due to concerns around its readiness. But there had been no communication to indicate it was a sprint priority. The dependency wasn't surfaced during refinement or captured in our Nexus forums. It had slipped through every safeguard we thought we had.

Now we were in recovery mode.

We initiated development mid-sprint to mitigate the gap, but it was impossible to complete it in time. The best we could do was deliver it early in the next sprint, enough for them to begin integration late. Thankfully, there was no downstream fallout. It was an upstream reconciliation issue, not a demo-breaker. It led to delays in their development kickoff, and naturally, some frustrations followed.

They picked alternate stories. We delivered the API. Crisis averted. But the process failure was apparent.

In hindsight, it was less about the framework or the delivery mechanics; it came down to a gap in dependency ownership.

The issue slipped through Nexus, not due to the framework itself, but because our facilitation had become inconsistent by then. The problem surfaced during a Scrum of Scrums, where we still had some space for actual problem-solving. The leadership didn't need to intervene; we resolved it collaboratively and constructively. But I walked away from that sprint with a hard lesson burned into memory:

CHAPTER 7 CONFESSION #7: SCALING NIGHTMARES—NEXUS, CHAOS, AND CUSTOMER CHALLENGES

Scaling without aligned ownership isn't really scaling; it's just synchronized confusion.

From that point forward, I created a dependency matrix, mapped across teams, and projected three sprints ahead. It became a single sheet of clarity. Teams were encouraged to flag dependencies proactively; if they didn't, the impact became their responsibility to manage. It brought much-needed predictability.

In the end, the incident didn't leave scars. But it did leave a blueprint.

Because even when the sprint survives, lasting impact is felt through weakened trust or missed opportunities to reinforce discipline.

Miscommunication wasn't limited to architecture, it also stemmed from the very individuals meant to align the vision.

The Split-Personality Product Owner

Two teams. Two Product Owners. One shared objective, and growing misalignment.

At first, the division of Product Ownership seemed harmless. Each PO supported a specific functional team, and both reported into the same business group. They worked on different slices of the same system, but the boundaries appeared clear. The model worked until the gaps began to show.

As the teams moved deeper into delivery, cracks began to emerge. Conceptually similar features started to evolve in conflicting directions. One team prioritized custom handling. Another pursued standardization. Both assumed they were solving the same business problem, but they were speaking different dialects of the same language.

Worse still, some commitments were made independently, without full cross-team coordination. One team decided to make a functionality generic, without fully communicating its dependency on the other team's module. The implicit assumption was that alignment would follow,

CHAPTER 7 CONFESSION #7: SCALING NIGHTMARES—NEXUS, CHAOS, AND CUSTOMER CHALLENGES

but it didn't. The result was parallel development on divergent tracks. Eventually, one side had to rework a good chunk of their solution. There was limited business intervention, possibly due to the cross-vendor structure. Two different teams were driving forward, and product leadership appeared to take a hands-off approach as the situation developed.

This wasn't about authority or influence; both Product Owners had similar standing. But both were being subtly pulled by the development teams they supported. Developers often prefer what feels right to their tech stack or area of expertise. And when both teams disagreed on approach, it should have triggered a broader architectural discussion. Instead, the issue dragged on until a shared platform team had to weigh in and validate the correct direction.

The team should have resolved all of this during a Nexus dependency discussion. But by that point, the framework was no longer being applied with the discipline it required. What was supposed to be a space for proactive alignment had become reactive noise.

Business stakeholders observed the divergence and recognized early signs that one approach might not succeed. It wasn't just a missed opportunity; it led to rework that could have been avoided with earlier alignment.

From my seat, I did what I could. I coached my team to present the solution clearly and concisely. I initiated broader discussions to bring the issue to the surface. But I didn't have the power to force alignment. The POs weren't blocking progress, but they weren't fully connected to the technical nuances that ultimately caused rework. Their teams were burning stories with no guarantee of delivery.

Looking back, the bottleneck wasn't technical. The gap was not technical; it stemmed from a lack of early intervention and clear product direction.

If I could rewrite that structure, I wouldn't necessarily collapse it into one Chief Product Owner. While a reporting structure was in place, decision-making didn't always reflect cohesive product leadership. What we needed wasn't new roles. It was stronger engagement, a broader perspective, and more proactive judgment to question decisions before they reached implementation.

In a scaled setup, every Product Owner must embrace this one mindset:

Don't shy away from technical decisions just because they're uncomfortable. What you avoid today might quietly undermine everything you deliver tomorrow.

As the roles blurred, so did accountability, and the deeper causes started revealing themselves away from the daily boards and stand-ups.

Behind Closed Doors: The Real Bottlenecks

On the surface, everything seemed fine.

The team ran sprints, updated the boards, and held planning ceremonies. However, anyone paying close attention could sense that something else was shaping our direction, something not visible on JIRA or in the retrospectives.

Key decisions were often made outside of team visibility. They weren't malicious, but relatively routine.

Leadership conversations happened outside the Scrum rhythm, often with good intent but limited transparency. Priorities shifted without warning. One day, the team was heads-down building a workflow; the next, they were asked to pivot without explanation. Changes were relayed post-fact, often framed as top-down directives without context. No context. Just a course correction.

CHAPTER 7 CONFESSION #7: SCALING NIGHTMARES—NEXUS, CHAOS, AND CUSTOMER CHALLENGES

Our tools didn't capture these shifts. JIRA reflected only the current sprint, while the longer-term vision remained undocumented. Release planning was underutilized, and any existing roadmaps were fluid and often undocumented.

Although frameworks like Nexus aimed to enhance transparency, they still could not shield us from decisions made during side meetings or one-on-one syncs. Decisions were often referenced as already finalized, but lacked visibility in team forums. Over time, this became part of the unspoken dynamics often found in service-driven delivery environments.

It wasn't always fair.

At times, a missed release was met with little visible reaction. At other times, a team's sprint struggles triggered escalations, lengthy email threads, and review meetings. Some people quietly absorbed the delivery struggles, while others brought them to the public's attention. Often, the difference lay in visibility, organizational alignment, and perceived strategic impact.

It wasn't always about who was right; it was often about who had influence or early access to context.

And influence doesn't always speak loudly. Sometimes it whispers. Quiet approvals. Nods in hallway conversations. Sometimes, decisions were already in motion before the broader team saw the problem clearly.

From my seat, it was deeply frustrating. I pushed back when I could. Sometimes, it led to clarifications. Most of the time, the train had already left the station. I guided my team as best I could: adjusting, shielding, and realigning sprint by sprint.

It became clear that the most significant bottlenecks weren't in our architecture. They were cultural.

If I could redesign this aspect of delivery, I wouldn't suggest more tools or meetings. I'd advocate for a single, empowered decision-maker, someone empowered to rise above competing interests, willing to resolve cross-team contradictions without bias. Someone who doesn't let silence masquerade as consensus.

And to every Scrum Master dealing with invisible decisions made outside their visibility: you're not alone.

In service-based environments, this is all too common. The best thing you can do is protect the integrity of your sprint. Pivot when needed, acknowledge what you can't control. Focus your energy where it matters: guiding your team, managing reality, and building resilience.

Some bottlenecks you can unblock. Others, you survive.

What appeared as misalignment in meetings soon showed up in code, proving that the system was following the structure it saw.

Conway's Law Isn't a Suggestion

We didn't draw lines in the system. The team structure did it for us.

Despite our clear architecture, the patterns of cross-team communication influenced how teams wrote, duplicated, or even overlooked code. Our team structure followed functional boundaries, an approach that seemed logical during the planning phase. But once dependencies entered the picture, that structure began to shape more than just meetings; it shaped the product itself.

There was one moment that captured it all.

Our team owned a key reconciliation component, a shared layer critical for multiple downstream processes. We had communicated clearly that teams should wait to integrate with the refactored version, but one team proceeded independently. They decided to proceed with their own version of the logic, even while acknowledging that rework might be needed later. Their justification? "It's complex to consume. We'll build it ourselves for now."

It wasn't a disaster, but it introduced duplication that could have been avoided. It created parallel logic, potential maintenance debt, and avoidable confusion. We didn't suffer because of unclear ownership. On the contrary, ownership was clear. But the follow-through wasn't consistent.

CHAPTER 7 CONFESSION #7: SCALING NIGHTMARES—NEXUS, CHAOS, AND CUSTOMER CHALLENGES

It wasn't an isolated case. In a few places, communication broke just long enough for features to get rebuilt in silos. One team believed that the delay was due to implementation issues, while another team thought that alignment was optional. By the time reconciliation happened, the code had diverged.

Was the system brittle? No. But it was becoming uneven.

My team was assigned the responsibility of refactoring, and we successfully upheld that responsibility. But alignment with that vision wasn't always shared by others. In one situation, a technical discussion turned into a disagreement. We aligned on the architectural direction during discussions, but the implementation path later diverged, likely due to perceived complexity.

I realized then that Conway's Law isn't just an observation. It's a warning.

The system will mirror your team structure, whether you plan for it or not. When teams lack alignment with the system's goals, no amount of documentation or strategy can prevent them from diverging from the intended direction. Even when architectural discussions are held, without consistent reinforcement and shared ownership, teams may fall back to what feels most achievable under pressure.

Leadership wasn't blind to this. When I raised the concern, the response was diplomatic: "Let's hear from both sides." It wasn't resistance, it was neutrality. However, in moments like these, neutrality can unintentionally contribute to misalignment.

My advice to other Scrum Masters?

Don't assume your team's discipline is enough to preserve architectural intent. Ensure every team understands the system goals and holds the line.

If you notice duplication, report it promptly. If shortcuts emerge, surface the trade-offs. If your structure is silently shaping your codebase, it's your responsibility to raise awareness.

CHAPTER 7   CONFESSION #7: SCALING NIGHTMARES—NEXUS, CHAOS, AND
            CUSTOMER CHALLENGES

Conway's Law doesn't have to be a trap. It can be a tool if you choose to design with it in mind.

Architecture mirrored structure, but the real surprise was how stakeholder behavior mirrored an even deeper strategy we hadn't anticipated.

Trust Wasn't Lost; It Was Never the Goal

The customer didn't lose patience in the way most people might expect.

There wasn't a loud outburst or argument. Instead, something more understated happened, a small change that could have gone unnoticed. But for those of us directly involved, it was apparent: the trust we'd built felt shaken.

This moment unfolded during a routine call in which two teams presented their parallel approaches to the same problem. Everyone was in the room. Everyone could see it. The two solutions didn't align. They weren't supposed to. The collaboration that should've happened never did. And yet, both teams moved forward, believing their work was the right path.

The customer listened. And then, without raising their voice, they made their position clear.

They weren't confused. They weren't surprised. They'd seen this dynamic building for a while. They were allowing the two teams to move forward, perhaps not out of faith in both, but out of a belief that pressure would reveal the right direction.

It wasn't about frustration with misalignment. It involves leveraging misalignment to drive progress.

I offered what I thought was the rational approach: let the team with ownership deliver, and avoid wasting effort on duplication. But that suggestion was met with neutrality. The customer didn't intervene to prevent redundancy; they were watching to see who would execute faster.

CHAPTER 7   CONFESSION #7: SCALING NIGHTMARES—NEXUS, CHAOS, AND CUSTOMER CHALLENGES

It was a subtle form of competition, one that didn't make itself apparent, yet still produced winners and losers.

That's when it dawned on me: this wasn't mismanagement; it was a deliberate strategy.

Letting vendors operate independently, perhaps even competitively. Allow the pressure to reveal the strongest team. Utilize overlapping efforts as a means to evaluate performance. It wasn't just about trust; it was about outcomes.

Leadership didn't intervene early; instead, they let it play out.

The cost? Morale. Wasted effort. A dynamic that unintentionally discouraged collaboration and deepened silos. The bigger loss occurred psychologically; teams began to stop aligning because the lack of rewards discouraged them from doing so.

Looking back, I don't think the customer ever lost patience. They simply focused less on alignment and more on delivery outcomes.

And that's a lesson I won't forget:

Sometimes, what looks like dysfunction is direction, though not the kind openly acknowledged.

As we tried to make sense of the dynamics, it became clear that even the framework we chose wasn't immune to being bent, or bypassed.

What Nexus Promised, and What We Denied It

I still recall one of our early Nexus sync meetings: eight windows illuminating the screen, each representing a team, a backlog, and a set of dependencies that rarely surfaced in time. We aimed for the meeting to function as the heartbeat of our scaled Agile approach. Instead, it felt more like a routine that continued more from habit than from impact. Status updates were often mistaken for collaboration. The real issues were left unsaid, either because no one owned them or because neither ownership nor decision-making power was clearly present.

We were aligned to the Nexus framework, but struggled with consistent practice.

Let's be clear: Nexus truly had a strong foundation, designed to foster consistency among Scrum teams and swiftly address integration challenges while establishing a clear Definition of Done. We have identified several opportunities to enhance our processes. There is a strong opportunity to make our work more flexible and fully use the strengths of our current system. By making strategic changes, we can enhance its effectiveness and achieve better results, ultimately leading to greater overall success.

The first crack was in the Product Backlog. Nexus teaches us that there should be a single Product Backlog, a unified stream of work feeding all the teams. In our world, each team had specific objectives. While aligned in intent, teams often operated independently in practice. Refinement was local. Priorities were local. Even dependencies were local, until they weren't.

We would often stumble upon integration gaps, not in planning, but in production. Handoffs were often implicit rather than formally coordinated. The Nexus Integration Team (NIT), designed to detect and resolve these issues, was present. However, it included stakeholders whose involvement was limited by competing priorities or role constraints, leading to deferred decisions. Ownership lacked clarity, and urgency often surfaced reactively rather than proactively.

There were daily Nexus syncs, far more frequent than the framework recommends. But rather than being the heartbeat of integration, they turned into noise. At times, they became repetitive, focused on past blockers rather than forward progress. We were all present, but rarely aligned. And I noticed something disturbing: people had stopped preparing for them. Participation became more procedural than purposeful.

CHAPTER 7 CONFESSION #7: SCALING NIGHTMARES—NEXUS, CHAOS, AND CUSTOMER CHALLENGES

One of the biggest missteps came in how we used the Nexus events. The Nexus Sprint Planning, for example, often felt more symbolic than collaborative in execution. Each team planned its sprint independently, hoping alignment would emerge organically, which didn't always happen.

I attempted to raise these concerns, first diplomatically, then more directly. I asked: "Why aren't we planning cross-team dependencies two sprints ahead? Why isn't integration discussed until it becomes a bottleneck?" The answers varied: time constraints, bandwidth, "we'll fix it next time," but the outcome didn't. Delivery challenges persisted, and over time, they began to feel routine.

Some argued we needed to be "practical," not "textbook." But this felt less like pragmatism and more like avoiding hard decisions under the guise of flexibility.

The framework offered tools, but our adoption was selective.

If I could do it over, I'd insist on three things. First, fewer Nexus syncs, but with purpose. Once a week, with face cameras on, only those who can decide and unblock are allowed. Second, a real shared backlog with visible cross-team dependencies, not fragmented plans appearing as a unified one. And third, NIT is empowered to make decisions, not just receive and relay concerns.

Most importantly, I'd make sure everyone understood this: frameworks don't save teams. Discipline does. Communication does. Courage does.

Ultimately, Nexus didn't fall short; we fell short in using it to its full potential.

Once the dust settled, the framework hadn't failed us. If anything, it revealed the discipline we didn't enforce.

CHAPTER 7 CONFESSION #7: SCALING NIGHTMARES—NEXUS, CHAOS, AND CUSTOMER CHALLENGES
What We Should Have Done Differently

Reflecting on our experiences helps us grow as individuals. It allows us to move past blame and judgment. When things get tough, it's key to make quick, wise choices. Celebrating what we've achieved also brings the team closer and sets us up for a more organized and meaningful future. Now that the chaos has settled and I reflect on that program, I no longer see it as a failure.

I see where we fell short in consistent execution.

We weren't lacking guidance. Nexus wasn't some trendy framework we adopted for appearances. We began with the right intentions. Shared planning, coordinated sprints, and a NIT on paper, we set things up as intended. But intention without consistency is just wishful thinking. We let the structure loosen. We let meetings become rituals. We let powerful voices bypass alignment. We allowed influence to override alignment at times.

If I had a reset button, I wouldn't ask for more time or more people. I'd ask for something far simpler:

Shared backlog, shared accountability, and shared truth.

We needed to stop believing each team could sprint toward a shared goal while navigating in different directions. We needed to face tough dependencies up front: not in the middle of a sprint, not after a demo that revealed misalignment. And we needed to respect the framework, not unquestioningly, but with a clear understanding of why it exists.

Scrum of Scrums should have been our early warning system. Instead, it became a weather report, informative, but powerless to change the storm.

The NIT should have been our alignment engine. Instead, it became a relay between teams that lacked shared context.

And the Product Owners, some of the most committed people I've worked with, should have operated with a shared vision, rather than

CHAPTER 7 CONFESSION #7: SCALING NIGHTMARES—NEXUS, CHAOS, AND CUSTOMER CHALLENGES

diverging priorities. We let structure mirror our silos, and the system mirrored us right back.

But here's the part I keep coming back to: this wasn't inevitable. We could have fixed it.

We could've paused, not just when QA chaos forced us to, but proactively, earlier. We could've asked more challenging questions in our planning rooms. We could've made Nexus a real boundary, one that enforced collaboration, not just suggested it.

And maybe most of all, we could've created space for honest retrospection, not just at the end of sprints, but at the end of patterns.

Because when you're scaling Agile, the most dangerous assumption is that things will work out if we simply keep moving.

It won't.

Not without course correction. Not without shared ownership. Not without the humility to say: "This isn't working, let's adjust before it causes greater impact."

That's what I wish we'd done differently.

Takeaway Confession The most challenging part of scaling isn't coordination, it's honesty. It's the willingness to acknowledge when things aren't working, even when it's uncomfortable. Nexus gave us a way to work together and build as one. However, having a framework doesn't guarantee **courage**. That responsibility is ours. If we delay tough conversations, we shift from preventing problems to reacting to them.

CHAPTER 8

Confession #8: How I Learned Velocity Isn't Everything

You can't improve what you don't measure, but not everything you can measure matters.

—Albert Einstein

There was a period in my work life when speed was the most important thing. We constantly discussed numbers related to our progress and the amount of work we completed during each cycle. If those numbers increased, we felt like we were successful. If they decreased, we felt pressure or concern. This emphasis on speed became a measure of our accomplishments, a symbol of our success, and the narrative we conveyed to our supervisors and ourselves.

Something didn't seem quite right. We made progress, and our results looked impressive, but we still fell short of our goals. Some projects were left incomplete, with important elements still pending, which delayed the benefits reaching customers. We celebrated our activity without truly considering whether we were heading in the right direction.

CHAPTER 8 CONFESSION #8: HOW I LEARNED VELOCITY ISN'T EVERYTHING

This chapter is about the slow unraveling of that illusion, the heavy focus on velocity, the ways teams adjusted how progress was shown, and the stakeholder praise for numbers that didn't always align with outcomes. It's also about the turning point: when we moved away from over-relying on velocity and started reframing it as just one signal in a larger system of delivery.

Velocity isn't everything. It never was. The real story lies in how we learned to see beyond it, to make progress visible in ways that mattered, and to rebuild trust between teams, leadership, and business through metrics that gave a clearer, more complete picture.

Our reliance on numbers seemed natural at first, but the moment velocity became the headline of every update, it took on a life of its own.

When Velocity Became the Gospel

The sprint review began as usual. As the meeting began, there was the usual mix of participants joining the video call, with a brief quiet pause before the presentation started. The first slide displayed our velocity chart, illustrating the progress we are making.

The chart displayed a straightforward line that was increasing, with the bars getting taller after each effort. From the outside, it presented an encouraging picture that was easy to appreciate.

The presenter highlighted the sprint as a success, pointing to the velocity achieved.

Yet I felt that the numbers didn't capture the full story; those positive numbers didn't capture the whole picture. Beneath those encouraging trends, we had no completed features ready to launch. Instead, we had partial work items across the backlog, but not yet a fully completed feature that was ready for use. The report showcases the progress made by the team in a given sprint, but it focuses on team progress and does not highlight what was actually delivered to the business.

CHAPTER 8   CONFESSION #8: HOW I LEARNED VELOCITY ISN'T EVERYTHING

I thought about speaking up, but it didn't seem like the right moment. The chart created a positive atmosphere, and I hesitated, concerned that raising unfinished work might shift the focus away from the positive energy in the room. So I didn't say anything, even though I felt uneasy about the gap between what the chart suggested and the actual state of progress.

I noticed that everyone focused on speed. No one asked about the quality, how well the team adopted the product, or whether it was ready for release. Those important metrics no longer appeared. As long as we met or exceeded points, the team celebrated. Success increasingly became associated with a single number.

In previous projects, I witnessed stakeholders sometimes assume that Agile practices alone would drive progress, focusing on ceremonies and terminology rather than outcomes. Now, we faced the same issue, but this time the emphasis rested solely on velocity.

In that moment, I realized that velocity had stopped being just a planning tool. It had become the one accurate measure of the project. And if we continue to treat it that way, we risk running into challenges down the line if velocity remains the sole measure.

That reliance on charts soon shaped the way we worked, as teams began to adapt their approach in ways that made the numbers look good, but didn't always reflect real outcomes.

Chasing Points, Losing Purpose

I still remember one example clearly. We should have handled a story as a single piece of work, but instead, we broke it up into a series of repetitive stories, each only a minor variation that could have been a task. Our backlog filled up with these fragments. Yes, our velocity numbers increased, but the actual value remained the same. It felt like progress was being measured mainly by the numbers on the chart.

CHAPTER 8   CONFESSION #8: HOW I LEARNED VELOCITY ISN'T EVERYTHING

The situation often felt frustrating, and it was clear that not everyone was comfortable with it. Those who tried to estimate honestly always ended up looking like they were lagging, while teams that estimated differently sometimes appeared to be performing better. Review meetings shifted from genuine discussions about progress to comparing charts, focusing on who had the steepest line and who could showcase the highest numbers. I tried to raise concerns and point out that this wasn't a genuine improvement, but my concerns didn't gain much traction at the time. The numbers overwhelmed everything else.

Some stakeholders strongly emphasized metrics as the main indicator of success. I recall a developer jokingly mentioning that "If we break our stories into smaller chunks, the report will make us look like superstars." What began as a lighthearted comment slowly turned into our new reality. Ultimately, even my team felt the pressure to keep pace with the perception created by the numbers.

For me, that was probably the most challenging part of being a Scrum Master. I pushed back against this, but my concerns didn't gain much attention at the time. When my team started following the same pattern, I realized something important was being overlooked. At that point, the focus had shifted; the focus had shifted from progress toward outcomes to sustaining numbers on the chart.

Planning stopped centering on delivering valuable features and shifted toward maximizing story point throughput. Instead, it became about how many points we could burn through each sprint. The bigger picture faded. Stories were scattered across the board, often disconnected, and it became harder to see how the scattered stories connected into a larger whole. Velocity, the one thing meant to help us understand capacity, lost its purpose.

In the end, the win felt incomplete. The numbers looked great, but the meaning was gone. The focus shifted away from value and leaned heavily toward points.

Over time, this focus on points created a hidden cost, progress that looked strong on paper but didn't translate into features ready for release.

The Hidden Cost of Fragmentation

Velocity painted a great picture. Sprint after sprint, our numbers looked strong, and the charts proved we were hitting (and even beating) our goals. From the outside, it appeared that our team was thriving, consistently delivering results above expectations. When I took a moment to ask an important question, "What can we use right now?", the response was surprising: nothing was fully ready for use yet.

What happened wasn't immediately apparent, but it created hidden challenges. We tended to pick up stories that were easier or already prepped, while all the leftover, connecting pieces were left behind. Those loose ends just sat in the backlog, remaining in the backlog, even as our metrics kept improving. It was progress on paper, not in reality.

Early on, leadership didn't immediately see the underlying issue. The team celebrated the upward trends, thinking the velocity meant we were almost ready to ship. Meanwhile, I grew increasingly concerned. Instead of getting closer to real value, it seemed we were moving further from achieving it. The core of Agile, rapid feedback from users, kept getting pushed off, sprint after sprint.

Even the developers didn't notice it at first. They concentrated on finishing their assigned tasks, without stepping back to assess whether the overall feature was launch-ready. Retrospectives were always positive; the numbers indicated we were winning, so everyone continued to believe it was true. It was only afterward, when a Product Owner pushed for the finalization of a feature, that the discrepancies became clear. It was evident that we could not ignore the fragmentation.

CHAPTER 8   CONFESSION #8: HOW I LEARNED VELOCITY ISN'T EVERYTHING

The main problem wasn't just about putting everything together or testing it out. It was really about how complete our work was. Every deliverable was a fragment of a feature; much of the functionality wasn't yet in a state that could be delivered to the business.

I began to worry about the direction we were taking. Without fully developed features, we were unable to conduct practical demonstrations or obtain genuine user feedback. As a result, we shifted our focus to metrics, and restoring the feedback loop was essential for improvement.

When I spoke up about this, it didn't land at first. I argued we needed to think in bigger blocks: look at epics, focus on finishing full features, and be more explicit about what "ready" meant. My concerns didn't gain traction for a couple of sprints. Then reality hit. When leaders asked to see what was releasable, it became clear that the positive charts didn't yet translate into a complete product.

That moment marked a significant change for us. We began to change the way we planned our work. Instead of glossing over details, we started to look deeper into our stories and big projects. We focused on picking stories that can allow us to complete a feature testable by the business team. We couldn't transform everything overnight, but the thought process shifted in that direction.

Looking back, the lesson is clear as day. Productivity has limited value if it doesn't translate into something users can actually use. Agile isn't about how busy we look or how many points we burn; it's about actually delivering value and learning quickly. Every delay in delivery is a lost chance to learn. Fragmented progress works against Agile's core principles.

If I could do it over, I would have pushed much sooner for clear rules around what's "ready": not just for stories, but for entire epics. And I'd make sure business and product teams worked closely together to deliver complete, testable work. Because no matter how good the numbers look, if we aren't releasing something usable, it's hard to call it real progress.

CHAPTER 8   CONFESSION #8: HOW I LEARNED VELOCITY ISN'T EVERYTHING

It wasn't just the teams who celebrated the numbers; stakeholders also applauded them, even when the results didn't add up to complete, usable features.

Stakeholder Euphoria, Team Disquiet

As we've seen earlier in this chapter, sprint reviews often highlight praise, with participants eager to emphasize that we're ahead of schedule or that the current sprint is a success. A closer look suggested we weren't making the forward progress the numbers implied.

The team was hustling, picking up whatever stories were ready, but we weren't consistently completing business-ready features. Many features appeared almost complete, but each had just enough missing pieces to prevent them from being released. The problem wasn't a lack of effort; it was a lack of focus on what truly mattered for delivery. Still, as long as the charts looked good, the celebrations continued based on the positive charts.

At the time, the developers had no doubts. Their work matched the charts, and with no reason to question the bigger picture, they assumed we were on track. It wasn't until someone pointed out the disconnect that people began to realize the truth. Quiet conversations started, and informal comments emerged, noting that strong numbers didn't always translate into strong results.

For me, those meetings were tough. I felt uneasy that the excitement in the room was based on an incomplete picture. It wasn't as if the team was asking me to speak up; they hadn't seen the issue yet. They'd started to take comfort in the same things the leaders did: if velocity was up, we must be doing something right. My frustration came from knowing that until people saw the gap for themselves, my concerns might not be taken seriously until the gap was visible to others.

CHAPTER 8   CONFESSION #8: HOW I LEARNED VELOCITY ISN'T EVERYTHING

The wake-up call came at a release milestone. Leadership expected finished, shippable features, but what emerged were partial features rather than fully shippable ones. Velocity had been high, but we weren't ready. That changed everything. Suddenly, not just the development teams but also business and leadership realized that the way we were working had to evolve.

After that, our conversations changed. We began mapping out work at the epic level and collecting, sizing, and prioritizing full features, rather than just focusing on stories. Business stakeholders became more involved, helping define deliverables and bringing greater clarity to the backlog. Story readiness became more structured, and gradually, the emphasis on velocity shifted toward delivering meaningful value.

Teams and leaders should celebrate the launch of features for customers, not just the completion of tasks. Otherwise, activity can sometimes be mistaken for progress, which may create challenges later.

If I had to offer one piece of advice to other Scrum Masters, I would be cautious not to equate velocity with value. Celebrate real outcomes, not just staying busy.

The wake-up call arrived when reality could no longer be ignored, and planning had to shift toward epics and complete features instead of fragmented tasks.

Breaking the Spell (One Epic at a Time)

As discussed earlier in this chapter, pursuing stories that don't align with completing features may look like success in sprint reviews, but they don't necessarily move the product closer to release.

I suggested a different approach. Before finalizing the current release, I emphasized the importance of identifying features for the next release. This planning allows us to align the features effectively, ensuring we are well-prepared rather than starting a new release without a clear direction.

CHAPTER 8   CONFESSION #8: HOW I LEARNED VELOCITY ISN'T EVERYTHING

At first, I wasn't sure how leadership would respond. But after the hiccups of the last release, where limited epic-level readiness made it difficult for everyone to adjust quickly, they were ready to listen. Together, we started listing out the features, separating the must-haves from the nice-to-haves, and mapping them into release milestones.

The change became visible in the sessions that followed. Business analysts began preparing stories in line with prioritized epics, rather than spreading effort across less connected work. If an epic was part of the release, its stories had to be refined, ready, and aligned. Developers noticed a change, too. Instead of jumping between unrelated stories, they could now see how their work connected to a bigger goal. The Product Owner played a crucial role in this process, connecting business priorities with IT delivery and helping ensure that story readiness remained a consistent focus.

For the first time, the team helped ensure that story readiness remained a consistent focus. The real breakthrough came with the first epic we delivered under this new approach. I'll leave the specifics anonymous, but I'll never forget the feeling. Instead of showcasing a partial flow, we demonstrated a complete feature end-to-end. The business tested it long before user acceptance testing, and the atmosphere in the review was highly positive and energized. It felt different from past sprint demos; it showed what the team could achieve when working with clear focus and alignment.

Stakeholders responded differently, too. Instead of congratulating velocity numbers, they were celebrating outcomes. They could see and touch a finished feature, interact with it, and envision how users would receive it. That sense of early engagement provided more meaningful insight than the charts we had relied on before.

For me, the lesson became clear: focusing on what matters makes the real difference. Epic-level focus brought earlier feedback, reduced rework, and finally reconnected us with the core of Agile, delivering value, not just activity.

CHAPTER 8   CONFESSION #8: HOW I LEARNED VELOCITY ISN'T EVERYTHING

If I had to give one piece of advice to another Scrum Master, it would be this: spend more time forecasting at the epic level. It enables you to align requirements and execution with what the business truly needs, keeping your teams focused on outcomes that matter. In the long run, stakeholders are less focused on points burned and more on the features delivered.

Once epics became the foundation of our planning, it was clear that we needed to expand our view of metrics to track what truly mattered.

The Metrics We Weren't Measuring

Velocity is a big deal in our work. We had charts, graphs, and progress reports that showed we were putting in a lot of effort, sprint after sprint. However, I soon realized that these figures could be misleading if taken at face value. While a report may look great at first glance, many of the features we were working on were incomplete. That's when I understood an important lesson: velocity shows how fast we're working, but not necessarily whether we're heading in the right direction.

Things changed when I took on the Scrum Master role and realized we needed to see more than just numbers. We needed to connect all that effort to real business progress. Instead of only tracking story points, I began measuring progress at the epic level. The shift wasn't dramatic, but it created meaningful change. Now, we started monitoring actual progress toward fully completed features that delivered value.

The impact was almost immediate. Developers liked the new approach because it made their work easier to connect with bigger goals. People began to feel more engaged in their work. Instead of just completing individual tasks, they recognized how their efforts contributed to larger goals. This clarity helped the team better see how individual tasks contributed to the overall goals.

Meetings to review progress became more open and straightforward. Epic-based tracking turned conversations from speed to real, working results.

Planning sessions became more purposeful as we focused on what was needed to complete an epic, rather than only what could fit into the sprint. Retrospectives became more effective, and the team began discussing how to deliver complete features, rather than just focusing on speed.

Because we made this change early, we avoided some common pitfalls. We saw the warning signs as soon as gaps surfaced. Making our progress visible, even when it meant highlighting challenges, kept us focused on what mattered.

Looking back, my advice is simple: Scrum Masters can consider creating or adjusting metrics if standard dashboards don't reflect what matters. Agile tools can surface a lot of data; it's up to us to shape it so that it drives tangible business outcomes. A chart showing story points might look good for a while, but a chart showing completed features or epics builds long-term trust.

It's like shooting without aiming or moving quickly without a clear target. You put in effort without real direction. The important thing is to make sure you're on the right track. When we shifted our mindset, we stopped just focusing solely on how quickly we were moving and started focusing on making real, significant progress.

This broader view helped me recognize that velocity wasn't useless, it just had to be reframed as a signal, not the finish line.

Velocity As a Smell, not a Goal

Back then, I wasn't responsible for justifying the numbers, but I couldn't ignore my concern. I didn't feel any urge to celebrate velocity, and I didn't feel comfortable joining in the enthusiasm around velocity. It was

CHAPTER 8   CONFESSION #8: HOW I LEARNED VELOCITY ISN'T EVERYTHING

frustrating to watch as the culture placed more emphasis on numbers than outcomes. Teams started focusing more on boosting story point totals, instead of asking the more important question: Are we delivering business value?

Instead of measuring story points for planning, it became something to win. I saw estimates edge higher, work rushed to finish the sprint, and partial features sometimes being celebrated as though they were complete wins. Stand-ups and retrospectives never directly called out the competition. Still, in leadership meetings, it was clear: teams were often compared primarily on their numbers, with less focus on the impact of what they delivered.

Once I became a Scrum Master, I knew this mindset needed to change. The first thing I did was reframe velocity for the team. I used metaphors before data, describing velocity as "smoke," a signal to investigate, not a target to chase. Later, I introduced tools like Epic dashboards, feature burndowns, and additional tracking focused on real delivery. The goal was to turn the team's focus away from speed and toward finishing real, usable outcomes.

The real focus shifted to completing epics, declaring features as done, and ensuring the business could utilize what we delivered.

Looking back, one lesson stands out to me. Velocity provides traction; it indicates speed but not necessarily the destination. It works best as an early warning sign, but it's the progress on epics and features that tells you if you're going in the right direction.

Reframing velocity opened the door to new ways of thinking, where different metrics began to reshape mindsets and expectations across the teams.

CHAPTER 8   CONFESSION #8: HOW I LEARNED VELOCITY ISN'T EVERYTHING

New Metrics, New Mindsets

When I first started sharing progress using epics instead of just velocity, it felt like I was taking a different approach. No other Scrum teams around me were tracking things that way; most other teams continued using story points and burndown charts. But I wanted a better measure, one that showed how close we were to delivering something the business could use.

To my surprise, there wasn't any pushback. The new reports were well received, despite being the only team to use them. Leadership appreciated the clarity, and business stakeholders finally had visibility into progress in ways that mattered to them. They shifted focus away from story point totals and could see at a glance which epics were nearly complete and which ones weren't moving.

The impact was immediately apparent. Our planning sessions changed. Instead of focusing on how many points could fit into the next sprint, we started talking about which stories would bring an epic over the finish line. If an epic was already nearly complete, it made sense to finish it, close it, and deliver tangible value. The whole conversation shifted from numbers to outcomes.

Retrospectives didn't change much, but elsewhere the cultural shift was noticeable. The connection between business and IT has grown stronger. Business leaders could now see real progress on features earlier in the process, which helped create more confidence around deadlines and shifting priorities. What could have become a complaint was often caught and addressed early, because our new view made bottlenecks stand out before they escalated into bigger challenges.

From a Scrum Master's perspective, this change barely took any extra time, only a short amount of time each week to update dashboards. Those few minutes made a big difference in the credibility of my role. Beyond simply facilitating meetings, I was providing leadership and stakeholders with a clear, up-to-date picture of the value delivered. That new level of visibility made my contributions more meaningful to the business.

CHAPTER 8   CONFESSION #8: HOW I LEARNED VELOCITY ISN'T EVERYTHING

The most surprising thing was the way these metrics revealed hidden issues. By tracking at the epic level, we began to notice dependencies that we hadn't seen before.

Even though it started with one team, it sparked a broader realization: Agile metrics work best when they provide genuine clarity, Beyond simply facilitating meetings.

As these metrics gained traction, their real power emerged when delivery itself became visible and progress could be seen in terms of features and epics.

When Delivery Became Visible

For a long time, all our reporting focused on velocity, how many points we burned, and how many stories we closed. That changed the first time I started reporting on epic-level progress. Suddenly, stakeholders weren't just following numbers on a chart. Now, they could see where the team stood in the larger plan. Weekly updates, which I shared with other Scrum Masters and IT leaders, highlighted not only what we'd finished, but also how early other teams could align with us and what capacity the team still had to take on new work. How many points were completed, and how many stories were closed? Instead, we start the discussion on how it impacts the existing epics.

The team could immediately tell the difference. The visibility gave the team a sense of pride. Motivation grew, not because the team hit sprint targets, but because they completed something meaningful.

Stakeholders noticed, too. Demos and reviews now emphasized complete features, rather than partial fragments. Their feedback became sharper and more helpful because they were finally seeing and responding to deliverables that made sense for the business. One leader even told me it shifted their perspective. The goal wasn't just to close a sprint anymore; it was to move closer to releasing real value.

CHAPTER 8   CONFESSION #8: HOW I LEARNED VELOCITY ISN'T EVERYTHING

This new level of transparency also made a cultural difference. Although I shared the latest report within IT, they soon began to inform business decisions. With clearer epic burnup and burndown charts, dependencies became apparent sooner, escalations decreased, and planning sessions proceeded much more smoothly. The uncertainty was greatly reduced.

Looking back, the lesson became very clear. Visibility makes planning possible. Without it, planning often relied on assumptions. With it, teams and leaders can align earlier, prioritize more effectively, and make decisions with greater confidence and less pressure.

If I could sum up my advice to other Scrum Masters, it's this: don't just show how fast your team is moving. Show where they are going. Proper visibility isn't about tracking performance for its own sake; it's about making progress clear and meaningful for everyone.

In the end, visibility taught us the right balance; velocity still mattered, but only as one piece of a much bigger picture.

Velocity Didn't Disappear, It Evolved

Velocity was never the problem by itself. It was just incomplete. It measured motion, but not direction. It showed activity, but didn't guarantee achievement. In the early days, we treated it as the final word. We chased higher numbers, celebrated speed, and overlooked the risks that were building up—fragmented delivery, unmet goals, and growing concerns. At one point, velocity became more like a competition, a marker of success, until we realized it was leading us in the wrong direction.

The real change occurred when we began to view velocity in a new light. It stopped being the objective and became a warning sign. If features stalled, defects increased, or stories failed to come together into real value, velocity would alert us. On its own, velocity could be misleading. But when combined with tracking at the epic level, burnup charts, and precise delivery metrics, velocity started to serve us again. It became a signal, not a prize.

This shift changed the culture in ways that were visible and meaningful. Teams became more focused and gained pride from completing full features, not just story points. Stakeholders began to ask about progress in terms of complete epics, rather than point totals. Leaders were able to make decisions faster and with more confidence, because they could see how work connected to business results. My responsibilities grew, too, and overlooked the risks that were building up: fragmented delivery, unmet goals, and growing concerns.

Velocity didn't disappear; it just took its proper place. Now it's one measure among several. It's useful when used wisely, but limiting if treated as the whole story.

If I had to give one piece of advice from all this, it's simple: be cautious not to focus only on numbers. Velocity shows how fast you're going, but only tracking epics and features shows whether you're truly moving toward delivering value.

Takeaway Confession Avoid treating velocity as the measure of success. Measure progress by the features you finish, not just the points you close. By focusing on epics, Scrum Masters can give their teams and stakeholders real, meaningful visibility. Ultimately, it's less about the numbers and more about demonstrating how close you are to achieving meaningful outcomes. That's why velocity shouldn't be everything. It's just a signpost along the way, not the goal itself.

CHAPTER 9

Confession #9: Customer Feedback in IT—The Forgotten Metric

> *The important thing is not to stop questioning. Curiosity has its own reason for existing.*
>
> —Albert Einstein

Real progress focuses on value rather than velocity. Users define that value through their experiences with what we create. However, in many projects, customer feedback can slip into the background. It comes late, or too many layers filter it. Teams may deliver software that meets documented requirements but doesn't fully align with user needs.

I learned this the hard way. In one release, the absence of feedback after launch gave us a false sense of achievement. Another time, a single support call highlighted gaps between what we delivered and what people actually needed. Things only started to improve when real users had a voice. When our demos became opportunities to discover, and feedback became a regular part of our process, we finally started to understand the fundamental goals of Agile.

This chapter is about putting feedback back where it belongs, as the key metric. Feedback helps turn delivery into value, speed into clear direction, and software into practical solutions. Through times of uncertainty, moments of defensiveness, and eventually, curiosity, we learned an important lesson. Feedback doesn't slow Agile down. If anything, it's the quickest way to move forward.

Those early reflections set the stage for what came next, the silence after our first release, a silence that carried its own lessons.

The Post-Go-Live Silence

The first release wasn't a victory lap. It felt like a hurried push to the finish line. We worked hard, made quick decisions, and did whatever it took to hit a critical deadline. The system went live as planned and remained stable enough to handle the load. From a pure delivery perspective, we had succeeded. However, we encountered a lack of response nearly immediately after we launched.

Within the team, the atmosphere was more like a quiet moment after a long stretch of effort, mixed with a sense of uncertainty. We had worked quickly, but did we build the right thing? We set up a war room, ready to handle any issues or tickets that came in, but very little activity came in.

Leadership held off on celebrating as well. Some areas experienced activity, while others saw barely any engagement. A few features saw little to no usage after launch. Nonetheless, no one was willing to voice any issues regarding it, which was considered a positive sign.

At that time, I wasn't a Scrum Master yet; I was the architect. I couldn't shake the feeling that something was wrong. Silence didn't mean we had done the right thing. It could just as easily mean that users weren't connecting with the product or weren't getting value from it. Eventually, a few escalations made that reality clear. Our efforts to deliver quickly came with trade-offs. We hadn't established the proper feedback channels, and that first release left us unsure about what users truly wanted.

Looking back, that release changed my thinking. I learned that early silence shouldn't be mistaken for a compliment; it's better treated as a signal to seek feedback. It doesn't prove that the product works; it simply indicates that important feedback is missing. From the second release onward, when I assumed the Scrum Master role, our process changed. We made feedback a core part of our delivery. However, the lesson from that first release has always stuck with me: meeting a deadline matters less if user voices aren't heard and real value isn't being delivered.

The quiet after launch eventually gave way to updates, but these arrived indirectly, filtered through others rather than directly from users.

Feedback by Proxy

After the first release, we were eager to find out how the product was being received. Instead of hearing directly from the people using the system, though, the team mostly relied on updates from key stakeholders. These were leaders who joined meetings and then shared what they heard about usage. They didn't intentionally filter or soften the feedback; they passed along what was reported. It didn't provide the same clarity as hearing from users directly or observing their interactions with the system.

In those early meetings, stakeholders honestly relayed the issues they had heard from a wide range of users, not just sponsors or power users, but also from the broader community. This gave the team a sense that we had the whole story after the pressure of the first release, which felt sufficient at the time. Developers accepted the feedback at face value. They were both fatigued and proud of what they had accomplished. The energy was focused on maintaining momentum, rather than questioning whether anything important might have been overlooked.

CHAPTER 9 CONFESSION #9: CUSTOMER FEEDBACK IN IT—THE FORGOTTEN METRIC

As the architect, I didn't push back either. The top priority was to stabilize the system, respond quickly to issues, and get fixes out as needed. It was understood that certain trade-offs had been necessary to meet the deadline, so hearing about problems wasn't surprising. It was expected, and our team applied interim fixes while preparing for a more stable follow-up release. At the same time, we planned a more stable follow-up release.

There wasn't a big, dramatic moment when indirect feedback failed us. The real challenge was baked into the nature of the first release itself. To meet the deadline, we emphasized speed, with plans to refine usability in later iterations. When feedback finally started coming in, it mostly confirmed what we already suspected: the core product functioned as intended, though it lacked the level of refinement we hoped to achieve.

In hindsight, the bigger lesson was about context, not just communication. When speed dominates decision-making, feedback often highlights gaps that were already anticipated. The product functioned, but it wasn't polished, and users naturally noticed that.

If I could go back, I would resist the urge to spend time perfecting the interface too early. Rather than trying to add polish up front, I'd focus on delivering the essential functionality first. User experience improvements can be introduced in later iterations once the basics are in place. When I coach teams facing similar deadlines today, I tell them this: if you can't reach your users directly, make sure you at least see raw, unedited feedback rather than polished summaries. Feedback doesn't need to be polished; it's most valuable when it's candid and direct.

Even as feedback trickled in, another challenge emerged, realizing that not every feature we invested in was truly needed.

CHAPTER 9   CONFESSION #9: CUSTOMER FEEDBACK IN IT—THE FORGOTTEN METRIC

The Feature Nobody Wanted

Not every feature starts with a clear customer need. Some exist because of architectural choices or technical requirements, requirements driven by system design, even if not directly requested by users. In our first release, one such feature required weeks of effort. It wasn't flashy or exciting, but was marked as essential and considered non-negotiable. The developers built it as asked, though some were skeptical.

After we launched the new feature, it became evident that usage was minimal, even after the considerable effort invested in development.

The team felt some disappointment about the outcome. They all knew the reality: when it was time to review upcoming tasks, no one advocated for making any changes or improvements to the feature. As a result, it gradually moved out of focus and was deprioritized.

Eventually, we had to acknowledge the reality. We realized that the feature was not helpful to the user, which opened our minds and led us to dive deeper into the lined-up features and take a closer look to see if they were necessary to the business.

Looking back, the lesson stands out as a clear reminder. Technical requirements by themselves rarely create value. If a feature doesn't help users or solve a business problem, it's unlikely to be a worthwhile investment. The actual test is return on investment: Does the feature drive meaningful results for the business? If not, it shouldn't be high on the backlog.

When I work with teams, I always encourage them to measure both effort and business benefits. Which features create value? Which ones help the company grow, reduce pain points, or promote adoption? Those are the ones we should focus on.

If I had to sum it up in one question, I'd put it like this: before you spend weeks of effort, ask, "If we never built this feature, would the business or our users truly miss it?" If the answer is "no," it may not deserve

CHAPTER 9   CONFESSION #9: CUSTOMER FEEDBACK IN IT—THE FORGOTTEN METRIC

a place in the upcoming sprint. In Agile, value is what matters most, not volume of code, not speed, and not just technical perfection. I learned this through experience with a feature that ultimately wasn't needed.

It wasn't until a support escalation arrived that the real impact of missing voices became impossible to ignore.

The Support Call That Changed Everything

The silence that followed the launch, accompanied by unexpected challenges, prompted the support team to seek feedback from the business team. It was a flow that impacted users, which identified a gap. Everything went well on time. When we thought all was going well, the feedback from the business made it evident that we were missing something crucial.

Inside the team, the reaction was instant. The team felt disappointed. Developers who had worked hard under pressure recognized that their effort hadn't translated into the value users expected. People rushed to suggest fixes, but initially, only short-term adjustments were possible. At the same time, the larger issue—the difference between what is delivered and what is needed—persisted.

Leadership acknowledged the issue but treated it as one among many items to manage, not as a warning about our understanding of user needs. For them, it was a problem to be solved; for the team, it highlighted that delivering software alone wasn't enough if it didn't address real user needs.

We realized that we needed to broaden the scope of UAT participation; we needed to broaden our approach to gather early feedback from users so that users can identify any gaps before the release.

The lesson I took with me is clear: early user feedback is essential. It's not just for catching defects or filling gaps; it serves to prevent wasted effort and help ensure the team's efforts align with user needs. When I later became a Scrum Master, I ensured that I built these feedback loops into the process sooner.

Now, when I coach other Scrum Masters, I always remind them that constructive feedback, even when critical, is valuable. Teams often only get input when things have gone wrong, and that can hurt morale, but it's still beneficial. The key is to treat these moments not as signs of failure but as guidance for what to do next. That challenging support call reminded us of the importance of listening closely and seeking out feedback early and often.

That call made it clear that we had to change our approach, and the answer was to bring real users into the process earlier.

Integrating Real Voices

Until then, most of what we built was evaluated indirectly: by stakeholders, business leads, or select testers during acceptance testing. Most end users only interacted with the system late in the process, when the development was nearing completion. Everything changed when we started inviting users to earlier demos.

The difference was immediate. We received direct feedback from users of our system, which was extremely helpful. We believed we had a good grasp of how they worked, but once they started using the app, it became clear that our assumptions didn't fully match reality. They interacted with the app in ways that none of us, not even our testers, had expected. Observing them use the app was both surprising and eye-opening for the team.

Stakeholders expressed caution about exposing features that were still incomplete. Knowing that real users would be observing their work encouraged the team to prepare more thoroughly. They began to use realistic examples that truly represented how users would interact with the product. The demonstrations shifted their focus to real use cases.

CHAPTER 9 CONFESSION #9: CUSTOMER FEEDBACK IN IT—THE FORGOTTEN METRIC

The guidance was to involve users once features were considered sufficiently ready. Balancing that caution with the need for authentic input was a challenge. Still, every time users joined, the value was clear. Business leaders saw firsthand how direct engagement uncovered problems and potential improvements no one else had noticed.

One demo sticks with me. Users attempted to use a workflow in an unexpected manner, which our tests hadn't covered. On paper and in testing, everything appeared to be fine. But under real-world use, the process broke down. We caught a critical flaw that would have gone live and caused significant challenges later. Catching and correcting it early saved us from bigger trouble down the road.

That moment made a big impression on me. It was the missing piece. User feedback didn't just confirm our work, it changed what we built next. By listening early, we found and fixed issues that would have become major support issues later. We also made changes that encouraged better adoption.

Looking back, the most significant benefit was prevention. Instead of scrambling to fix problems after launch, we addressed them before they hit production. This experience convinced me that relying only on business analysts or a small stakeholder group can leave important gaps. Involving a wider group of users always brings new insights. Their feedback is essential for building truly successful products.

Now, when I coach Scrum Masters, I encourage them to advocate for user involvement as soon as features are ready to be shown. Not when everything is perfect, but not so soon that it's incomplete, either. Just a few real user sessions can influence priorities more than any amount of documentation. My rule is simple: make space for users early. Their feedback isn't optional; it's what helps transform software into solutions that truly meet your needs.

Yet involving users came with its own tension, as the team had to learn how to handle feedback without slipping into defensiveness.

CHAPTER 9   CONFESSION #9: CUSTOMER FEEDBACK IN IT—THE FORGOTTEN METRIC

From Defensiveness to Curiosity

When users started sharing their feedback, the scrum team initially responded defensively due to the hard work spent on building that feature. It was instinct to defend what the team had developed, but an opportunity to listen to valuable feedback was overlooked.

The team focused on defending the system, while the users concentrated on their actual needs. Neither side was wrong, but the gap between perspectives became clearer.

As the architect, I decided to step in. I reminded everyone that this kind of direct discussion with business users was rare, and it was important to make the most of it. I asked the users to show us their actual process, even the undocumented steps. That shift from justifying our choices to being genuinely curious changed the mood. The team began to hear new details and learned things that hadn't come up in any requirements or test scripts.

The real lesson was clear: users pointed out where the design did not match real-life practices. They showed where the design failed to align with the real world.

If I were the Scrum Master, I would have asked the team to approach feedback with openness instead of jumping to explain. Users don't need to be told why a system works a certain way; they need to see that their feedback can make a difference.

That experience reinforced something essential for me: defensiveness can reduce opportunities to learn. Whenever a user shows how the product falls short, they provide insight into their reality, offering perspectives the team may not otherwise see. A defensive stance pushes that gift away. However, a curious team welcomes it and, as a result, builds trust as well as better solutions.

Now, when I work with teams, I stress this: defensiveness can limit opportunities, while curiosity helps create them. Changing to this mindset is challenging, but it's what enables a team to move from merely delivering software to creating genuine value.

Once curiosity replaced resistance, the question became how to make feedback sustainable, not just a one-time adjustment.

Building Feedback Loops

Initially, the feedback we received was inconsistent. Sometimes we would face pressure to change things, other times we'd have meetings to showcase our work, and occasionally, unanticipated gaps would surface during testing. It made things challenging for the team to assess whether we were fully aligned with user expectations.

The change didn't occur immediately. We established a process to gather early feedback from users, who initially saw it as an added step, but later began to experience the benefits.

As the team recognized that constructive feedback could significantly mitigate rework and provide clarity regarding project requirements from the outset, their attitudes shifted positively. Feedback has evolved from being seen as extra work to being viewed as a valuable opportunity to enhance product quality. It helps find potential issues early in the development process, instead of having to rush to fix problems after the product is released.

This change showed up in how we worked together. Testing scenarios became more focused. Acceptance criteria got clearer. Instead of working in isolation, teams began writing user stories and test cases that aligned with actual business practices. We didn't invent a new process. We just let feedback become part of the routine.

CHAPTER 9 CONFESSION #9: CUSTOMER FEEDBACK IN IT—THE FORGOTTEN METRIC

There were still challenges. Getting business users involved regularly wasn't easy. It was never realistic to have them join every session, and sometimes only a few could attend. The challenge was never overwhelming feedback; more often, it was the limited amount available. Even so, the team found ways to connect what feedback they did get with how they checked and validated their work.

The results showed up in later releases. We saw fewer problems after launch. Where previously we had to implement quick workarounds, our systems now run more smoothly. In one case, a feedback session addressed a business scenario that had previously caused trouble, handling it perfectly. Even limited feedback loops made a real difference.

Looking back, I saw more than just fewer bugs. Feedback built alignment. It made business users feel like partners in the process, active contributors rather than distant observers. People adopted the system not because it was flawless, but because their voices had shaped it. That feeling of ownership was just as important as any feature we released.

Today, I always tell teams that spending time on validation with business partners is essential; it's at the core of Agile. Feedback isn't something you gather at the end. It's what energizes the whole process. And it's not just about hearing from IT proxies. It's about making room for real customers, business leaders, and end users, so everyone is responsible for both the problem and the solution.

If I had to sum it up in one principle, this: feedback loops are central to Agile, keeping the process active and aligned. Without them, the process looks active but isn't truly healthy. With them, the product gets stronger, more people embrace it, and the team delivers something of real value, not just code.

Over time, those loops did more than prevent issues; they began shaping how we thought about strategy and value.

CHAPTER 9   CONFESSION #9: CUSTOMER FEEDBACK IN IT—THE FORGOTTEN METRIC

Feedback As Product Strategy

During our first release cycle, feedback played a critical role in shaping our process. It helped us identify usability gaps, clarify how workflows should work, and find issues before they became serious problems. Although feedback didn't always change the roadmap or shift priorities, it was still significant beyond just fixing bugs. As time went on, it became clear that feedback was more than just information; it was a sign of whether our actions matched the core values of our business.

To their credit, the leaders began incorporating this feedback into their strategic decision-making. They didn't have to change their plans or budgets completely, but they began to see feedback as a way to understand better how we were doing. Team speed can be measured through metrics like task completion rates or issue counts. However, it's the feedback from users that shows whether that work is making a difference for the business. This understanding is fundamental.

During a feedback session, users shared insights about more efficient ways to interact with the system. We did not need to rebuild the product, but the small changes made the system feel more suited to their daily work. As a result, adoption rates climbed, not because of new features, but because the product started to feel natural for users.

For developers, this was a valuable lesson. The feedback did not disrupt our plans, but it showed us that user input can shape the results in ways that testing alone may not capture. We changed our focus. Instead of only asking if we were working quickly, we started asking if we were going in the right direction. Even minor adjustments based on feedback helped build trust with stakeholders and improve the product.

Users showed higher satisfaction and greater adoption because they felt their input was valued and mattered. Stakeholders gained confidence as they noticed their feedback led to real improvements. This connection built a stronger relationship between the team and the business, something that metrics alone could not achieve.

CHAPTER 9   CONFESSION #9: CUSTOMER FEEDBACK IN IT—THE FORGOTTEN METRIC

Looking back, I realized something key: metrics highlight execution, but feedback highlights relevance. A burn-down chart shows efficiency, while feedback helps reveal whether the team is working on the right problems. You can move quickly and still be off course.

Even if it doesn't always lead to significant changes, it helps guide the team and keeps everyone focused on what matters to users. Metrics can show how fast the team is working, while feedback helps ensure the work stays aligned with user needs. Ultimately, a good strategy is about knowing where we're headed, not just how quickly we arrive.

What started as tactical adjustments soon revealed something larger: feedback could actually fuel innovation.

When Feedback Sparked Innovation

Feedback is typically seen as a tool for correction, highlighting shortcomings, and resolving confusion. The feedback we have received has identified a pattern based on the user's use case. Instead of expecting users to change their habits, the product team, especially the user experience specialists, chose to follow their lead.

The effect was more than just a minor improvement. Feedback not only identifies issues but also creates opportunities for improvement. Rather than avoiding criticism, the team started to welcome fresh ideas and insights from users.

Leadership soon saw the benefits. The changes prompted by user feedback not only addressed existing gaps; they also helped shape the product's direction. These insights became a key part of longer-term planning and future roadmaps. Business stakeholders noticed, too. As they saw real user behavior influencing not just fixes but priorities, trust in the development process grew.

The practical benefits were clear. Adoption increased because the product became more intuitive to use. Processes that had previously been slow and cumbersome became much more efficient, saving time for both users and teams. It wasn't just a technical achievement; it translated directly into measurable improvements for the business.

Often, genuine innovation arises from the surprising ways that people use and respond to what you've built. The gap between design intentions and users' real experiences may feel challenging, but it is often where new ideas and breakthroughs emerge.

Now, when I coach teams, I ask them to view feedback as more than a list of issues to resolve. It's a source of ideas and a window into knowledge you can't get from requirements alone. Metrics and plans will get you only so far. It's feedback that reveals how users interact with your product. That experience taught us that innovation often emerges not only from invention but from attentive listening.

Ultimately, these experiences showed that feedback was not a side activity, but the very driver of direction and trust.

Feedback Is the Fastest Way Forward

The first release felt stable but lacked meaningful engagement; users weren't speaking up, and the team assumed that meant it was successful. Over time, it became clear that feedback relayed through stakeholders proved insufficient on its own. Their reactions, workflows, and surprises revealed gaps we hadn't identified, and at times challenged our understanding of how the system should work.

At first, the team initially reacted with resistance. The instinctive response was to defend existing work rather than immediately accept the critique. But with deliberate effort, curiosity replaced resistance. We began to listen more than explain. That change improved acceptance criteria, reduced production defects, and ultimately built trust between the team and business users.

CHAPTER 9 CONFESSION #9: CUSTOMER FEEDBACK IN IT—THE FORGOTTEN METRIC

What started as a way to prevent issues grew into something bigger; feedback became a source of innovation. Leadership now views feedback as a crucial component of strategy, enhancing adoption rates and overall satisfaction.

Takeaway Confession Metrics show speed, but feedback shows direction. Agile thrives not by avoiding problems but through open conversations. Every loop closed with users saved time, strengthened trust, and gave the team clarity about what mattered most.

CHAPTER 10

Confession #10: Siloed Teams, Stalled Delivery

> *Collaboration is not about gluing together existing egos. It's about the ideas that never existed until after everyone entered the room.*
>
> —Unknown

Every team I've worked with has faced a common, mostly unspoken challenge: silos. You won't see them on process diagrams or sprint boards, but they're always present. Development, QA, UX, and integration teams often operate in parallel rather than fully integrated. Each group focuses on its piece of the puzzle, but the larger picture often gets lost in the space between them.

Initially, the problems are easy to overlook. A bug can remain in the backlog when ownership is unclear. A design may look great, but it can't be built on the chosen framework. A release might go live, only to later reveal that a test was missing. These issues don't happen because anyone is lazy or doesn't care. They happen when collaboration is limited and teams focus more on their individual contributions than on the shared outcome.

CHAPTER 10   CONFESSION #10: SILOED TEAMS, STALLED DELIVERY

I've learned, sometimes the hard way, that Agile challenges are less common within a single team and more likely to emerge where teams interact, dependencies accumulate, and ownership is unclear. Those gaps can lead to bottlenecks, extra rework, delays, and gradual erosion of stakeholder confidence.

This chapter is about those in-between spaces and the ways we learned to close the gaps. The stories include missed connections, unexpected breakthroughs in chat threads, the frustration of duplicated effort, and the satisfaction that comes from swarming problems and mapping out dependencies. They highlight the messy but essential work of breaking down silos.

Because collaboration isn't just a principle in a manifesto, it's the everyday effort to make sure no team becomes isolated or drifts too far from the rest.

The first cracks in collaboration often showed up at the edges, and nowhere was this more visible than in the way integration gradually became our biggest obstacle.

When Integration Became the Bottleneck

Integration problems don't emerge overnight; they build up progressively over time. Initially, processes may experience a slight slowdown, causing only minor concerns. Over time, however, everything comes to a standstill, leaving the team uncertain about how it had escalated to that stage. This is exactly what happened in our project when integration became our biggest challenge.

The warning signs had been there for weeks. Teams continued to develop features that relied on APIs that had not been tested correctly together. QA teams had limited ability to start their work since testing environments were not yet ready. Developers would mark their stories as done, moving tickets on their boards, only to realize that "done" didn't mean the feature worked in the bigger system. We kept making progress on paper, but the goal kept slipping away.

We tried to address it in the usual way. We set up meeting after meeting, holding lengthy sessions with people from every team to discuss dependencies, blockers, and responsibilities. These sessions went well beyond stand-ups, with much of the time spent on updates rather than collaborative problem-solving. After every meeting, the same issues would resurface. The larger the meeting, the less we achieved. The crucial connection between teams, the "handshake" that could have aligned us, never took place.

Ironically, our real breakthroughs came from much smaller, less formal moments. A small group of developers and testers had a casual discussion and came up with a solution that hadn't been thought of in larger meetings. Everyone was focused on finding an answer, without the pressure of formality or the need for approval. This experience served as a valuable reminder that sometimes, straightforward and honest conversations can lead to better outcomes than lengthy, formal discussions.

Integration exposed how fragile cross-team alignment could be, but the quieter friction between development and QA revealed another invisible barrier.

The Wall No One Saw—Dev vs. QA

It all started innocently enough, as most walls between teams do. Development and QA appeared to be aligned. Features were being built, tickets were getting closed, and stand-ups were happening as expected. But underneath, issues were building up. I first saw the problem when defects appeared in unusual ways. They weren't logged with the features

CHAPTER 10   CONFESSION #10: SILOED TEAMS, STALLED DELIVERY

where they belonged. Instead, they became new user stories in the backlog, or sometimes weren't clearly linked to the features they affected, leaving ownership unclear.

The acceptance criteria, which had started sharp and clear, began to blur. To keep sprints moving, the requirements became less detailed. Developers kept working ahead, expecting QA would fill in the gaps once a feature was "ready." QA, meanwhile, felt they could only do their job when everything was finished. The result was that essential test scenarios got pushed from one sprint to the next, never really getting the focus they needed.

Tension started to grow, and it was most evident in daily stand-ups. QA repeatedly highlighted concerns about missing test scenarios and unresolved issues. Developers would respond that the features were built and stories were done. These weren't angry exchanges, but you could feel the frustration mounting. Both sides expected the other to bridge the gap, but nobody owned responsibility for closing it.

As a result, the backlog became heavier with bugs. QA's list of open defects grew, and developers were frustrated when new stories emerged for issues they believed had already been addressed. It was never a matter of effort; everyone was working hard. But the invisible wall between teams meant the effort wasn't translating into the progress everyone expected.

Leadership eventually noticed the growing problem. It became clear that the issue wasn't a matter of technical skill, but rather a mismatched set of expectations. The turning point came during a stand-up when the discomfort was evident. QA repeated concerns they'd raised for weeks, and this time, everyone listened. Silence replaced the usual back-and-forth, and it became clear that a gap between teams existed.

The solution wasn't drastic. We didn't need a new tool or an entirely new process. Instead, we made a simple but significant change: testers joined backlog refinement and played an explicit role in prioritizing scenarios. The team began planning features not only based on business needs, but also on the completeness of testing. Stories weren't called "done" until all testing scenarios were covered, even if it meant delivery took a little longer. The thinking was that it's better to pause up front than to fix problems later.

With testers shaping what went into the sprint, the wall between teams began to fall. Developers began to view QA as partners earlier in the process rather than only at the end. Testers felt empowered to raise gaps early, and the results showed quickly: fewer bugs, more transparent accountability, and a release that felt much less risky.

When I reflect, I realize that the most significant risk wasn't the defects, but the tendency to prioritize speed above all else. You can work quickly, but if you don't focus on quality, you are just heading for bigger problems. Agile isn't just about finishing tasks for the sake of it; it's about delivering work that can hold up under examination.

Ultimately, we discovered that agility without quality risks becoming movement without meaningful progress. Giving testing scenarios equal weight with business features became part of our DNA, and it changed the way we delivered, making our releases stronger and our results more reliable.

Even as we improved the connection between developers and testers, the pressure of release cycles reminded us how easily gaps could still surface.

A Release Held Together by a Workaround

The day of the big launch is always a bit stressful, but this time felt more intense than usual. No one needed to say it out loud; everyone could feel the added pressure. The deadline for the quarter was approaching fast, and once again, the stories about what users needed were clarified only after the work had already begun. This meant that development and testing weren't progressing together; instead, both were racing against the

CHAPTER 10   CONFESSION #10: SILOED TEAMS, STALLED DELIVERY

clock. In the stand-ups, team updates were brief and focused on business matters. Everyone was feeling the crunch, but nobody wanted to be the one to call out the risks.

When the release finally went live, a fragile sense of relief settled over the team. Everything was going well at first. A team member identified a critical issue during testing that caused a significant failure in the system. This problem was not minor; it was a significant challenge affecting a crucial aspect of the user experience.

There was no immediate rollback, but fixing the defect proved to be a challenging task. The issue hadn't been documented. It had no corresponding user story or acceptance criteria; instead, it turned out to be a missed scenario that had slipped through because integration testing was conducted too late, and quality checks had been deferred until later in the process.

Leadership responded quickly, and the disappointment was evident. This problem went beyond being a typical bug; it created a noticeable strain on trust. Customers became aware of the issue, and although the maintenance team quickly implemented a temporary solution, the impact had already been felt. Users might accept sporadic outages, but a flawed release can weaken confidence in the overall process.

Everyone on the team felt a sense of responsibility, even if no specific person could be blamed. This wasn't due to carelessness; it reflected a gap in planning. The absence of thorough scenario mapping, the late start for integration testing, and the rushed acceptance criteria had all contributed. The real issue was the siloed approach that left gaps outside anyone's direct ownership.

Afterward, the team held a candid postmortem. With emotions cooled, they dissected the mistakes. The conclusion was clear: scenarios were missed because integration testing had been delayed until late in the process. By then, the time needed for thorough QA was already gone. The missed scenario wasn't an isolated oversight; it pointed to a broader issue.

CHAPTER 10   CONFESSION #10: SILOED TEAMS, STALLED DELIVERY

The fix was straightforward. QA was brought into the planning process earlier, integration testing was moved up, and review of scenario coverage became a key point in planning rather than an afterthought. This didn't erase the mistake, but it ensured that the same gap wouldn't appear again.

The immediate workaround was put in place, closely monitored by the maintenance team, and the project was able to move forward. Still, the lesson lingered. Releases rarely stumble due to a single overlooked test; more often, pressure and silos combine to create gaps that aren't visible until too late.

The main takeaway for the team was simple: make integration testing an early priority, and never assume missing scenarios will resolve themselves. While a workaround may patch a release, early QA involvement was the change that ultimately transformed how every subsequent release was handled.

The release taught us about timing and testing, but the next challenge came from another direction, when design vision and technical reality drifted apart.

UX in Orbit, Dev on the Ground

From the outset, a quiet gap existed between the UX team and the developers. It wasn't caused by conflict, but by a difference in priorities. The UX group worked independently, creating designs that were visually polished and appealing. The problem wasn't their creativity; it was that the designs weren't grounded in the technical framework the developers were using. When those designs finally reached backlog refinement, the team had to face the mismatch.

The first issues appeared during refinement meetings. Screens and workflows were presented as though they were ready to build, but developers knew immediately that some features would require significant changes. Some controls weren't available in the platform, and others would need weeks of custom work. This wasn't just additional effort; it highlighted a disconnect between design ambitions and the platform's capabilities.

But the designs already had customer approval, which made them feel non-negotiable. Even when developers raised concerns early, they learned that the designs had already been signed off. There was often an assumption that developers could adapt the designs, while UX expected adjustments could be made later if necessary. In practice, neither side's assumptions proved true.

The problems quickly became visible. Developers had to add exceptions to the backlog and get approval from IT and business leaders to keep moving forward. Sprints slowed down as prototypes were built, only to show that specific ideas just weren't possible. The cycle kept repeating: delays, repeated discussions with stakeholders, and eventual workarounds.

Emotions began to show up in meetings. Developers were frustrated when asked to deliver items that were not feasible within the framework. Meanwhile, UX designers felt sidelined when their work was changed or reduced without early involvement. Since technical experts weren't brought in from the beginning, UX only learned about technical limits when the Product Owner relayed feedback, which left them less connected to the process.

The situation escalated during a sprint demo. Developers used workaround controls, but the result differed from the initial UX mockups. Stakeholders sought explanations, and the framework team acknowledged that the original design was not feasible within the framework.

Leadership responded by adding a new checkpoint: from then on, UX designs would be reviewed by business, the Product Owner, and technical specialists before anything got approved. This early review gave UX a chance to receive crucial feedback before their designs were sent to customers. It didn't prevent every conflict, but it made a significant difference in reducing wasted cycles and redesigns.

It wasn't a perfect fix. Developers still sometimes had to use workarounds that fell short of the UX vision. However, everyone now understands the limitations up-front. Compromises were apparent before sprints started, not after a demo failed. It wasn't always the refined experience envisioned by UX, but it kept the project moving and helped the whole team stay aligned.

The practical solution was to stick to controls available in the framework, even if that made the experience less ideal. It wasn't perfect, but it provided UX and developers with common ground to build upon and made delivery more predictable.

Misalignment with UX showed how damaging late involvement could be, and it set the stage for a broader truth: critical alignment often never happened at all.

The Handshake That Never Came

Some failures are apparent, a stalled release or a demo that falls apart under tough questions. Others are quieter and harder to spot at first. Misalignment between teams is one of those subtle failures. In our project, there was never a formal kickoff. No one sat down to confirm dependencies or clarify roles. The expectation was that integration, QA, and UX would align on their own as the work progressed. However, the handshake that should have united us never actually occurred.

The cracks only appeared later. Teams moved ahead in parallel, each confident about their progress. But when it was time to bring everything together, we discovered duplicated work. Two groups had solved the same problem in different ways, leading to duplicated effort that could have been directed more effectively. Developers and QA based their work on different interpretations, and UX had advanced designs before confirming they were feasible. The rework ultimately fell mainly on the developers.

CHAPTER 10   CONFESSION #10: SILOED TEAMS, STALLED DELIVERY

Nobody came right out and said, "We missed alignment." Instead, frustration surfaced in small ways. Stand-ups began to reflect growing tension. Developers prepared for changes, QA raised concerns about mismatches, and UX felt stuck in the middle. During demos, stakeholders noticed the confusion; simple questions about system flows often lacked clear answers. Some leaders weren't part of those early conversations that might have helped alignment. By the time alignment was finally forced, it was after we'd already spent a lot of energy on struggles that we could have avoided.

The tipping point was a UX gap that made the problem impossible to ignore. Developers couldn't implement some controls with the framework, QA couldn't validate what UX had designed, and the customer, having already approved the designs, expressed resistance to change. At this point, the issue stopped being just technical. It highlighted the risks of starting without clear alignment.

When we started to fix things, the solution was straightforward. We didn't need a significant change or an official policy. Instead, we set up smaller, informal syncs. Developers, testers, and UX designers held cross-team conversations outside of the large formal meetings. Agreements were captured in a shared decision log, with contributors from each team noted. We used that log as our new way to track agreements; it helped everyone stay informed and kept us accountable.

It wasn't a perfect solution, but it was effective. Instead of confusion and duplication, we created a clear record of responsibility. Teams could check back and see, "Here's when we made this decision, and who agreed to it." That cut down on repetitive debates and helped prevent teams from drifting too far apart.

The key change was practical: decisions moved from individuals' memories into a shared record. It couldn't fully replace the kickoff that hadn't happened, but it gave us all a clear point of reference and helped keep everyone aligned as the work continued.

CHAPTER 10   CONFESSION #10: SILOED TEAMS, STALLED DELIVERY

The missed handshake created confusion, but an unexpected breakthrough showed us that sometimes the simplest channels offer the fastest clarity.

The Teams Thread That Saved Us

For weeks, the same issue kept resurfacing in our meetings without resolution. Each time we reached that agenda item, the conversation came to a halt. Ownership wasn't clear, and instead of converging on a solution, the group raised more questions. Meetings that were meant to move the project along often circled back without resolution. The issue remained unresolved on the table, growing heavier with every sprint.

The breakthrough didn't come during a meeting, but in a Teams channel. I had created dedicated chat spaces with all the necessary voices: developers, testers, integration experts, and cross-team collaborators. Unlike meetings, where someone was always missing or distracted, the channel let everyone participate on their own time.

One day, a developer posted the lingering question in the integration channel. Within minutes, someone responded. Then another teammate added their take, and soon someone from a different team jumped in with more context. What took two weeks of formal meetings was resolved in just half an hour of chat messages.

The difference was noticeable. In meetings, people hesitated, feeling the weight of formality and conscious that every comment carried more weight. In chat, the conversation was lively. People made side comments easily. Ideas were shared and explained right away. The lack of a rigid structure made it easier for the group to keep things moving.

By the time the next regular meeting came around, the blocker had already been removed. The team reported that integration was sorted out and work had resumed. Leadership didn't need to step in; they were happy to see progress.

CHAPTER 10   CONFESSION #10: SILOED TEAMS, STALLED DELIVERY

What surprised everyone most was the speed. A short burst of open, collaborative messaging replaced weeks of stalled debate. People admitted, a bit sheepishly, that it was surprising how quickly the chat solved what meetings hadn't been able to. But that feeling soon gave way to recognition; this was a better approach.

After that, the new habit stuck. Instead of waiting for a scheduled call, team members just posted questions in the channel and tagged whoever could answer. If someone were slow to respond, others would chip in. Issues that previously took several emails or delayed meetings could often be solved with a simple question. The change spread fast, becoming the natural way to address blockers within and between teams.

Teams discovered that they often didn't need another meeting to solve problems. Instead, they just needed someone to start a genuine conversation. From that point on, sending a quick message in a shared channel became the usual way to get aligned, making it easier and faster for everyone to collaborate.

What started as a single conversation in a chat channel soon inspired a bigger experiment—bringing whole teams together to swarm on problems.

From Siloes to Swarms

For weeks, making progress felt like pushing forward with something essential missing. Even though we had decision logs and active Teams channels, silos still hindered our progress. Each team moved forward on its backlog, but whenever dependencies crossed team boundaries, everything slowed significantly. Priorities never quite aligned; something urgent for one team could be of low priority for another. We felt frustrated waiting around, even after some small wins.

So, we decided to try a new approach. Instead of working alone and delaying tasks, we gathered everyone to focus on one job at a time. There was no formal process or big announcement. We agreed to stop saying tasks were seen as belonging to one team or another and made them everyone's priority.

The experiment started small, with backlog items inside the Scrum teams. Developers, QA, and UX all worked together at once, and it was satisfying to see stories move forward without bouncing between roles or waiting for handoffs. Then we invited external integration teams into the mix, collaborating in the same channel to address issues that had lingered unresolved. For once, there were fewer unnecessary handoffs and less duplicated work happening in parallel.

The change in energy was immediately noticeable. Where our old process felt like handing off tasks one by one, this new approach felt like everyone building together in real time. It could have been chaotic, but it wasn't; roles blended naturally. Developers wrote code while testers validated scenarios immediately, and UX jumped in to adjust designs as needed. Everyone brought their expertise, everyone contributed actively without waiting for their part.

The results were precise. Turnaround times were shortened, and misunderstandings were identified early. Testing took place in parallel with development, not weeks afterward.

For the team, the emotional shift was even more significant. What began as a simple experiment became a revelation. People were surprised by how well it worked to swarm around a single priority, even when several teams were involved. There was a new sense of pride, but even more, there was relief. It was a relief to move past waiting and the tension of unclear responsibilities and instead get the work done together.

It became a new, flexible habit. Whenever a backlog item crossed team boundaries or priorities clashed, swarming became our go-to response. Sometimes it lasted a few hours, sometimes a few days, but the principle stayed the same: gather the right people in the same space, and let actual ownership emerge through collaboration.

The habit stuck. Whenever a challenge needed contributions from more than one team, we avoided spending extra energy debating backlogs; we just brought everyone together and solved it as a group.

Swarming proved the value of focused collaboration, but it also reshaped how we saw our routine syncs and what they could actually deliver.

Sync Meetings That Weren't a Waste

For a long time, sync meetings felt like an item to check off a list. People would attend, share brief updates, and then the discussion would taper off. The routine was familiar: status updates that often felt repetitive and led to limited progress. For many, attendance and brief updates felt like the main expectation, with less emphasis on problem-solving.

Only a few voices focused on problem-solving, but those contributions sometimes struggled to gain traction. Frustration quietly built over time, peaking when I attended a session where the same integration decision remained unresolved across several meetings. Clear ownership was missing, and the issue continued without resolution. The lack of progress became frustrating for both me and the members of the customer team. You could see the exasperation. It didn't feel like true collaboration, more like routine without meaningful results.

But what changed everything wasn't a flashy new meeting format or a different agenda. The real breakthrough came when we started moving actual problem-solving out of the meeting and into our Teams channels. I set up channels with the necessary participants, ensuring that the right cross-team members were included, people who typically didn't attend meetings. In these chat spaces, the issues that had stalled suddenly began to move forward. Threads would start, responses would come quickly, and clarity would come without having to wait for the next scheduled call.

CHAPTER 10   CONFESSION #10: SILOED TEAMS, STALLED DELIVERY

This shift completely changed what sync meetings meant to us. They shifted from being the main venue for solving problems to serving as a helpful backup, there for anything that couldn't be sorted out in the channel. If a problem still needed discussion, it might arise during the sync; however, the expectation was clear: someone would take it back to the channel and shepherd it to resolution after the meeting. Syncs became shorter, more focused, and considerably more energizing.

The overall atmosphere improved, too. Fewer unnecessary updates meant less talking and more action. When discussions did happen, they were sharper and more focused, about real decisions rather than repetitive looping. This change made delivery smoother: fewer surprises, earlier resolution of dependencies, and fewer late-stage bottlenecks.

For the team, this brought relief. Instead of feeling weighed down by long, unfocused sessions, people now saw syncs as a valuable checkpoint. Stakeholders noticed a shift: progress was reflected in how quickly issues were resolved rather than how long meetings lasted. This new approach enhanced time management and reignited motivation.

We achieved a good balance by reducing the workload of sync meetings. Quick clarifications were handled in the chat, reserving syncs for more significant alignment needs. Everyone adapted, and the meetings became productive.

The lesson was lasting but straightforward: avoid bringing problems to meetings that can be solved with a quick message. Value people's time, keep calendars clear, and reserve meetings for tasks that require a group. That respect for time is what finally made our syncs worthwhile.

As syncs became more purposeful, we still faced recurring misunderstandings—until visual maps made alignment visible to everyone at once.

CHAPTER 10   CONFESSION #10: SILOED TEAMS, STALLED DELIVERY

The Map That Made It Clear

No matter how many conversations, syncs, or chat threads we went through, one problem kept coming back: people often left with varying interpretations. Some followed the process as agreed, while others reverted to prior ways of working, and a few were still uncertain about what the process was intended to cover. By the time we realized there was misalignment, it would show up in sync meetings, usually when it was too late, and the team had already been working under different assumptions.

That's when I turned to a habit I'd picked up as an architect: making the invisible visible. Instead of revisiting the same points in multiple meetings, I opened Visio and created a process flow diagram. It wasn't complicated or overly technical; it was a high-level visual map showing the steps, decisions, and handoffs as they were supposed to happen. My goal was to turn all the spoken explanations into something official and tangible, something people could reference and agree on.

When I first shared the diagram with the team, it wasn't a big unveiling. Most of what I mapped out was already familiar, with just a few tweaks. Still, the impact was greater than I expected. Even with only minor changes, people wanted a walkthrough. Seeing the process mapped out made things clear in a way that talking about it never had. What once felt confusing or abstract suddenly became concrete and clear.

Instead of surprise, the reaction was one of recognition. People nodded as we went through the flow, realizing their perspectives had been slightly different. Now, instead of debating what the process should be, everyone could look at the same map. It became a shared point of reference, something more consistent than memory or individual notes.

Conversations started to shift right away. Instead of repetitive discussions, people referred to the diagram, leading to better alignment and more productive meetings.

The emotional impact was small but significant. With a shared map in front of them, people felt more oriented. The process became easier because they could trust the visual tool and go back to it, which turned tension and confusion into clarity and relief.

Over time, the diagram evolved, updating as workflows changed. It wasn't filed away somewhere and forgotten; it became a tool everyone on the team and in stakeholder roles used for planning and alignment. Instead of repeatedly seeking clarity each sprint, we had a solid foundation to build on.

The habit that lasted was simple: always visualize dependencies before making commitments. Putting the process into a visual format didn't just make it easier to follow; it also made it more effective. It helped make alignment a natural, ongoing part of the team's workflow.

The map gave us clarity sprint by sprint, and in hindsight, it revealed the central truth behind every struggle: agility succeeds or fails in the spaces between teams.

Agile Isn't Just Inside a Team, It's Between Them

Looking back, I can trace every struggle in this chapter to the exact underlying cause: the gap between teams. Integration bottlenecks weren't the result of laziness or lack of skill. The wall between development and QA wasn't there because people weren't trying. The release that required a patch with a workaround wasn't the fault of a single developer or tester. The UX feeling of disconnection didn't happen because designers ignored technical constraints. The real issue in every story was the same: when teams worked in silos, things slowed down, became fragmented, or lost cohesion.

The missing handshake showed us what happens when alignment is assumed instead of being explicitly established. Without explicit coordination, duplicate work and confusion quietly grew until the problems became obvious. In contrast, that Teams thread proved that

CHAPTER 10 CONFESSION #10: SILOED TEAMS, STALLED DELIVERY

sometimes a quick, informal conversation can resolve issues faster than multiple structured meetings. Swarming demonstrated what's possible when silos are broken down, even for a short time: sudden speed, clarity, and shared ownership. Sync meetings, once draining, found a new purpose by acting as the backup for fast-moving, informal channels. The process map also made it clear that accurate alignment happens when everyone can see the same picture.

The main lesson I took away is that Agile's real challenge isn't making a single team efficient. Many teams can achieve that. What's harder is getting multiple teams, each with different goals and workflows, to stay in sync without losing momentum. Agile practices within a team are about speed; Agile practices between teams are about coordination. Without the second, the first quickly loses its impact.

This is the insight I wish I'd understood sooner: Agile isn't just about what happens inside a Scrum team. It's about the spaces in between. It lives in the partnerships we don't form, the conversations we postpone, and the shared understanding we overlook. When we ignore those spaces, even the best frameworks can't stop silos from growing.

The fundamental responsibility of a Scrum Master isn't just encouraging agility within a single team; it's about connecting teams. Only then can the whole organization truly move forward as one.

Takeaway Confession For a long time, I measured agility inside the walls of a single team. But every struggle reminded me that the real test is outside those walls, in the spaces where teams intersect, or fail to. My confession is this: until you bridge those spaces, Agile will only ever feel incomplete.

CHAPTER 11

Confession #11: The Human Side of Scrum—People Skills that Make or Break Teams

> *You don't build business. You build people, and then people build the business.*
>
> —Zig Ziglar

In technology, it's easy to think that success comes down to frameworks, tools, or code quality. But time and again, I've learned that the most challenging problems aren't technical, they're human. Teams rarely struggle because of tools or testing alone. More often, they break down because someone is afraid to speak up, an email thread turns negative, or managers may overlook the human side of teamwork.

CHAPTER 11 CONFESSION #11: THE HUMAN SIDE OF SCRUM—PEOPLE SKILLS THAT MAKE OR BREAK TEAMS

Agile is built on principles like transparency, collaboration, and adaptability. However, these principles only come to life when people feel safe enough to use them. If a developer remains quiet about a blocker, if a QA team member feels discouraged or disengaged, or if a retrospective drifts into unproductive blame, the problem isn't in the process. It's in the missing people skills, the unseen force that keeps teams working together.

This chapter examines those moments when empathy mattered more than efficiency, when coaching was more effective than commanding, and when a simple apology altered the course of a sprint. It examines how psychological safety helps teams innovate, how buddy systems bring out hidden talent, and why people sometimes move on due to leadership challenges rather than project work. The reality is that building soft skills is much harder than running ceremonies, but without them, Agile risks becoming an empty routine.

Because collaboration isn't just a line on a manifesto, it's the complex, everyday task of making sure no team becomes isolated or drifts out of sync.

The Developer Who Stayed Silent

In the modernization project where developers and QA were working under different delivery groups, one developer became exceptionally skilled at staying silent. Every morning in stand-up, his update was always the same: "No blockers." Nothing more, nothing less. At first, this seemed efficient, as it meant one less voice to manage in an already tense room. But weeks later, when deadlines slipped and critical gaps became visible, we learned the real story. He hadn't been "all clear" at all. He had been struggling in silence, afraid that admitting difficulty might expose him to criticism. In an environment where transparency often felt risky, keeping quiet felt safer than being honest.

CHAPTER 11   CONFESSION #11: THE HUMAN SIDE OF SCRUM—PEOPLE SKILLS THAT MAKE OR BREAK TEAMS

It took time for this to become clear. For weeks, I believed the outward calm, trusting the daily updates and the rhythm of the ceremonies as a sign of progress. However, when a missed deadline revealed hidden integration issues, everything fell into place. His silence was not a sign of laziness or lack of effort; it was a survival tactic. He knew that speaking up in an environment where accountability often turned into blame would only result in criticism. The setup of the project, with two vendors each held accountable in different ways, created conditions where fear grew and honesty suffered.

When I finally spoke with him one-on-one, I expected to feel frustrated, but what I felt instead was empathy. His admission was heartbreaking and straightforward: "If I admitted I was blocked, I knew they'd blame me. So, I just kept saying I was fine." When the delivery is slipped, the cost of silence spills out; it's a warning signal, but not a neutral sign, which is often missed until it is too late.

As a Scrum Master, this forced me to face a hard truth: I had paid too much attention to the structure of the ceremonies, and not enough to the human signals happening in between. Stand-up only works when people feel safe speaking honestly. In this case, the ceremony appeared fine on the surface; everyone said the updates were shared, but the true spirit of openness was gone.

After that, I changed my approach. I created more space for quieter voices, not by forcing them to speak, but by recognizing and appreciating honesty when it appeared. I praised transparency in front of the team, showing that reporting a blocker was a sign of strength, not weakness. I also made it clear in broader syncs that stakeholders could not bypass me to blame anyone on the team directly. If feedback was needed, it came through me. This wasn't about hiding problems, but about protecting the environment that made it safe for them to raise their concerns.

The impact of silence in Agile can be significant. One blocker, hidden behind "no issues," can ripple out into delays, rework, and even distrust between teams. The deeper danger is cultural. Each time silence feels safer than honesty, a piece of Agile value is lost. Transparency should always be a strength, never a risk.

The lesson I took forward is simple: transparency should always be supported. When a developer admits to being blocked, the response should always be gratitude, never blame. Anything else works against the spirit of Agile.

A Scrum Master's role is to set and defend this tone, even when leaders or clients become impatient. By shielding my team from blame and framing honesty as a form of courage, I created an environment where silence was no longer necessary for self-protection.

If I had to give one line of advice to another Scrum Master, it would be this: help your team navigate blame in high-pressure situations, not from accountability, but from environments that punish openness. Otherwise, your best people will learn to stay quiet, and silence can become the most difficult blocker of all.

Silence showed how fragile openness can be, but just as quickly, words spoken or written without care can create barriers of their own.

The Comment Thread That Broke Trust

If silence can slowly derail a project, careless words can break it in an instant. In our modernization project, in the same setup where developers and QA operated under separate groups, an underlying tension was always present. Eventually, it surfaced: not through code, but through comments.

It started with an email from QA. The message seemed intended to highlight a problem, but it was worded in a way that felt accusatory. However, the tone of the message felt sharper than the issue itself. A remark was phrased sarcastically, which made it difficult for others to

CHAPTER 11　CONFESSION #11: THE HUMAN SIDE OF SCRUM—PEOPLE SKILLS THAT MAKE OR BREAK TEAMS

accept. The developers, who were already feeling stressed and under fire from their supervisors, perceived the message as overly critical in a public setting. In that moment, their frustration quickly gave way to a defensive response.

The negative feelings continued into team meetings. What should have been a simple problem to solve turned into another barrier between two groups that already felt more like rivals than teammates. Ultimately, that email caused more harm than the original issue itself.

When I stepped in, my focus wasn't to assign blame or figure out who was technically correct. I had to make it clear; this wasn't just a developer problem; it was everyone's issue. Code doesn't break because of one missed step, and quality doesn't collapse from a single oversight. Problems often span across team boundaries, and without collective ownership, a culture of blame can grow instead of a culture of delivery.

That experience left a lasting impression. Written words can be misunderstood in Agile teams if not handled carefully. Unlike spoken conversations, they lack tone, body language, and context. Sarcasm that feels like lightheartedness to one person can be perceived as criticism by another. A blunt comment can be interpreted more critically than intended. Once an email is sent, it can be reread and misinterpreted long after the fact, often in the worst way.

After that incident, I asked the team to handle tense disagreements by discussing them directly, rather than letting lengthy email chains escalate. The new rule was simple: if things start getting heated, pause the email and have a direct conversation. I won't lie, it was hard for all of us to adjust, including me. We had to break old habits and learn to have honest conversations instead of going back and forth over endless emails. But every time we replaced a tense message thread with a direct discussion, things improved. Tension dropped, understanding increased, and progress was faster.

CHAPTER 11   CONFESSION #11: THE HUMAN SIDE OF SCRUM—PEOPLE SKILLS
             THAT MAKE OR BREAK TEAMS

The real lesson was simple but powerful: communication isn't just about sending information; it's about maintaining trust. A poorly phrased message can quickly undermine weeks of teamwork. As Scrum Masters, we have to model and reinforce the discipline of assuming positive intent, and when things go wrong, guide people back to direct, human conversation. Because when frustration enters written communication, it rarely solves the problem. More often, it adds to the tension within the team.

Communication taught me how quickly trust can falter, and it set the stage for another lesson: why empathy often matters more than raw efficiency.

Why Empathy Outperforms Efficiency

In service industry projects, there's always pressure to move quickly. Deadlines appear before we even know exactly what we need to do, plans keep changing, and whenever the team puts in extra hours, expectations for the next cycle often grow. Everyone keeps talking about being efficient: getting things done faster, delivering sooner, and working harder. At first glance, this appears to be progress. But beneath it all, the human cost becomes visible: signs of burnout appear, quality can decline, and engagement may suffer. I witnessed this pattern repeatedly across several service projects I joined.

Leadership often celebrated the numbers. Hitting a milestone on time was praised in emails and status reports. However, those reports never revealed what was truly happening, such as people looking worn out, missing meals, or staying up too late. You'd never see those things in the numbers. Back then, looking out for each other was not emphasized as much as delivery. However, the truth is that overlooking well-being was ultimately affecting our work more than helping it.

CHAPTER 11 CONFESSION #11: THE HUMAN SIDE OF SCRUM—PEOPLE SKILLS THAT MAKE OR BREAK TEAMS

As a Scrum Master, I found myself caught in this contradiction. Talking back to leadership rarely worked. In service delivery, caring about people was sometimes misinterpreted as being unable to handle the pressure. So, I changed how I talked about it. Instead of asking for time off, I would ask how we can keep this pace week after week. I suggest that we avoid burnout, not just for the team but for the work itself. By putting it this way, I was sometimes able to steer the conversation in a more positive direction.

Within the team, I took a more direct approach. I made sure to celebrate small wins and acknowledge individual contributions in retrospectives and stand-ups. I shielded team members from client feedback that was expressed strongly, transforming criticism into actionable improvements rather than personal criticism. I ensured the team had time to recharge by avoiding late-night meetings and respecting everyone's time zone. These small steps showed the team I cared, and it encouraged them to step up and take more ownership.

I learned that when people feel appreciated, they become more involved, share their thoughts, and recover more quickly from challenges. Without empathy, teams may still meet deadlines, but the effort often feels forced and ownership can diminish. When you show empathy, people can keep going, and the work feels more real and meaningful.

For any Scrum Master in a similar environment, my advice would be this: don't frame empathy as just kindness. Present it as a strategy. If you want a team that can truly sustain high performance, start with empathy. It turns simple compliance into real commitment and transforms status updates into genuine ownership. Without empathy, what looks like efficiency can actually mask exhaustion.

Empathy reshaped how I thought about team well-being, and that same mindset carried into my own leadership style when I had to shift from directing to coaching.

CHAPTER 11 CONFESSION #11: THE HUMAN SIDE OF SCRUM—PEOPLE SKILLS
THAT MAKE OR BREAK TEAMS

When Coaching Replaced Commanding

During the modernization project, I found myself slipping back into the role I was most comfortable with: that of an architect. When problems came up, I didn't wait for the team to find solutions; I told them what to do. I believed I was helping. To me, this meant greater efficiency: fewer errors, quicker resolutions. But for the team, it felt more like I was acting as an architect than as a Scrum Master. They listened politely, followed instructions, and moved on. On the surface, it looked like progress, but something important was missing. Their voices grew quieter, responding with compliance rather than genuine engagement.

It took me longer than I'd like to admit to see what was happening. The team wasn't resisting or tuning out; they were following my directions. Things were getting done, but people weren't really taking ownership anymore. By frequently stepping in with solutions, I unintentionally limited their chance to think for themselves and take ownership. If I'd continued in that way, the technical work might have been finished, but the team's growth and ownership would have suffered.

Realizing this was tough, but it was important. That's when things started to change for me. I gradually transitioned from giving instructions to coaching. Rather than handing out answers, I began asking questions. If there were problems with integration, I'd ask, "What ideas do you have?" Instead of constantly bringing in the right expert myself, I connected the team and let them take the lead in figuring things out. My role shifted from being the fixer to being the enabler.

This change was messy at first. The team stumbled and tested out solutions that didn't always work. At times, I felt the urge to step in and resolve issues myself. But when I didn't, something extraordinary happened: the team stepped up. People who used to stay quiet started speaking out, taking the lead, and learning as they went. It didn't always look quick, but it helped them take responsibility seriously.

This change also had a significant impact on me. I realized I didn't need to have all the answers. Being a coach means being patient, humble, and trusting others. It reminded me of guiding children; stepping in to solve everything prevents them from learning. People truly grow when you support them, encourage them, and allow them to learn from their own mistakes.

For the team, the result was genuine ownership. They no longer relied on me to prescribe solutions. The team began moving projects forward on their own, engaging in productive debates, trying new approaches, and taking pride in their accomplishments. I realized my job as Scrum Master was clearer now; I wasn't there to give orders or fix everything myself. My role was to coach and create the right environment so the team could succeed on its own.

If I could give one piece of advice to a new Scrum Master, it would be this: Telling people what to do can feel quicker in the moment, but it often limits the team's growth. Coaching seems slower, but it helps the team grow and stand on its own. The real value of a Scrum Master is less about having the answers and more about asking the right questions.

Moving from commands to coaching revealed the value of ownership, and I soon saw how a simple act of honesty, an apology, could rebuild trust just as powerfully.

The Designer's Apology That Shifted a Sprint

In one service industry project, everything was going smoothly until the design deliverables created an unexpected pause in the sprint. The team had received mockups, built the pages, and moved ahead with confidence, only to get a new set of designs that looked nothing like what they had just completed. Frustration was immediate. Developers and testers who had worked late into the night now realized they would have to redo their work. The sprint went from steady progress to visible frustration.

The real story surfaced later. One of the designers had used a different style due to constraints outside the team's control. No one had communicated that these were only interim deliverables, and by the time the correct designs arrived, it was too late. The sprint backlog was scattered, rework loomed large, and team morale dropped. What hurt most wasn't the extra work, but the lack of openness.

When the problem was escalated, the customer's leadership raised the issue with the design team. Something unusual happened next: the design team shared an open apology with the team. They took responsibility and admitted that the team should never have been left in the dark about the incomplete assets. The apology didn't get back the lost hours, but it made a real difference; it defused the tension in the room. Developers now felt heard, and their frustration eased, allowing the team to regroup.

Instead of asking who caused the problem, we wondered how to fix it. Acknowledging mistakes turned a challenging situation into an opportunity to work together.

Looking back, I've learned that accountability in Agile is less about avoiding mistakes and more about how you respond to them afterward. A genuine apology can clear the air, rebuild trust, and help everyone feel safe to speak up when something goes wrong. Without that kind of honesty, the team might have stayed frustrated. But because of it, we were able to move forward together.

If another Scrum Master asked why apologies matter, I would say this: mistakes can strain trust, but apologies can help repair it. Teams don't need perfect execution; they need honest communication. Acknowledging mistakes can sometimes move a sprint forward more effectively than a week of flawless code.

CHAPTER 11 CONFESSION #11: THE HUMAN SIDE OF SCRUM—PEOPLE SKILLS THAT MAKE OR BREAK TEAMS

Accountability through apology strengthened the team, and it reminded me that in retrospectives especially, the way we speak can make or break collaboration.

Learning Nonviolent Communication in Retros

Retrospectives are designed to be a safe space for honest discussion and improvement. However, during one particularly challenging project, ours was the opposite. We were falling behind, outcomes weren't meeting expectations, and morale was low. Instead of working things out, the team turned to blame. Arguments arose, fingers were pointed, and confidence in each other's ability started to drop. What should have been a forum for growth became a place of unproductive accusations.

The tension didn't go away after the meeting. It carried into our stand-ups and planning sessions. Every update felt tense, with team members sounding defensive and anticipating criticism. Teamwork began to weaken, and trust between people started to erode. The retro missed the point; instead of bringing us together, it just pushed us further apart.

What eventually changed things wasn't my own action, but the leadership team stepping in. They skillfully shifted the conversation by reminding everyone to focus on the problem, not the people. The moment they distinguished between systemic issues and individual performance, it took the spotlight off blame and placed it on real impediments. The effect was immediate. The tense, accusatory tone softened. Discussions shifted from blaming individuals to discussing process gaps and shared obstacles.

I didn't lead that intervention, but I learned a lot from it. I saw how quickly a retrospective can derail when emotions run high, and how crucial it is to communicate calmly and respectfully. It's not about pretending things are fine; it's about how you say the hard stuff. If people feel blamed, they either shut down or get defensive. However, if you frame problems as tasks that the whole team can work on together, feedback becomes easier to accept and more likely to help the team improve.

That lesson gradually changed the way we ran retrospectives. Instead of pointing fingers, people began speaking in terms of shared responsibility. Instead of accusations, statements shifted to "I'm struggling with..." or "We could improve by..." Even team members who had previously held back started to contribute, confident that their comments wouldn't be used against them.

The difference between a blame-focused retro and a constructive one is significant. In the first, energy fades, morale declines, and teamwork weakens. In the second, issues are addressed sooner, ideas multiply, and solutions surface. The key is simple but powerful: focus on solving problems, not judging people.

If I could give one piece of advice to another Scrum Master, it would be this: intervene the moment finger-pointing emerges, step in to reset the tone. Remind your team that retrospectives are for learning, not judgment. You might not be able to fix everything in one meeting, but you can ensure that people feel safe sharing their concerns. Just having that safe space helps the team keep going, even when things are hard.

Once retrospectives became constructive, the door opened to experiment with new practices like buddy systems that built confidence and spread knowledge.

The Buddy System That Built Confidence

Our promise to deliver projects has been both critical and challenging from the start. We have many tasks that need to be finished by specific dates, and the pressure to deliver quickly led to problems accumulating faster than we could resolve them. The workload has been distributed unevenly; some team members were handling more complex user stories

CHAPTER 11 CONFESSION #11: THE HUMAN SIDE OF SCRUM—PEOPLE SKILLS THAT MAKE OR BREAK TEAMS

while others worked on simpler ones, which created an imbalance. Continuing along this path risks burnout for our most experienced team members and may jeopardize our ability to meet delivery deadlines.

That's when we decided to try a buddy system. The developers were paired up to assist each other offline, support each other, and deliver user stories. It was initiated to fast-track delivery, reduce recurring mistakes, and create cross-skilling (knowledge sharing). We thought it would be a challenge at first, which might slow them down. Still, surprisingly, they started supporting each other, supporting each other's deliveries, and it became a shared responsibility.

The biggest surprise was how quickly pairing brought out hidden strengths. Seniority stopped being a dividing line; what mattered now was the ability to step up, grasp new concepts, and contribute to moving work forward. Sometimes, newer team members spotted gaps that more experienced ones had missed. Their fresh perspectives led to creative ideas. Our group moved from being divided by experience to being united by contribution.

The effects showed up right away. The imbalance in the user stories assignment was addressed, where team members who initially took on simple user stories began contributing to their paired-up developers, sharing innovative solutions, reducing repeated work, and paving the way for more knowledge. They then took on complex user stories. The long nights that had become common for the team gradually disappeared, and adopting an innovative approach led them to achieve a better work–life balance.

Naturally, there were bumps at first. Not every pair clicked immediately. Some people hesitated at first, preferring the comfort of familiar routines. However, as the improvements became apparent: fewer late nights, faster problem-solving, and better teamwork; the resistance waned. The buddy system moved from something new to something valued. It changed the way everyone saw the team.

CHAPTER 11 CONFESSION #11: THE HUMAN SIDE OF SCRUM—PEOPLE SKILLS
THAT MAKE OR BREAK TEAMS

The inspiration came partly from Extreme Programming, where pairing is a fundamental principle. But here, it was less about code quality and more about building confidence and trust. The buddy system became a multiplier for both of them. It sent a message to every team member: you're not alone, and your contributions matter.

The lesson I carry forward is simple: buddy systems aren't just for onboarding; they are genuine confidence builders. It challenges traditional structures, cultivates ownership in individuals, shares knowledge, and helps shift the team from survival mode toward innovation.

Pairing teammates boosted confidence, and it highlighted a larger truth: when safety is present, innovation can thrive far beyond immediate delivery.

How Psychological Safety Sparked Innovation

Fifteen years ago, I was part of an initiative, a proof-of-concept that shaped my understanding of innovation. It was challenging to develop a solution that was distinct from competitors' ideas and novel enough to be patent-worthy. Our task was to innovate, not just deliver. In that product-based environment, innovation was valued even more than quick results.

The mindset was open from the beginning; team members shared their ideas freely without worrying about immediate consequences, even the ones that sounded far-fetched. It allowed us to experiment, to fail, to suggest anything, and actually changed everything. We pursued an unconventional and bold idea, but the ecosystem spun up provided that space for us.

We didn't stop at the idea. We developed a working algorithm and advanced the proof of concept beyond our expectations. For our internal demo, what we had went well beyond a throwaway prototype; it became something that could really set us apart. Leadership embraced the approach. Instead of demanding, "Will this be ready for production?" they asked, "What can we learn from this?" That one simple question changed everything. Instead of trying to be perfect, we started thinking about what was possible.

That was a significant turning point in my life. I realized that psychological safety isn't extra; it's what sparks real creativity. When people know they won't be punished for trying and failing, they aim higher, take more risks, and sometimes come up with genuinely new ideas. Our approach went on to influence practices beyond our immediate project. But the most valuable lesson was not the technical outcome; it was the culture that had allowed it to happen.

In that environment, we didn't shy away from risk. Each idea was explored on its own merits. If a test failed, it meant a trip back to the drawing board, not a sign of shame. If something showed promise, the team rallied around it. The excitement of discovery replaced the fear of failure. In that setting, safety was less about comfort and more about creating the conditions where real discovery could happen.

Looking back, I often compare this experience to service industry projects where the push for fast delivery frequently stifles curiosity. In those environments, fear of failure silences creative ideas. Survival usually becomes the focus, and innovation tends to take a back seat. The difference is dramatic: product companies that foster innovation make room for mistakes; service companies that emphasize deadlines too heavily risk leaving new ideas behind.

Suppose another Scrum Master asked me about psychological safety. In that case, I'd say this: If you don't let your team try things, make mistakes, and learn, you're not fostering real innovation; you're only sustaining delivery. Getting by might help you finish a sprint, but feeling safe is what enables people to come up with ideas that truly make a difference.

CHAPTER 11 CONFESSION #11: THE HUMAN SIDE OF SCRUM—PEOPLE SKILLS THAT MAKE OR BREAK TEAMS

Psychological safety fueled creativity, but its absence in other contexts revealed a different reality, people often leave environments that neglect it.

Why People Quit Managers, Not Codebases

On a challenging project, I observed something familiar happening. The technology was modern and enjoyable, and the team was talented and cared about their work. But even with all that, our best people started leaving. It wasn't the work itself; it was the surrounding environment that influenced their decision.

The pressure never let up, but that wasn't the actual problem. It was how that pressure was handled. Team members felt micromanaged, their contributions under-recognized, and mistakes highlighted publicly. Recognition was infrequent, while accountability for mistakes was emphasized more quickly. Expectations continued to rise, but support and stability never materialized. In this environment, the leadership could have done more to retain high performers, but instead they left quietly, one by one.

As associates started leaving, the work slowed us down significantly, and we lost knowledge; deadlines had to be adjusted. Despite this pattern, we successfully added new hires to the team with minimal impact on the existing environment. When high performers are treated as easily replaceable, it raises the question of what incentive remains to go above and beyond.

The experience left a significant impression on me. I realized that employees rarely resign because of intricate or poorly organized codebases. More often, they leave when the work environment feels unsustainable or unappreciated.

This lesson changed my leadership perspective. When I became a Scrum Master, I learned that protecting the team wasn't just about stopping distractions or outside demands. It meant creating a place where talented people actually wanted to stay and be satisfied.

CHAPTER 11   CONFESSION #11: THE HUMAN SIDE OF SCRUM—PEOPLE SKILLS
THAT MAKE OR BREAK TEAMS

If I had to sum it up for another Scrum Master, I'd say this: people can work with complex codebases, but they struggle to stay in environments with ineffective management practices. A passion for technology is what attracts talented people to the door, but only recognition, respect, and reasonable expectations will keep them. If that balance is lost, the risk isn't just losing individuals, but also the spirit that drives the whole team.

The departures of strong team members showed the high cost of weak people skills, and it reinforced one of the hardest truths: soft skills don't scale by accident.

Soft Skills Are the Hardest to Scale

Scaling processes is comparatively simple. You can add more tools, introduce new frameworks, and schedule additional ceremonies; on paper, it looks like progress. However, scaling soft skills, such as trust, empathy, communication, and psychological safety, is the real challenge. No Jira workflow or Nexus guidebook can replace the need for team members to feel heard, valued, and safe. Yet it is precisely these invisible skills that ultimately determine whether delivery succeeds or fails.

Looking back at the stories in this chapter, a clear pattern stands out. The quiet developer who was afraid to share blockers taught me that people are only honest when they know it's safe. A tense conversation between developers and QA showed me how fast trust can fall apart if people don't choose their words carefully. In high-pressure projects, I found that if you only care about speed and results, and not the people, the risk is burnout and the possibility of losing valued team members. But even small acts of support or coaching can help people feel responsible and grow stronger.

I've seen how just one apology from a design team can turn a tense sprint into a time when everyone is willing to work together. I've experienced retrospectives that shifted toward unproductive blame, but then they turned around when leaders showed the team how to give feedback in a thoughtful and helpful way. I've seen buddy systems turn new team members into confident, valued people. It reinforces that talent often grows stronger when knowledge is shared. In product companies, I've learned that psychological safety is what makes big innovation possible; it can have an impact that goes way beyond just one project.

But the hardest lesson of all came from environments where empathy was missing, where talented people left not because of complex code, but because of the way they were managed. People rarely leave because of codebases; more often, they step away because of how they are managed, and once trust is lost at that level, even strong processes or framework struggle to hold a team together.

Soft skills are the toughest to scale because they can't be implemented through tools or procedures. They live in people, how we communicate, how we listen, and how we choose to act under pressure. Scaling soft skills takes daily effort, reinforcement from every leader and team member, and most importantly, intentional action. They don't scale automatically; they grow through design, commitment, and by setting examples.

If there's one truth I've learned, it's this: Agile success depends on the soft skills we too often consider secondary. You cannot scale trust with a framework or force empathy with a workflow. Teams thrive when people feel safe to be honest, take risks, and support one another. They risk breaking down when silence, blame, or unhelpful leadership patterns take over.

Takeaway Confession Agile stands or falls on these invisible skills. Encourage honesty, even if it means going at a slower pace. Protect your team from blame so transparency feels safe. Demonstrate empathy yourself, rather than focusing solely on efficiency. Remember: frameworks can scale ceremonies, but only leadership can truly scale trust.

CHAPTER 12

Confession #12: Surviving Meetings That Should Have Been Emails

> *A Meeting without a clear purpose is just a tax on everyone's time.*
>
> —Unknown

Agile was never designed to center around meetings. The ceremonies we started with: stand-ups, sprint planning, retrospectives, were designed as light, focused tools to keep teams aligned and moving forward. Yet somewhere along the way, meetings began to take a central role. Instead of enabling collaboration, they started to consume it. Hours that should have been spent on building, problem-solving, and cooperation were lost to calls, syncs, and frequent status updates.

I have experienced calendars so full that there was barely any time left for real work. I've seen stand-ups extend into lengthy working sessions, planning sessions stretched into detailed grooming sessions, and alignment meetings sometimes result in less clarity than intended. I've watched offshore teammates stay up late at night to attend calls that probably could have been handled with a quick message. I've also seen what happens when meetings lack clear ownership, often drifting or repeating, which reduces confidence in their value.

This chapter offers an honest assessment of how meetings can either foster or hinder agility. It's about recognizing the cost of overused, poorly managed sessions, and the benefits that come when teams regain control of their time. The stories here chart the move from endless discussion to purposeful action, from just maintaining appearances to actually achieving outcomes, from simply "being present" to truly delivering value.

Ultimately, Agile is not about the number of hours teams spend in meetings. It's about how much momentum and progress those conversations generate.

The Eleven-Hour Monday

Some days, your calendar doesn't just help you plan; it can sometimes take over the day. On one project, every day was packed with calls, meetings, and "working sessions," leaving very little time for focused work. Since our team was split between onshore and offshore, the little time we had together quickly filled up with meetings. By the time the last call ended, there was no space left for focus, creativity, or even clear thinking.

At first, the constant overload seemed unusual, a temporary disruption. However, it soon became the norm. Daily stand-ups grew into lengthy problem-solving workshops. Program-level ceremonies often ran long, covering topics beyond their original scope. Customers requested more alignment sessions, internal stakeholders added extra checkpoints, and before long, workdays filled with back-to-back extended meetings. Finishing a meeting with enough energy to focus on design or problem-solving became increasingly difficult.

CHAPTER 12   CONFESSION #12: SURVIVING MEETINGS THAT SHOULD HAVE BEEN EMAILS

At that time, I wasn't a Scrum Master; I was an architect. My primary role was to oversee the technical direction and design. Most days, I sat in meetings where only a few people talked and everyone else just listened. I often found my presence wasn't critical; it sometimes felt more about representation than contribution. After a while, I started asking before joining: Do you really need me in this meeting? If the answer wasn't clear, I said no. That became my way of making space for the responsibilities I was directly accountable for.

What baffled me was how easily teams sometimes extended meetings without realizing the impact on others' time. They often keep meetings running longer than scheduled, often because discussions lacked structure or focus. Most of the time, when one team member shares their screen and works, others watch, some contribute, and many participants remain passive, with limited opportunity to contribute. It became the norm to include everyone in every meeting, ultimately draining their time and energy.

If I could redesign those days, I would start with a different approach: trust the team. Rather than pulling everyone into the same call until the time is gone, set a clear direction, empower individuals or small groups to work, and only reconnect when there is real progress to discuss. Making every task into a group meeting wasn't true collaboration; it was just an activity that looked like collaboration but lacked real effectiveness.

This lesson became even clearer as remote and hybrid work continued after the pandemic. What started as an unusual overload gradually became the default, simply because no one questioned it.

The takeaway from those long, meeting-filled Mondays is simple: meetings should create momentum, not drain it. Without this discipline, a team can start its week already exhausted, before meaningful progress on deliverables has even started.

Those marathon Mondays revealed how unchecked meeting habits could set the tone for an entire week. The following symptom appeared in the very ceremony meant to bring focus, the daily stand-up.

CHAPTER 12   CONFESSION #12: SURVIVING MEETINGS THAT SHOULD HAVE BEEN EMAILS

Stand-Up or Stand-Still?

The daily stand-up is meant to be the heartbeat of an Agile team, a fifteen-minute session of quick alignment and energy to kick off the real work. But on one project, that rhythm began to slip early on. What should have been a short check-in regularly stretched to an hour, sometimes even two, and on the worst days, it would extend well beyond the morning. Instead of acting as a spark, the stand-up became a marathon.

The causes were clear. Instead of a brief exchange of updates, the meeting turned into a detailed oversight of individual tasks. Team members were asked to explain every detail of their work, and they were often asked in real time to pick up additional tasks while everyone watched. Developers were paired up with testers during the call and encouraged to resolve issues immediately during the call, so the stand-up morphed into a working session while the rest waited in silence. For the offshore team, this was especially challenging; it was late at night, and they were drawn into extended discussions that could have unfolded differently.

This pattern didn't appear all at once. Minor changes began with meetings that ran longer and addressed small issues together. Over time, these adjustments became the norm. Stand-up meetings lost their effectiveness, making people anxious instead of focused. People began to expect lengthy meetings characterized by detailed review, rather than a brief discussion about priorities and blockers.

At that time, I was still in an architect role. I tried setting time limits and occasionally spoke up to get us back on track, but lasting change rarely followed. I often felt like the odd one out, pushing against a drift into detailed task oversight. It wasn't until I moved into the Scrum Master position that I had the authority to reset our approach truly.

With that opportunity, I made the shift: stand-ups were time-boxed to fifteen minutes. The focus was on blockers because that's where group presence makes a difference; one person's roadblock could quickly be solved by someone else. Actual problem-solving, though, had to wait. We created a "parking lot" to capture side issues and handled them afterward, either in smaller groups or asynchronously. Occasionally, I experimented with offline updates, such as Friday stand-ups via chat so that people could catch their breath at the end of the week. Surprisingly, this improved alignment, because people felt trusted and empowered in how they shared updates.

Reflecting on it, I realized that the difference between a real stand-up and a status meeting is small but significant. A stand-up is meant to create momentum. A status meeting often focuses on monitoring progress. The real difference comes down to trust, not just how the meeting is run.

Improving the stand-up helped restore rhythm, but structure alone couldn't fix everything. The real strain surfaced when longer ceremonies, such as Sprint Planning, began to mirror the same drift.

Sprint Planning Derailments

If stand-ups are the heartbeat of a team, Sprint Planning is its compass. It's where the team decides on direction and plans the work. On one project, though, these meetings frequently drifted off focus. A meeting scheduled for ninety minutes would often last more than two hours. With a hybrid team spread across time zones, some people dropped off as the session dragged on, but the meeting often carried on. This cycle repeated every sprint until no one even questioned why it was happening.

Several issues led to these derailments. Sometimes, the backlog hadn't been prepped, so planning veered into grooming. At other times, stakeholders made last-minute changes to the scope. Leadership often asked the team to do more work than they could handle. Many items were labeled "critical," making prioritization difficult. Meetings were too full; discussion was widespread, but decisions and ownership were unclear. Any one of these issues might have been manageable on its own, but together, they created a perfect storm.

CHAPTER 12 CONFESSION #12: SURVIVING MEETINGS THAT SHOULD HAVE BEEN EMAILS

As an architect, I tried to set boundaries. I reminded the group to time-box, avoid technical deep dives, and focus on accurate deliverables. Unfortunately, my suggestions were often not adopted. "This is too important to rush" was the constant refrain.

In reality, the planning session had shifted from being a time to align on execution to becoming a forum that reflected underlying concerns. My focus on long-term design and sustainable pace was often in tension with the pressure to add more work.

The impact on the team was clear. People became quieter, their body language grew tense as additional tasks were assigned. Cameras went off. Side chats popped up. No one openly disagreed, but everyone could sense that many of the commitments were unlikely to be met, and indeed, some carried over. Stories rolled into the next sprint, velocity dropped, and frustration set in. The inefficiency hurt, but worse was the strain of trust; every sprint began with a compromise everyone understood but no one acknowledged.

It wasn't until I became a Scrum Master that the lesson clicked. Sprint Planning is not the place to debate "what might be ready"; it's for making commitments about what is already prepared. At that point, I focused on groundwork: stories were refined before the meeting, not during. I kept offline notes to help balance skill sets and learning while avoiding putting anyone on the spot. During planning, as items were claimed, the board was updated immediately to keep momentum. If no one volunteered for a story, I waited and followed up privately, giving people space to consider rather than placing them under immediate public expectation.

If I condense what I learned into one rule, it would be this: preparation is everything. Without clear agendas, refined backlogs, and defined roles, Sprint Planning can quickly lose focus and weigh down the entire sprint. When that happens, the impacts are obvious: missed commitments, low morale, and progress that struggles to build momentum.

CHAPTER 12   CONFESSION #12: SURVIVING MEETINGS THAT SHOULD HAVE BEEN EMAILS

Looking back, I see that the root cause wasn't bad intentions; everyone wanted alignment. However, without structure, what appeared to be alignment often lacked real follow-through.

Planning sessions showed how misalignment begins, not with disagreement, but with quiet acceptance. That illusion of agreement would soon become one of the most persistent challenges I encountered.

The Mirage of Alignment

Some of the most unproductive meetings aren't the ones with arguments, but the ones where everyone seems to agree. We conducted several planning meetings and conversations that appeared to be fruitful, and everyone left believing we were in consensus. However, it soon became apparent that we hadn't reached any conclusions. Underneath, however, people hesitated, remained silent, and often deferred decisions to those not present.

Whether the meeting was for sprint planning, inter-team dependencies, or technical choices, the rhythm was always the same. Ideas were raised but not thoroughly discussed, and decisions were often postponed, occasionally assigned to stakeholders not present. Instead of achieving clarity, we produced only the appearance of consensus. That appearance was convincing because it felt like progress, even though nothing was truly settled.

The root causes were subtle but significant. Few people were willing to risk open conflict in the moment. Some people were afraid of being wrong, others didn't want to commit, and many just waited for someone else to speak up. Now and then, someone brave would share their concerns, but most disagreements got discussed in private messages after the meeting. The silence wasn't only because people were tired. It often stemmed from fear, hesitation, or uncertainty about responsibility.

CHAPTER 12 CONFESSION #12: SURVIVING MEETINGS THAT SHOULD HAVE BEEN EMAILS

As the architect in the room, I immediately noticed the gaps. I asked for clarity: What exactly are we agreeing on? Who's responsible? What are the next steps? However, the answers often drifted back to general referrals, such as "Let's wait for X" or "We'll cover it in the next meeting." It wasn't that people didn't care. They just avoided making decisions, so meetings frequently circled back without closure.

The results were not surprising, as the teams implemented with different understandings. The delivery was impacted, causing rework, and inefficiencies began to feel like the new norm; even people accepted that it is how things work here.

Over time, I learned to distinguish what I now call "apparent consensus" from real alignment. Consensus theater appears to be an agreement, but it rarely produces outcomes. It consumes time and impacts morale because no one's input is truly absorbed. Absolute alignment, on the other hand, depends on participants' willingness to listen, speak up, and commit, even imperfectly. It is not about everyone smiling in the meeting, but about everyone leaving with a clear and shared understanding of what they own and what to deliver next.

That perspective changed how I handled meetings once I became a Scrum Master. If the team couldn't decide in one or two sessions, it meant either the right people weren't present or the group wasn't ready to commit. I stopped holding meetings with the same participants and focused on involving those prepared to make decisions, rather than only adding discussion. More voices were not the answer; commitment was.

If I could set one principle to guard against the illusion of alignment, it would be this: Only include people in meetings who can both listen and make decisions, not just those who can discuss. Otherwise, alignment can appear real from a distance but fall apart under closer scrutiny.

Someone can still manage false alignment if they take ownership, but when no one does, meetings lose direction entirely. That absence of steady facilitation defined the next experience.

CHAPTER 12   CONFESSION #12: SURVIVING MEETINGS THAT SHOULD HAVE BEEN EMAILS

Meetings Without a Pilot

Some meetings don't fail because of conflict. They falter when no one is clearly guiding them. On one project, this became the norm. Status checks, workshops, and stakeholder syncs often started without a clear facilitator. On paper, the meetings had a purpose. In practice, they often drifted without clear direction.

Each time the customer representative led the meeting, the approach varied. Several sessions focused on documentation, discussion, and maintaining order, but outcomes hinged more on the leader than the agenda. Teams often postponed sensitive topics until a familiar leader was present, and the significance attributed to written decisions varied with leadership. The lack of consistency gradually reduced confidence in outcomes.

The issue was evident: ownership kept shifting. Leaders were stretched thin across teams, causing meetings to feel like they were handed off frequently without clear direction. Facilitators had differing approaches, and participants often attended more out of obligation than active engagement. Without guidance, discussions frequently became circular.

I recall stepping in as an architect to bring some structure when a meeting started to drift. I was told it wasn't my duty, emphasizing the importance of avoiding disruptions to the chain of command, even at the expense of effectiveness. My efforts were ignored, and the meeting resumed its repetitive routine with limited outcomes. This experience highlighted how ineffective facilitation can harm both productivity and team spirit.

The outcome was predictable. Instead of action items, we left with more meetings. We were left with placeholders rather than tangible progress. Participation declined as people skipped sessions or logged in with cameras off, leading to time lost and reduced energy. Morale fell as the team realized that these meetings weren't advancing work, but instead filling time.

Later, as a Scrum Master, I ensured that I applied that lesson. Every meeting I ran had a clear agenda and a clear owner. If I couldn't attend a meeting, I rescheduled instead of handing it off. I set a clear rule: meetings required an agenda and purpose. Every meeting ended with decisions and assigned owners, not just notes.

Because without someone guiding the process, meetings don't just drift; they multiply, circling without closure, gradually reducing confidence in the process.

Too many leaderless meetings taught me that more calls weren't the answer. Real efficiency came only when we learned to replace repetition with smarter, asynchronous communication.

Asynchronous Is Strength, Not Slack

The turning point came when our weekly meetings became less effective. We heard the same updates repeatedly, but made very limited progress. Teammates overseas had to stay up late for long calls, and they began speaking up about how little was being accomplished. It became apparent that we need to make a real change.

We began using asynchronous communication by transitioning to dedicated team channels for updates, clarifications, and quick decisions, rather than holding more meetings. Initially, people were used to live calls for participation, but as the benefits became clear, excitement grew over time.

The issues were obvious: nonstop meetings, exhausted offshore teammates, and discussion that lacked outcomes. Out of this frustration, the team started using more asynchronous communication. I supported this change by highlighting small wins, providing quick answers, and offering clear, straightforward explanations. By modeling the practice and sharing our successes, I helped establish this new habit.

CHAPTER 12   CONFESSION #12: SURVIVING MEETINGS THAT SHOULD HAVE BEEN EMAILS

The impact was immediate. The team had more time for actual work, documentation improved, and response times decreased. Meeting fatigue was reduced, and collaboration with offshore teams became much easier because team members no longer had to extend into late evening hours. Asynchronous channels created a level playing field; team members who were quiet in meetings felt more comfortable contributing in writing, and updates were visible to all, with no need to repeat information across multiple calls. Rather than lose momentum, we gained it.

Interestingly, both leadership and customers were adaptable as long as results continued to be achieved. Their primary focus was on making progress, not on whether updates were shared through a call or a channel.

I realized that choosing the right way to communicate is very important. Meetings are most effective for sharing ideas, solving problems, and making difficult decisions. For updates, clarifications, and tracking progress, it's better to handle these in separate parts. Once we eliminated the confusion between the two, our team became more agile and effective.

When I eventually became a Scrum Master, I kept that lesson at the forefront of my mind. I treated asynchronous as the default, not just a fallback. It saved teams hours every week, energized focused work, and removed the pressure of attending meetings that were not essential.

If I could offer one guiding principle to every team, it would be this: default to asynchronous unless face-to-face interaction truly adds value. Agile is less about time spent in meetings; it's about how quickly a team moves together.

Adopting asynchronous habits revealed to me how I was genuinely spending my time. Looking closer, I realized that a team's calendar itself told a deeper story about its culture and priorities.

CHAPTER 12 CONFESSION #12: SURVIVING MEETINGS THAT SHOULD HAVE BEEN EMAILS

Calendars As Cultural X-Rays

If you really want to know how a team works, don't just ask for reports; look at their calendars. I came to realize this over time. Time after time, I found that a team's shared calendar showed the real story of a project. Days were packed with back-to-back meetings, from morning to night. People were constantly double-booked and jumping between calls. There was no room to breathe and no time set aside for undisturbed work. Instead of a schedule, what I saw was an X-ray, revealing challenges in how the organization functioned.

Listening to conversations about these calendars, another story emerged. Team members weren't proud of being so busy; they were frustrated and discouraged by the overwhelming nature of their schedules. The unspoken norm was that everyone was expected to attend every meeting. Declining was discouraged and sometimes viewed as a lack of commitment. As a result, calendars were filled with events that gave the appearance of activity but contributed little to progress being made.

Specific patterns appeared quickly. Meetings were scheduled with no context, added to calendars with vague titles, and lacked a clear agenda. Focus time was rarely respected, except by a few leaders who quietly blocked off hours for deep work, something most team members didn't feel empowered to do. Rather than being the result of planning, most meetings were reactionary, scheduled reactively to address ongoing issues, making reactive work the norm.

Back then, I was still an architect. My calendar was full of meeting invites, many of which were not directly related to my core responsibilities. I began reviewing agendas and only attended meetings where I was required. Sometimes people understood, but a lot of the time they'd say, "That's just the way we work." Even when I managed to block out time for myself, it felt like the same problem was dragging everyone down.

CHAPTER 12   CONFESSION #12: SURVIVING MEETINGS THAT SHOULD HAVE BEEN EMAILS

The consequences were real. When days were packed with meetings, actual work happened late at night. People multitasked to keep up, half-listening to calls while typing away on deliverables. Offshore team members suffered most; overloaded onshore calendars left virtually no time for genuine collaboration. Productivity, focus, morale, and trust all declined. It was clear the approach wasn't sustainable, but change was difficult to achieve.

A team's calendar often reflects its culture. An effective team provides runway for focused work and collaboration, as opposed to packing their calendars with nonstop meetings. It can give the impression of micromanagement, create stress, and blur work–life boundaries.

When I became a Scrum Master, I made sure our calendars didn't become a trap. I set up no-meeting days so the team had time to focus on getting real work done. All ceremonies were kept short and started with a clear agenda. Focus hours were blocked off, and everyone respected that time. Most importantly, I limited meetings to no more than two hours a day. If we went over that, we were drifting away from Agile principles and losing momentum.

Calendars often reveal whether a team is empowered to manage their own time or heavily scheduled by others. Once you recognize them as a kind of cultural X-ray, you can't help but see the truth they reveal.

Calendars exposed the pattern; the meetings within them confirmed it. The emphasis shifted from meeting frequency to the actual decisions made, highlighting the need for discussions to yield tangible outcomes.

Decisions, Not Dialogues

Silence can make it appear as though everyone agrees, but excessive noise can give the impression that real progress is being made. I've seen meetings full of energy: people talking over each other, whiteboards covered in notes, heated debates, but little tangible progress was made.

CHAPTER 12 CONFESSION #12: SURVIVING MEETINGS THAT SHOULD HAVE BEEN EMAILS

These weren't fake moments of quiet agreement. Instead, they were long, energy-draining cycles of discussion, where every angle was considered, but no decisions were made.

This pattern showed up in planning sessions, technical design debates, and dependency discussions. The room would come alive with conversation: arguments, counterarguments, and endless "what if" scenarios. But as the hours dragged on, it became clear that resolution often wasn't actively pursued. The group was circling, hesitant to take on the risk that comes with making a decision. Taking ownership would mean accepting accountability. Sometimes it was the fear of being wrong, sometimes a lack of authority, and occasionally simple leadership hesitation; each factor contributed to keeping choices unresolved.

At some point, someone is bound to ask, "What should we do next? Who is responsible for this situation?" The answers often fall short: "We need more information; let's wait for input from so-and-so; we can talk about this again at our next meeting." As a result, the process begins again. The same issue would emerge in the upcoming meeting, accompanied by the same repetitive conversation and the same lack of closure. This wasn't alignment theater, but rather extended dialogue, creating the impression of progress while delivering limited outcomes.

The outcomes were significant. Delivery suffered because teams had unresolved dependencies. As deadlines approached, teams made rushed decisions. The main challenge was the delay in decision-making, rather than the complexity itself. Team morale decreased, and people became disengaged, as meetings felt less productive. Frustration gradually turned into mistrust.

As an architect, I often tried to drive discussions toward concrete next steps, but answers would be vague or delayed. My attempts usually revealed a bigger issue: the people in the room either lacked the authority or the willingness to make decisions. Meetings sometimes continued

CHAPTER 12   CONFESSION #12: SURVIVING MEETINGS THAT SHOULD HAVE BEEN EMAILS

more for visibility than for outcomes, allowing leaders to point to "active discussions" as proof of progress. In reality, this was an activity without real progress.

When I became a Scrum Master, I approached meetings differently. I made a clear distinction between discussion and decision. Discussions were intended to explore options, but every meeting had to conclude with a choice, an owner, and a timeline. If the same topic carried over for more than two meetings, I changed the participants, because revisiting the same issues with the same people was not collaboration; it reflected a lack of progress.

The principle I enforced was simple: every meeting ends with a decision, a responsible owner, and a clear next step. Without these, the meeting was unlikely to be a productive use of time. The decisions might not always be perfect, but taking action beats endless indecision every time.

Agile is about movement. Endless dialogue might feel collaborative, but unless it results in a genuine choice, it becomes an activity without meaningful outcomes.

Once decisions began to take shape, a new question emerged: how do we actually preserve the time to act on them? The answer lay in protecting focus as a shared team discipline.

Protecting Focus Time Together

Agile promises focus, but the team still finds it challenging to achieve this due to a packed schedule. When I proposed setting focus time for uninterrupted work, it was received with skepticism. The days were so fragmented that even setting aside dedicated focus seems unrealistic.

The need for change was evident. Too many meetings and constant interruptions had become normal. This situation forced people to work late into the night to finish their tasks. Teammates in other countries often

CHAPTER 12   CONFESSION #12: SURVIVING MEETINGS THAT SHOULD HAVE BEEN EMAILS

had to deal with late-night calls, which made them rush their work. This pattern happened nearly every cycle, impacting both productivity and morale. Efforts to address it were often difficult to sustain. Management and clients connected constant availability with commitment. Protecting focused, uninterrupted work time felt very challenging.

At that stage, I was still an architect and could only advocate for change. But without authority, my suggestions fell flat. The culture held firm: presence in meetings was sometimes equated with engagement, and actual deep work was neglected.

Years later, as a Scrum Master, I finally had the authority to make changes, and I acted. Fridays became no-meeting days, even the stand-up moved to an asynchronous format, giving everyone a whole day for deep thinking or an early log-off. All ceremonies were strictly time-boxed, and I encouraged asynchronous updates to reduce the need for live calls. Offshore team members were encouraged to log off after stand-up, avoiding scattered follow-up meetings. Suddenly, hours that had been lost to meetings were reclaimed for real progress.

The results were precise. Productivity improved, but so did creativity and morale. With fewer interruptions, people solved problems more quickly and with greater focus. Offshore colleagues no longer had to work late nights. The reduced overlap became more purposeful, and team members invested their energy in tangible deliverables, not just attending meetings.

What I learned is that collaboration is powerful, but only when intentional. Not every task benefits from having the entire team in a meeting. True agility empowers people to contribute meaningfully, not simply attend. Protecting focus time doesn't decrease collaboration; it ensures that when collaboration happens, it truly counts.

Looking back, I saw how these changes allowed focus time to become a natural part of our routine. Work flowed with less noise and more clarity. Meetings gained value because they were no longer constant.

CHAPTER 12   CONFESSION #12: SURVIVING MEETINGS THAT SHOULD HAVE BEEN EMAILS

If I could offer one guiding principle for every team, it would be this: every sprint should include at least one day without meetings; each day should provide two to three hours for deep, uninterrupted work; teams should also aim for at least two hours of complete focus. Anything less can often signal micromanagement or reduced trust.

Focus time is not a luxury; it is the engine of delivery. Without it, Agile risks becoming dominated by conversation rather than progress. With it, Agile fulfills its promise of sustainable, meaningful progress.

That brings us to the core truth of this chapter: Agile is less about how much we talk and more about how those conversations help us move forward. That is the principle I want to close on.

Agile Isn't About Talking, It's About Moving

After years of packed calendars, endless stand-ups, long planning sessions, and meetings with no clear owner, one thing stood out: we often spent more time in discussion than in making tangible progress. Agile was never supposed to be just a series of meetings. Its ceremonies were meant to create focus and flow, not keep teams in prolonged discussion. At some point, habits and routines sometimes took precedence over real progress.

The stories throughout this chapter, from eleven-hour Mondays to the illusion of alignment, from endless status updates to planning sessions bogged down in debate, highlight a clear pattern. Meetings themselves weren't the problem; it was how we used them that caused the issue. We let fear, hierarchy, and familiar routines turn essential conversations into rituals that consume time without delivering value. We mistook discussion for action, attendance for productivity, and formality for genuine alignment. In the process, we lost track of what Agile is supposed to protect: our momentum.

CHAPTER 12   CONFESSION #12: SURVIVING MEETINGS THAT SHOULD HAVE BEEN EMAILS

Here's my confession: I accepted it for too long without challenging it. I sat in those rooms, nodded along in countless meetings, and let my energy, and everyone else's, drain away. I even convinced myself that showing up was part of "doing the work." It wasn't. It took stepping into the Scrum Master role and feeling firsthand the weight of the team's frustration to realize how I had unintentionally reinforced some of the very patterns I wanted to change.

I started to see meetings as tools for progress rather than just calendar entries. Stand-ups focused on obstacles, while planning sessions evaluated readiness. We shifted to asynchronous updates when possible and protected our focus time. Slowly, we regained our momentum.

If there's one lesson I would share, it's this: Agile is not sustained by the amount we talk, but by how much we move. Talking without making decisions, holding meetings without purpose, and maintaining calendars without breathing room are signs of over-caution or reduced trust. Real agility is built when trust minimizes the need for micromanagement, when results replace appearances, and when teams are trusted to spend most of their time delivering value instead of only reporting on it.

Takeaway Confession   I used to think that more meetings meant better team alignment, but I've learned that absolute alignment shows up in the results, not in the number of hours we spend talking. Agile works best when we focus on actual progress, rather than just the number of conversations we have.

CHAPTER 13

Confession #13: The Costs of Cultural Blindness

Culture eats strategy for breakfast.

—Peter Drucker

What's strange about workplace culture challenges? It doesn't slam into your team like a freight train. Instead, it slips in subtly, such as an offhand remark during stand-up, someone quietly shouldering way more than they signed up for, or leadership making decisions that may yield short-term results but strain the team in the long term. At first, you think, "This is fine. We can handle this." But that's the thing about these patterns: they build up like compound interest, except in reverse.

I've seen this play out too many times. Teams that looked bulletproof on org charts started falling apart, not because people couldn't do the work, but because the work environment gradually eroded trust within the team. Management celebrated feature releases while overlooking the fact that many team members were disengaging.

CHAPTER 13   CONFESSION #13: THE COSTS OF CULTURAL BLINDNESS

The consequences eventually surface. People quit, engagement tanks. Everyone's running on fumes.

In this chapter, I want to delve into those hairline fractures that can turn into complete breaks: the high performer who is given disproportionate accommodation, the daily micro-cuts that we've all learned to overlook, the resignations that blindside leadership, and all those costs that never make it into any spreadsheet. Here's what I've learned the hard way: culture isn't some fluffy HR thing you can push to next quarter. It's the foundation on which everything else sits. If neglected, even strong teams can weaken over time.

Look, I'm not writing this to throw stones. I'm writing this because I've made the same mistake myself. When I truly reflect on these situations (being brutally honest about my own mistakes), I see how this cultural debt accumulates, how trust is eroded one paper cut at a time, and how paying attention to this issue can make a significant difference. Here's the truth that took me embarrassingly long to accept: you can't separate culture from delivery. If culture is undermined, delivery quality will inevitably decline.

The Star Performer Everyone Feared

Early in my career, I became the go-to person for fixing problems. Deadlines slipping? Complex integration that scared everyone? Last-minute critical defect? Somehow, these always ended up in my lap. I'd find a solution or pull an all-nighter if it were crucial to get things done. Essentially, I served as the reliable backup for the team, ensuring projects were completed on time, regardless of the circumstances.

Some team members attempted to replicate my methods and seemed confident about it, while others were curious about how I approached problems. But the leadership team didn't celebrate what I produced; they just came to depend on it. Eventually, I figured out this wasn't a blessing but actually a burden.

CHAPTER 13 CONFESSION #13: THE COSTS OF CULTURAL BLINDNESS

What made things worse was how I communicated back then. I didn't soften my feedback. When mistakes happened, I pointed them out directly. If something seemed clear to me, I'd ask why others couldn't see it. My communication style was blunt, maybe too blunt. I wasn't trying to intimidate anyone, but that's often how it came across. The team rarely pushed back, partly because they appreciated my results, and partly because my certainty could feel pretty final. Some colleagues hesitated to challenge me, concerned that my certainty left little room for discussion.

Strangely, this tension didn't stop us from delivering our message. Projects launched, customers got what they needed, and leadership could relax each time. Everything appeared successful on the surface. However, underneath, the imbalance continued to worsen. About 20% of us were handling 80% of the workload. Others tended to step back or take on smaller roles. They did contribute, but opportunities to take on bigger challenges often went to a few of us because everyone expected "the star" to jump in and handle things eventually.

Back then, I couldn't see the cultural problems I was creating. From my perspective, I was doing what needed to be done. But now I understand how this created two harmful patterns: leadership depending too much on a few individuals rather than investing in the whole team, and those few people (myself included) taking on too much without realizing it couldn't last.

After giving this considerable thought, I've come to realize something important. I used to believe that sharing everything I had and stepping in when others hesitated was the best way I could help my team. Now I see that sometimes my actions disrupt our balance. I want to learn from this experience and improve our collaboration. By jumping in too frequently, I took away opportunities for others to learn from mistakes. This hindered our growth and led the team to rely on a handful of strong performers instead of developing a sustainable approach to collaboration.

CHAPTER 13   CONFESSION #13: THE COSTS OF CULTURAL BLINDNESS

If I met someone like my younger self today, I would approach it in a completely different way. I don't load them up with more work just because they can handle it. Instead, I protect their time, give them room to guide others, and make sure their contributions strengthen the whole team rather than replace it. The reality is straightforward: a star performer alone can't create a healthy culture.

That was my first absolute acknowledgment of culture, understanding that high performance without balance masks deeper problems. A team might look successful temporarily, but the culture suffers. And when culture breaks down, the people relied on most heavily are often at greater risk of burnout.

This brings us to the more subtle warning signs we overlooked, the subtle behaviors and small interactions that seemed harmless but gradually influenced how team members related to one another.

When Microaggressions Become the Norm

Unhealthy cultural patterns rarely emerge suddenly with a dramatic event. Instead, it stealthily creeps in, camouflaged in everyday habits, sarcasm masquerading as humor, selective tolerance of mistakes, or seemingly insignificant dismissals. These seemingly harmless actions, at first, blend into the background of the team's routine. But the team always notices, even if it's not immediately apparent.

In one project where I served as the architect, I observed these patterns becoming ingrained in our daily routine. Some mistakes were overlooked, while others were criticized more severely. Casual sarcasm in stand-ups or evaluations influenced the atmosphere more than many realized. The team's reaction was quiet but consistent, with an underlying resentment. They didn't respond with laughter, nor did they voice any objections. Instead, they internalized it.

CHAPTER 13 CONFESSION #13: THE COSTS OF CULTURAL BLINDNESS

What made it worse was how invisible it felt at the time. No sprint failed because of sarcasm. No release was slipped because management excused one person's mistakes while amplifying another's. Delivery continued smoothly, so leadership may not have recognized an intervention. But underneath it all, morale started to slip. People stopped sharing ideas as openly. Trust faded bit by bit. The atmosphere in the room became more subdued, although no one could quite put their finger on why. This erosion of trust and openness decreases productivity and innovation, ultimately affecting the team's long-term success.

Looking back, I realize there was a trigger point, not one dramatic event, but the gradual recognition among the team that these behaviors weren't temporary. They weren't accidents. They had become part of how we worked. Yet the tension stayed unspoken. Team members shared their frustrations, but not outside the circle. By the time leadership recognized it, the pattern was already embedded in the team's ways of working.

At the time, I let it pass. I noticed the sarcasm, the uneven treatment, the quiet frustrations, but I didn't address them directly. Instead, I escalated my concerns to management, which were politely acknowledged but then set aside. Months later, when the problems finally reached a breaking point, leadership acknowledged the situation, but by then the damage had already been done. That hindsight didn't repair the damage already done.

What I learned was that microaggressions, despite their "micro" prefix, don't stay small. They build up gradually, like small frictions in a system, eventually affecting how smoothly the team works. If left unaddressed, they can foster resentment and reduce motivation, even among committed team members. Over time, those "small things" shape the entire culture, sometimes with long-lasting consequences.

If I were to guide a team through this now, my approach would be different. I'd call out sarcasm early, not with confrontation but with curiosity: "Can we reframe that?" I'd advocate for professional neutrality: everyone is treated fairly, feedback is given consistently, and mistakes are handled as learning opportunities instead of judgment. Because when professionalism erodes, it doesn't just affect the target of the behavior; it also affects those around them. It shifts the tone for the entire group, and eventually, those who receive disrespect begin to mirror it. To address these issues, consider implementing regular team feedback sessions and training on respectful communication.

The takeaway for Scrum Masters is critical but straightforward: don't overlook the small stuff. Culture is shaped less by grand statements and more by the everyday exchanges between teammates. Addressing microaggressions at the root, before they become normalized, is crucial. It preserves trust and equality in the team. Everyone deserves to feel respected, not some of the time, not depending on who they are, but every day, from everyone. It's important to address these issues early, before they become embedded in the team's culture.

And when we ignore the small things long enough, the consequences may surface quietly, such as the unexpected departure of a valued team member.

The Silent Exit Nobody Saw Coming

Some departures affect a team deeply, not because they're dramatic, but because they happen quietly and unexpectedly. I'll never forget when one of our most dependable team members suddenly resigned. Nobody saw it coming.

They weren't someone struggling or on the periphery. They were a colleague we all respected, someone who consistently delivered and had our backs. The team relied on them more than we fully recognized at the time.

Looking back, the warning signs were definitely there. Nothing dramatic: no heated meetings, no blown deadlines, no apparent frustration. Instead, it was this gradual pulling back that most of us didn't

CHAPTER 13 CONFESSION #13: THE COSTS OF CULTURAL BLINDNESS

notice: speaking up less in discussions, seeming less enthusiastic about new projects, and going quiet in spaces where they used to bring real energy. At the time, we assumed they were simply focused or tired. In hindsight, it was an early sign of disengagement.

When the resignation finally came, there was no big moment, no dramatic exit interview. A brief, professional message stating they were moving on. The resignation caught leadership off guard, and the rest of us scrambled to pick up the pieces. Our delivery timeline went sideways almost immediately.

The work this person handled wasn't just busy work; it was critical stuff. Without them, dependencies began to cascade, creating delays in unexpected areas, creating delays in places we never expected. We had come to take their contributions for granted, and their absence revealed just how central their work was to our success.

I was working as an architect at the time. Keeping people wasn't technically my job; that was the manager's responsibility. But since I had a decent relationship with this teammate, I reached out to understand what happened. Their answer was difficult to hear but very clear: they felt completely burnt out. The constant overload that had become routine on our project had worn them down, not just mentally but physically, too. Their health had to come first, and the job no longer fit with that priority. They didn't want to fight about it; they just chose to walk away.

That conversation stuck with me. It showed me that the biggest threats to team stability aren't always the apparent conflicts. Sometimes the quietest person in the room is already planning their exit, and by the time you notice, it's over. Overwork, especially when framed as "being reliable," can have serious effects on individuals that may not be apparent in sprint reports or velocity metrics. When it finally surfaces, it's in the form of a resignation letter.

CHAPTER 13   CONFESSION #13: THE COSTS OF CULTURAL BLINDNESS

If I could do it over, I'd push back harder against the overload culture. I'd remind leadership that just because someone can handle more doesn't mean they should have to. Sustainability isn't optional; it's what helps keep teams functioning over time. When someone's health gets compromised, the whole project pays the price.

For Scrum Masters, the key lesson is never to take quiet dedication for granted. Watch for those subtle signs of withdrawal, those moments when someone's energy drops without explanation. Shield your people from constant overload, regardless of how capable they appear. Because once work starts costing someone their health, their decision to leave may already be made, and last-minute actions often come too late.

Quiet exits often leave us with lessons we only recognize in hindsight. The real trick is spotting them before they happen, and building a culture where leaving isn't the only way to survive.

Culture Debt: The Backlog We Never Logged

In Agile circles, everyone talks about technical debt. The metaphor is familiar: shortcuts today lead to costs tomorrow. Teams track it, estimate it, and debate how much debt is acceptable in pursuit of delivery. What struck me later in my career is how little attention we give to a parallel kind of debt, the debt created when cultural issues are ignored.

I saw this play out in one particular project. From the beginning, there were patterns that we all recognized: uneven workloads, where the same people carried the heavy lifting; accountability that was inconsistent across the team, and subtle patterns of favoritism that weren't addressed. Everyone noticed, but the justification was always the same: delivery first. We told ourselves we'd address those things "after the release," just as developers sometimes say they'll refactor "after go-live." After each release, another deadline quickly followed, and the cycle continued.

CHAPTER 13   CONFESSION #13: THE COSTS OF CULTURAL BLINDNESS

For a while, nothing seemed broken. The sprints produced results, the backlog moved, and leadership considered the team successful. But culture debt can work much like technical debt: it often builds quietly until a major release exposes it. For us, that moment came when the project hit a critical delivery milestone. Those who carried the heaviest load for months began to burn out, while others were less prepared to step in. Frustration began to grow within the team, expressed not in confrontations but in subtle ways: reduced energy in meetings, reluctance to take on tasks, and a noticeable slowdown in momentum.

I was an architect at the time, and I had raised concerns about the imbalance on multiple occasions. Each time, my feedback was acknowledged but not acted on. Delivery targets overshadowed cultural signals. By the time the impact was felt, it didn't just affect morale; it affected delivery itself. Deadlines slipped, handoffs broke down, and the goodwill that had carried us through earlier crunches had diminished.

What disappointed me most was realizing how preventable it all had been. A more balanced distribution of work could have been achievable. More transparent accountability could have been built into the process from the start. However, because cultural debt wasn't tracked in the same way as technical debt, it lacked visibility, clear priority, or a plan for resolution.

The lesson I took from that experience is simple: if you only track technical debt, you're only looking at half the story. Culture debt can disrupt teams much like technical debt can disrupt releases. You can't ignore it just because it doesn't show up in Jira or on a burn-down chart. If accountability gaps, favoritism, or overloading persist too long, they will eventually erode the team's most valuable asset: motivation.

For Scrum Masters especially, this is a reminder not to measure success solely by delivery. Delivery without sustainability is fragile. Culture without accountability becomes fragile. If you want a team to thrive in the long term, treat cultural debt with the same urgency as technical debt: log it, discuss it, and address it before it compounds.

CHAPTER 13 CONFESSION #13: THE COSTS OF CULTURAL BLINDNESS

When culture debt surfaces, it affects not just systems or schedules, but also the people who carry them. And unlike code, people can choose to step away.

The Informal Escalations That Went Nowhere

Culture rarely changes overnight; it can gradually unravel when concerns are repeatedly deferred with responses like, "We'll look into it." I learned that lesson in a project where the cracks were visible to almost everyone, but the reactions from leadership were always the same polite deferral. The issues weren't unusual: chronic overload on a handful of reliable people, perceptions of favoritism that influenced how leniency was applied, and accountability that appeared inconsistent across the team. None of it was dramatic enough to explode into a formal escalation. Instead, we raised them in one-on-one meetings, hallway conversations, and quiet side chats with leaders. Each time, the feedback was acknowledged. Each time, the promise was given: "We'll look into it." And then nothing happened.

Initially, I believed the promises. The wheels of change were just slow. But release after release, informal feedback clearly wasn't moving the needle at all. The very patterns we flagged: overloading, favoritism, and lack of accountability, kept repeating, like an issue that was continually deferred to "the next sprint." The message was subtle but unmistakable: if it didn't threaten immediate delivery, it wasn't important.

As an architect at the time, my approach to raising concerns was direct. I spoke to leaders in one-on-one meetings, provided candid feedback in side conversations, and attempted to identify the risks. Without action, however, my feedback began to feel like it was lost in the system. Over time, my motivation shifted. I stopped expecting change from the top. Instead, I watched the team learn to adapt in their own way: by lowering expectations, tolerating patterns they couldn't control, or eventually moving on. Turnover increased, and the team struggled to build the sustainable cohesion the work required.

Looking back, informal escalation often feels like speaking without being heard. It might feel safer, but it rarely sticks. Leaders may acknowledge it in the moment, but without follow-through, the concern fades away. Culture problems, left in the realm of the informal, dissolve without resolution. The cost surfaces later: increased turnover, risk of burnout, and diminished trust. By then, the damage is already done.

If I had to give one piece of advice to Scrum Masters, it would be this: don't stop at raising concerns. Document them. Make them visible. Treat them like backlog items that require tracking and closure. Even leadership should be accountable for outcomes, not just delivery. Without that discipline, culture problems drift into the background until the team stops believing change is possible.

My confession here is straightforward: I let too many issues slip into informal channels, trusting that they would eventually be addressed. They weren't. And every time nothing happened, it trained the team to believe nothing would happen. Silence gradually became the default response.

Eventually, the retrospective, the one place where we couldn't ignore voices, assumed a whole new significance. It became less about process improvement and more about a release valve for a team that had struggled to find other outlets.

Retrospectives As Therapy Sessions

Retrospectives are supposed to focus on process: what went well, what didn't, and what we'll try next time. However, sometimes they evolve into something entirely different. I'll never forget one retro where our usual structure just fell apart and became something much more emotional. The atmosphere was tense, raw, and surprisingly open.

CHAPTER 13   CONFESSION #13: THE COSTS OF CULTURAL BLINDNESS

The trigger wasn't a single missed sprint or a minor defect. It was all these long-ignored issues piling up: leadership remaining focused on delivery without addressing underlying concerns, constant overloads, and the frustration of problems that had been raised but never addressed. What really pushed it over the edge was an email from QA, highlighting that quality issues were starting to affect the team's work. It was the kind of message everyone felt but no one had said out loud. Once it was voiced, others felt freer to speak openly.

As Scrum Master, I felt the weight of the room. Usually, I would guide the conversation back toward process improvement, but in that moment, I knew steering too quickly would shut people down. So, I let the venting happen. Some comments were candid, while others were emotional, but all of them were genuine. At the same time, I had to protect the space, ensuring the discussion remained professional enough to be constructive. When someone crossed the line, I suggested taking that part offline, but I never dismissed the underlying concern.

What happened next was surprising. Team members who had previously been quieter or struggled with output spoke up with genuine passion. Their frustrations revealed blockers we hadn't acknowledged before. Being heard shifted something in the room. Even when solutions weren't immediate, the act of showing empathy (of saying, "I hear you, and I'll help where I can") brought energy back into the team. Within weeks, some of those who had struggled most began showing new levels of ownership. Not because the work had suddenly become easier, but because they felt acknowledged and supported.

That retro taught me something I hadn't expected: sometimes the best thing you can do is pause the focus on productivity metrics. Instead of loading up on more action items, people need to know their struggles matter, that what they're going through is real. When you make room for the challenging, candid conversations, trust starts to build. And once that trust is there, the performance usually follows.

Now, I'm not saying this approach doesn't have risks. A retro without boundaries can risk becoming an unstructured venting session that leaves everyone more frustrated than before. You've got to find the sweet spot: be open to feedback that might sting, but keep steering toward lessons rather than finger-pointing. Address any unprofessional behavior promptly in one-on-one settings; unresolved issues can quietly build tension.

I'll be honest, I once feared retros turning into therapy sessions. However, I've come to view those moments as some of the most crucial in a team's development cycle. They reveal the human dimension of delivery: the emotions and struggles that don't neatly fit into story points or burndown charts.

For Scrum Masters, my approach is simple: give everyone the space they need. Listen without rushing. When you show genuine empathy, it actually improves how people perform. Even if you can't fix every problem immediately, making the effort to address it and showing that the team's voice matters builds a culture where people want to keep showing up.

And sometimes, the follow-up conversations that emerge after an emotional retrospective can change everything, reshaping not just the sprint, but your role itself.

The 1-on-1 That Changed My Role

As a Scrum Master, I knew ceremonies mattered: the stand-ups, the reviews, the retros. But I completely underestimated how much one conversation could change everything. A single 1-on-1 reshaped how I see my role.

The person who requested it? Not someone I expected to shift my perspective. They often pushed back in planning sessions, raised concerns without clear alternatives, and rarely committed to full capacity. I saw them as resistant, as if they were holding back while others moved ahead. When they asked for a 1-on-1, I prepared for excuses.

Instead, I got raw honesty. They told me, "I don't want this ownership just because I have experience. I need time to learn. This framework is new. Leaders expect too much, too fast."

That moment hit me hard. I'd misread everything. Their reluctance wasn't due to laziness; it was a fear of failure. They weren't holding back due to a lack of motivation; they were protecting themselves. No room to learn when expectations are assumed based on unrelated experience. That pressure had significantly diminished their motivation.

After that 1-on-1, everything shifted for me. No more pushing harder, I started asking better questions instead. What kind of support do you actually need? Would you like me to outline the steps, or would you prefer that I provide the general overview and let you work it out? Let's slow down a bit so you can learn this material without missing our deadlines. It felt like such a small change, but in truth, it reshaped my approach. Finally, someone was listening to them instead of just measuring them against assumptions that didn't reflect their reality.

The results were not immediate, but they were undeniably real. With space to learn, they started contributing regularly. Everyone on the team noticed. Others began requesting clarity in their own ways (one person wanted detailed steps, another thrived with big-picture guidance). My tech background helped me bridge these different needs. I gave each person the right kind of input without overwhelming them. Our team has become stronger, not because of my direction, but because we learned to support each person in a unique and individualized way.

The biggest lesson from that conversation was a humbling one: very few people intentionally perform poorly. Someone seems disengaged or underperforming? It's usually circumstances, not character. Expectations are unrealistic. The context may be unfamiliar. The fear of failure can sometimes overshadow the motivation to try. Sometimes, one honest conversation in private can change everything.

I now view 1-on-1s as mirrors for reflection, outlets for pressure, and opportunities for growth. They reveal what people won't say publicly, allowing me to address unspoken frustrations. They also serve as pressure valves, releasing tension and creating a safe space for development. I'll never underestimate their power again.

Here's my simple confession: I thought resistance was the enemy. That 1-on-1 showed me resistance is often a symptom. Give people space to speak honestly; even brief conversations can pivot both individual and team dynamics.

I learned something even more significant: when leaders overlook these dynamics, damage spreads beyond individuals; it can erode the culture.

Leadership Without Awareness, Leadership Without Trust

One of the hardest truths I've learned is that teams don't break only because of missed deadlines or failed releases. They break just as often because leadership sometimes overlooks cultural cracks when delivery takes priority. I experienced this firsthand in a project where leadership's attention focused on one thing only: the first release.

From the start, the problems were clear: overload concentrated on a few individuals, uneven responses to mistakes, and inconsistent accountability. These weren't invisible issues. Team members spoke about them quietly, sometimes directly to me, and sometimes among themselves. I raised them too, pointing out that the imbalance was starting to take a toll on morale. The message was clear: focus on the release first, and revisit concerns later.

But the pivot never came. The release did go live, but instead of the celebration leadership expected, the team's morale collapsed. People felt stretched, not fully supported. Some grew resentful; others disengaged entirely. Productivity dipped in the sprints that followed, not because of technical hurdles, but because trust within the team had weakened. The unspoken message was clear: as long as delivery looked good on the surface, the deeper issues didn't matter.

At the time, I was an architect. My role provided me with visibility into both the technical work and the team's struggles, but gave me little authority to change the culture. I could raise awareness (and I did), but without leadership willing to act, those warnings went nowhere. What frustrated me most was knowing that the cracks weren't fatal. With attention and care, we could have addressed them early.

The experience taught me a lesson I carry with me: leadership awareness isn't optional. It forms the foundation of trust. Teams can forgive strict deadlines or high stakes if they believe their leaders genuinely see, hear, and care about their well-being. However, when leaders ignore the early warning signs (those subtle signals of overload or resentment), they risk undermining the team's future by focusing only on short-term outcomes.

My confession here is that I once believed delivery was enough. As long as we hit the target, leadership and customers would be happy. And for a while, that was true. But delivery without trust is temporary: it may create quick wins but is unsustainable. Sustainable success requires more. It requires leaders who treat cultural health as seriously as delivery metrics.

For Scrum Masters, the principle is simple: pay attention to the early warnings. Don't assume a successful release means a healthy team. If you sense resentment in the room or a decline in morale, address it directly and openly. Delivery is only half the goal. The other half is building a team that can keep delivering (not just once, but consistently over time).

Because when leadership lacks awareness, the cost isn't just cultural: it can also affect the team's structure and stability over time.

CHAPTER 13 CONFESSION #13: THE COSTS OF CULTURAL BLINDNESS

Burnout Is More Than Just Overtime

Burnout isn't always about clocking endless hours. Sure, those late nights and weekend sprints wear you down, but what really drains people is when expectations keep mounting without any balance, recognition, or empathy. I watched this unfold firsthand during a project where our management pushed the team beyond sustainable limits.

The math was unforgiving: mountains of work, impossible timelines. Our leadership had promised delivery dates that no realistic plan could meet, and questioning them wasn't even on the table. These weren't just tight deadlines; they were immovable deadlines. So, our team did what dedicated people always do: we pushed harder, stretched ourselves thinner, and somehow made it happen. To outsiders, we'd succeeded brilliantly. To us, it felt like we had survived, but at significant personal cost.

You couldn't ignore the warning signs. Colleagues who used to contribute actively in meetings went silent, not from lack of ideas, but from sheer exhaustion. Minor irritations turned into real friction. People started getting sick, some with minor issues, others needing actual medical leave. Our work quality slipped, not because we'd lost our skills, but because we were running on empty. Then came that moment when even our strongest team members said out loud what we all knew: "I can't keep doing this."

At the time, I was working as an architect. I could see what was happening, but seeing the problem didn't fix it. Leadership had already locked in their promises. We couldn't redistribute the workload; voicing our concerns made no difference. The team had to push through that timeline, and we did deliver, but the cost was severe. Team morale collapsed under the weight of those pressures. Everyone felt they'd poured everything into the project and received nothing in return, not even a basic acknowledgment. That stung the most: sacrificing so much of ourselves, only to watch leadership treat it as routine business.

CHAPTER 13   CONFESSION #13: THE COSTS OF CULTURAL BLINDNESS

Looking back now, I realize overtime wasn't the real villain. Teams will put in extra hours when needed, and most people will step up if they believe in what they're building and feel valued for their efforts. The real damage happens when working overtime becomes your standard operating procedure, and appreciation never materializes. Relentless pressure without empathy erodes motivation; it gradually wears down people's foundations. It doesn't just tire them out physically; it erodes their willingness to give extra effort in the future.

I'll admit something: I used to think burnout was about endurance, whether someone had the grit to handle long hours. My perspective has completely shifted. Burnout stems from unfairness, a lack of recognition, and treating people as resources rather than individuals. It's about whether your team feels seen and valued for their sacrifices.

For Scrum Masters, here's what I've learned: overtime will happen sometimes, but it should be the exception, not the rule, and leadership must acknowledge those extra efforts. When overtime becomes routine, that's your signal that planning and commitments are misaligned or unsustainable. And if leadership can't show empathy or give credit where it's due, you might hit your delivery targets on paper, but your culture will deteriorate beneath the surface.

That's what I've discovered about culture: it's not some "soft" concept. It's the hardest thing to build correctly and the easiest thing to damage if neglected.

Culture Isn't Soft: It's the Hardest Structure to Build

When people talk about culture, it's often dismissed as "soft." They view delivery as concrete, measurable, and undeniable, whereas they frame culture as abstract and optional. But I've learned the opposite is true.

CHAPTER 13 CONFESSION #13: THE COSTS OF CULTURAL BLINDNESS

Culture isn't soft at all; it's structural. It shapes how people show up, how they collaborate, and how long they stay. If this structure is weak, delivery eventually falters under its own weight.

This chapter has traced the different ways culture reveals itself, through star performers who get overloaded until they break, through microaggressions that teams tolerate until they become norms, through silent exits that no one sees coming, and through debts that accumulate invisibly until morale deteriorates. Leadership can ignore these signals for a time, but the cost eventually arrives, and it's often higher than expected.

As Scrum Masters, we may not control budgets, strategies, or executive decisions, but we do influence the one arena that matters most: how the team experiences its day-to-day work. And that influence is not small. By noticing the overlooked, surfacing the unspoken, and giving space for honesty, we protect the foundation that delivery depends on.

Culture doesn't build itself. It takes shape in every stand-up, every 1-on-1, every retrospective, and every recognition that we give or withhold. And once weakened, it's far tougher to repair than any system or process.

Takeaway Confession I used to believe culture was secondary, something that followed delivery. Now I know culture is delivery, because without it, the wins may be short-lived, and the losses can compound quickly. My confession is this: the most challenging work I've done as a Scrum Master wasn't about processes, tools, or frameworks. It was about culture. And the sooner we treat it like the structural discipline it truly is, the more sustainable our success becomes.

CHAPTER 14

Confession #14: You Can't Hold Everyone Accountable All the Time

> *You can delegate authority, but you cannot delegate responsibility.*
>
> —Byron Dorgan

If trust is the foundation of Agile, then accountability is the frame that holds everything together. Without accountability, trust collapses into fragility. But accountability itself is tricky. Too little, and delivery falters because no one feels truly responsible. Too much, and the weight often concentrates on a few shoulders, creating stress and the risk of micromanagement or burnout.

CHAPTER 14   CONFESSION #14: YOU CAN'T HOLD EVERYONE ACCOUNTABLE ALL THE TIME

Throughout my journey across various projects, I've observed accountability taking many forms, some of which are empowering, while others are destructive. I've seen high performers pushed beyond their limits while others drifted to the sidelines. I've watched leaders emphasize "ownership" but sometimes pair it with excessive monitoring rather than building trust. I've sat through retrospectives that shifted toward blame rather than constructive learning. And I've seen accountability slipped into a punitive pattern, where "ownership" sometimes meant having to explain outcomes beyond one's control.

Yet I've also seen the moments where accountability worked. When middle managers listened and acted, even within their limited power, teams felt heard. When teams clarified responsibilities and made agreements, friction gave way to flow. And when accountability was recognized, when effort was celebrated instead of punished, it became contagious, strengthening the entire team.

This chapter explores the fine line between accountability as empowerment and accountability as burden. Through stories of imbalance, micromanagement, blurred boundaries, and fragile agreements, I'll share what I've learned: that accountability is not about assigning blame or demanding updates. It's about creating the conditions where people want to own the outcome because they feel trusted, supported, and recognized.

Handled poorly, accountability risks reducing Agile to a ceremony without meaningful impact. Handled well, it transforms Agile into what it should be: a system where teams deliver not because someone forces them to, but because they take pride in doing so together.

The Overburdened High Performer

Every Agile team has them: the "go-to" people. Those who seem to hold the system in their heads, who can bridge gaps that others can't, who carry disproportionate workloads when timelines get tight. In one of my

CHAPTER 14 CONFESSION #14: YOU CAN'T HOLD EVERYONE ACCOUNTABLE ALL THE TIME

early projects, I found myself in that role alongside another developer. We weren't just building features; we were attempting the near-impossible: migrating a legacy system that had been in place for years, and doing it in an extremely compressed timeline. The rest of the team continued to meet their committed milestones, but the most complex and fragile pieces fell squarely on our shoulders.

At first, it felt like a badge of honor. Leadership trusted us, deadlines justified the intensity, and the team seemed relieved that "the experts" were taking care of the most challenging part. But the imbalance quickly became visible. While the two of us worked late nights untangling migration logic, the rest of the team continued with their deliverables, often without a clear connection to the migration effort.

The breaking point wasn't a production outage or a missed release date: it was a steady sense of fatigue that spread across the team. We had unintentionally created a two-speed team: the "core" doing the heroic work under pressure, and the rest waiting on outcomes they couldn't influence. Leadership, seeing the urgency of the migration, chose to hang on rather than intervene. They couldn't derail what was underway, even if it meant allowing frustration to build over time.

As the architect, I saw the imbalance clearly. But I let it continue. My rationale was simple: the migration was too significant to risk spreading across less experienced hands, and stakeholder expectations were heavily centered on the deadline. Yet, in reality, my choice reinforced the very problem I was worried about. By not redistributing work or creating space for others to step in, I deepened the dependency on two individuals. I undermined the sense of shared accountability that Agile encourages. The fallout wasn't burnout, though we brushed close to it. What emerged instead was frustration; team members who felt sidelined lost energy and ownership.

Chapter 14 Confession #14: You Can't Hold Everyone Accountable All The Time

Instead of a group moving forward together, we had pockets of people quietly questioning their effort, wondering if the hardest work would always land on the same few shoulders. That loss of motivation didn't show up immediately in metrics, but it eroded the sense of shared purpose that every Scrum Master and architect should be working to protect. Looking back, I realize we had slipped into a hybrid mode: part Agile, part shaped by dependency. We discussed collaboration, but the system was still relying on a few key players to keep it together. True Agile requires something different: empowering more team members to become genuine contributors, even if that means the work slows down at first. Without spreading accountability, the team never truly learns, and delivery becomes fragile.

What really struck me was this: yes, high performers are valuable; I get that. But I made them into the only thing keeping us afloat. My approach as a leader was misguided. Instead of giving the "stars" more work, which isn't really protecting them, I should have focused on sharing that knowledge around. Getting everyone involved in something they could actually own and feel proud of. That's when you stop having a few people carrying everything and start having a team that actually works together.

The imbalance of overburdened high performers often sets the stage for the next dysfunction: when leaders mistake micromanagement for ownership. Because when a few people hold all the accountability, the instinct is to control it even more tightly, and that's where things really begin to unravel.

Micromanagement Masquerading as Ownership

On paper, accountability and visibility are beneficial. Agile thrives on transparency, with daily stand-ups, sprint reviews, and retrospectives designed to keep work visible without slowing down the team. However,

CHAPTER 14   CONFESSION #14: YOU CAN'T HOLD EVERYONE ACCOUNTABLE ALL THE TIME

in one project, leadership took visibility and transformed it into something entirely different. What they called "ensuring ownership" felt more like being under constant scrutiny.

We weren't just doing the usual sprint or daily progress reports. Leadership wanted hourly updates. They expected developers to create separate task reports even though our tools already tracked everything. Testers had to develop additional spreadsheets that summarized work already visible in the dashboards. As an architect, I faced the same demands: frequent status calls, detailed explanations for decisions, and extra approval steps for tasks that were once simple. And here's the thing. It wasn't trust motivating these requests. It was fear. Leadership wanted to flood the customer with data points to keep them happy, and I found myself doing the same thing with my team. Before I knew it, that sense of distrust began to filter through the team.

The change was subtle but damaging. Meetings got quieter. People stopped sharing ideas openly because anything they said might be perceived as a weakness or used to delay. You could see the frustration in little things: cameras staying off during calls, one-word answers in retrospectives, those heavy sighs when yet another status report request came through. Engagement dropped, and people began going through the motions. Instead of actually solving problems, everyone was busy trying to prove they were working.

I tried pushing back, but honestly? I wasn't very convincing about it. Leadership kept saying it was all about "keeping the customer happy," and I went along with it, thinking that sharing information was better than starting fights. Looking back, I realize I was wrong about that. Productivity dropped noticeably as we spent hours each week on duplicate reporting. Team morale declined because nobody felt trusted anymore. Innovation slowed significantly. It's hard to try new things when every hour is scrutinized.

CHAPTER 14   CONFESSION #14: YOU CAN'T HOLD EVERYONE ACCOUNTABLE ALL THE TIME

Here's the thing that really gets me: leadership thought micromanagement would create ownership, but it did precisely the opposite. You know what actually creates ownership? Trust and letting people have some autonomy, basically knowing your work matters and having room to breathe while you deliver it. Look, all we needed was some basic stuff: dashboards that everyone could see, some metrics we'd all buy into, and team rituals that'd help us feel responsible together instead of scared of each other. If we'd had those things, we could've given the customer transparency without destroying trust within the team.

Look, this keeps bothering me: when you dress up micromanagement as accountability, you risk misleading everyone. It may appear professional on the surface, but underneath, it's draining energy, discouraging input, and weakening pride in the work. Absolute ownership only happens when there's trust. Without that foundation, accountability becomes performance; people appear busy, but real engagement fades.

And nowhere was that disengagement more evident than in retrospectives, where our supposed safe spaces had turned into blame sessions, with accountability completely off the rails.

Retrospectives That Became Blame Sessions

Retrospectives serve as the heartbeat of Agile spaces where the team can reflect honestly, identify patterns, and emerge stronger. We design them to be safe zones, shielded from hierarchy and politics, where the focus shifts from who failed to what we can improve. However, I've seen how quickly that intent can collapse when external voices dominate the room.

In one project, retrospectives included not only the delivery team but also external stakeholders who had a direct interest in the outcomes. On the surface, it's a good idea to include the customer in the spirit of transparency. But instead of enabling shared understanding, their presence shifted the purpose of the session. The moment discussions began, the tone was clear: the focus leaned less on learning and more on identifying fault. Each slip, each delay, each bug became an opportunity to identify a culprit.

The effect was immediate. Nobody argued back. How could they? Pushing against a customer's frustration only risked making things worse. Instead, the team disengaged. People stopped contributing, their eyes drifted to laptops, and silence grew with each comment. The ritual continued, but the spirit of the retrospective had died.

As an architect, I lacked the standing to intervene. My role was technical, and in that environment, the stakeholders' voices would likely have overshadowed mine if I'd tried to redirect. So I let it run its course, just as others did. Each session ended the same way: no outcomes, no action items, no plans for improvement. The only consistent result was a new layer of frustration, along with the sense that retrospectives were turning into rituals focused more on blame than improvement.

Looking back, the challenge wasn't in the team's willingness to improve; it was the lack of effective facilitation. A genuine Agile retrospective needs a moderator who understands both the mechanics of Agile and the dynamics of power in the room. When external stakeholders dominate, someone must have the authority to reset the tone, redirecting the energy from blame to learning. Without that, the retrospective loses much of its value.

The lesson for me was sobering: not every forum labeled "Agile" reflects the intent of Agile. Unless there is psychological safety, retrospectives become closer to audits than to learning conversations. The only way to protect their purpose is through strong facilitation, ideally with someone the customer recognizes as having the mandate to intervene, not just a symbolic presence with limited influence. Without that safeguard, retrospectives risk turning into far from what they are intended to be.

CHAPTER 14   CONFESSION #14: YOU CAN'T HOLD EVERYONE ACCOUNTABLE ALL THE TIME

When retrospectives collapse, the distinction between ownership and accountability becomes even more blurred. It raises a deeper question: what does it mean to hold someone "accountable" if they have no actual control? The collapse of retrospectives leads us to the next issue: the false equivalence between ownership and accountability.

Why Ownership ≠ Accountability

One of the most common misconceptions I've seen in Agile projects is the casual way we assign "ownership." On the surface, it seems empowering; someone is made the "owner" of a module or feature, giving the impression of responsibility and recognition. But too often, that ownership is hollow. Instead of being granted the authority to coordinate across roles, influence requirements, or negotiate priorities, the so-called owner is given only the responsibility to execute. In practice, it means they risk being blamed if things go wrong, without having the influence to shape outcomes.

I watched this unfold on a project where developers were routinely labeled as "owners" of modules. The leadership's intent was straightforward: to provide clarity. However, ownership was defined narrowly: write the code, deliver the feature, and be responsible for any delays. Decisions on requirements rested with business analysts, testers safeguarded acceptance criteria, and dependencies were managed in other teams' backlogs. If a module slipped, however, the developer often ended up singled out. The imbalance was stark: ownership without empowerment, accountability without support.

The cracks appeared quickly. Delivery slowed, not because people lacked effort, but because the so-called owner was left defending themselves in every review or checkpoint. Problems that should have been shared became isolated. If requirements shifted, it was still "the owner's fault." If testing revealed a gap, again, the owner often found themselves

CHAPTER 14   CONFESSION #14: YOU CAN'T HOLD EVERYONE ACCOUNTABLE ALL THE TIME

having to defend the outcome. The concept of collective responsibility, the developer, analyst, and tester as a unified delivery unit, was reduced to a single name on a report.

As the architect, I raised the issue directly: "We cannot call this ownership. If we want someone to own delivery, we must also give them the authority to drive it across all roles. Otherwise, we should be clear and call it what it really is, execution, not ownership." But the pattern was hard to break. Leadership valued clarity, even if it meant compromising fairness. And the developers, knowing the risks, carried the quiet frustration of being accountable for things outside their influence. Morale dipped. Instead of fostering pride, ownership became a burden.

Looking back, I see the solution clearly. Actual ownership can still exist, but only when paired with empowerment. Assign one person to lead, yes, but give them the authority to align analysts, testers, and supporting roles. Make accountability collective, with the "owner" acting as a driver, not a scapegoat. That's how modules succeed, through collaboration reinforced by trust, not through titles that mask an imbalance.

The lesson is simple: ownership without accountability becomes a dead end, but accountability without empowerment is even more damaging. Agile thrives when responsibility is shared across roles, yet directed by someone empowered to lead. Anything less reduces ownership to a hollow label and turns accountability into little more than a disguise for blame.

And nowhere is this imbalance more visible than in the forgotten space between teams and leadership, the middle layer of management that often amplifies pressure rather than resolving it.

The Forgotten Middle Layer of Leadership

In most Agile discussions, the spotlight falls either on leadership at the top or on the teams delivering at the ground level. But there's a middle layer, those managers caught between both worlds, who often end up

CHAPTER 14 CONFESSION #14: YOU CAN'T HOLD EVERYONE ACCOUNTABLE ALL THE TIME

shaping accountability more than anyone realizes. They don't write code or set strategy, yet their role can decide whether accountability becomes a shared discipline or a downward flow of pressure.

I recall one project where this layer's influence was clearly revealed. Initially, they served as messengers of pressure from above. Their updates sounded less like collaboration and more like transmission: deadlines, escalations, demands for output. It wore on the team to hear repeated echoes of leadership's concerns without any attempt at translation or protection. For a while, it felt as though the middle layer existed only to enforce, not to enable.

However, a persistent problem arose: the presence of team members whose contributions consistently fell short of expectations. It was apparent what was happening, and others picked up the additional work, keeping things moving somehow. For too long, nothing was done. The issue lingered, and frustration grew. When the middle managers finally took action, it marked a turning point. Despite pushback from those who questioned the need for change, "Why disrupt the team if delivery is happening?", they made the effort to bring in new associates to address the performance gap.

It wasn't a perfect solution, and it didn't erase the frustration that had built up over previous months. However, it revealed something more important: that our concerns were being taken into account. The act of even attempting a change restored a measure of trust. For the first time in weeks, the team believed that accountability wasn't just about delivering regardless of circumstance; it included creating conditions where individuals weren't left carrying disproportionate loads.

As the architect, I spent a lot of time with those middle managers. We'd sit together, brainstorm ideas, work through problems, and figure out possible fixes. I learned a lot from their experiences. They told me that meeting customer demands and changing deadlines were not possible for them. However, when they finally took action, even if it was late, it

CHAPTER 14   CONFESSION #14: YOU CAN'T HOLD EVERYONE ACCOUNTABLE ALL THE TIME

truly boosted the team's morale. It's striking how even the act of trying can matter. It reminded the team that their struggles weren't invisible, that someone was at least trying to make things fairer.

The lesson here is nuanced. Middle managers rarely have the power to transform the environment entirely. But they can decide whether to remain passive transmitters of pressure or to become advocates who amplify the team's voice upward. Even small actions, such as adjusting team composition when needed, acknowledging concerns, and pushing back where possible, can help build alignment and trust. The earlier those actions come, the stronger the effect.

The forgotten middle layer matters. When they step up, they become facilitators of accountability instead of channels of pressure. When they don't, misalignments grow quickly. In this project, their eventual intervention was sufficient to reset morale, but the delay highlighted how fragile accountability becomes when advocacy is lacking.

And fragility is exactly what teams face when boundaries blur, when accountability spills beyond its limits, and teams begin saying yes to everything without structure.

When Teams Lose Their Boundaries

I love working in agile environments where teams actually know what they own, what they deliver, and who they depend on. But I've seen what happens when those boundaries turn into a complete mess. One project really drove this home for me when our development team suddenly found themselves handling production support.

Here's the thing: nobody officially told us this was happening. The support team began struggling to meet their commitments, and instead of dealing with it properly, leadership quietly started sending us their work. It was frustrating. Suddenly, we were building features for the next release while also addressing production issues: same sprint timeline, no

CHAPTER 14 CONFESSION #14: YOU CAN'T HOLD EVERYONE ACCOUNTABLE ALL THE TIME

extra time, two completely different jobs. The release date wasn't budging, so now we're juggling yesterday's broken features while trying to build tomorrow's.

The chaos hit us immediately. Every time production blew up, our sprint work got derailed. Developers were ping-ponging between bug fixes and feature development, constantly switching contexts and showing signs of burnout. Testers were overwhelmed because bug fixes consumed the time they needed for validating new work. Operating in constant emergency mode was damaging our productivity and morale. Planning became this weird guessing game where we'd ask: "Okay, how much time would production issues consume this week?" It wasn't working, but customers still expected their items to be delivered on time.

So I pushed back. I told them production support had its own team, and we were being pulled significantly off track. But you know what they said? "Someone has to fix these issues, and we can't slip the deadline." It was a familiar pattern. The dependency had morphed into delegation without anyone acknowledging it. What should've been support's job became our responsibility. But here's the thing: nobody wanted to have that awkward conversation about how the boundaries had become so blurred. The harder conversation about boundaries was avoided. That's what really broke down whatever trust we had between teams.

But here's the real kicker: it wasn't just about missing goals. The team stopped believing that agile ceremonies actually protected our boundaries. Sprint commitments no longer felt reliable because we knew support work would come crashing through whenever it felt like it. Trust between teams fractured significantly. Developers resented being asked to support dumping work on us; they became defensive when we pointed out their mistakes. Instead of collaboration, we created an unhealthy environment. And trust, is everything in teamwork. Watching it fall apart like this really showed me how fragile it actually is.

CHAPTER 14 CONFESSION #14: YOU CAN'T HOLD EVERYONE ACCOUNTABLE ALL THE TIME

Now that I look back, the fix was staring us in the face. I mean, seriously, how did we miss it? Boundaries aren't walls; they're agreements between people. A basic RACI chart would've made it crystal clear who handles what, who jumps in to help, and who owns the outcome. Simple working agreements could've established proper escalation without throwing support work at development mid-sprint. Most importantly, the support team needed real empowerment and resources to handle their own issues, rather than treating development as their personal backup plan. Agile isn't about saying yes to every request; it's about creating sustainable workflows.

My takeaway? Blurry accountability undermines everyone. Teams without clear boundaries aren't more agile; they become more fragile. We thought we were helping in the short run. We destroyed long-term trust and our ability to deliver anything on time. True collaboration means respecting what each team brings while still having each other's backs. When that balance is lost, accountability dissolves, and good intentions can give rise to serious frustration. The only real safeguard is having crystal-clear agreements that define boundaries before someone decides to test them. Because without those ground rules, even excellent teams end up carrying work that was never intended for them. Looking back now, and I can't believe I'm saying this, I finally get why clear boundaries and solid agreements matter so much when you're trying to keep teams working together.

The Power of Clear Agreements

One of the most overlooked tools in Agile isn't a complex metric or framework; it's clarity. And nowhere does clarity matter more than in defining what "done" actually means. Without it, accountability becomes a moving target, and every role has a different story to tell.

CHAPTER 14   CONFESSION #14: YOU CAN'T HOLD EVERYONE ACCOUNTABLE ALL THE TIME

I saw this play out in a sprint where a feature was declared "done" by the development team. The team had committed code, builds were green, and the demo was ready. However, when testers examined it, they found that testing had not validated critical paths. From their perspective, it wasn't "done," it was incomplete. The business stakeholders agreed, asking, "If they can't use it in production, how is this done?"

The stand-up that followed quickly turned into a cycle of conflicting viewpoints. Developers said, "We finished our part." Testers pushed back: "We haven't tested the code, so it's not done." The business side added, "If we can't show it, it doesn't count." Each role was technically correct, but as a group, they were misaligned. No one set a shared definition or standard agreement. Accountability turned into defensiveness.

As an architect in that room, I didn't have the authority of a Scrum Master to reset the conversation. But I watched the tension escalate and the sprint goal unravel. By the end, nobody was satisfied. Developers felt unfairly singled out, testers felt unheard, and business stakeholders left questioning the team's credibility, largely because an explicit agreement was missing.

The fallout wasn't catastrophic: a sprint slipped, some rework followed, but the impact was cultural. Trust took a hit. What could have been a quick alignment became a tension that resurfaced in future ceremonies. People hesitated to call things "done" with confidence, concerned that expectations might shift again.

The lesson is straightforward but often ignored: agreements don't limit agility; they support it. A clear, written Definition of Done could have prevented the chaos by making expectations visible before conflict arose. Everyone (developers, testers, business) would know when a feature truly met the bar. Accountability would be less negotiable and more consistent; everyone would share it.

Since then, I've come to see agreements as the subtle guardrails of Agile. They don't attract attention like burn-down charts or flashy dashboards, but they help team avoid conflicts. Without them, accountability fragments. With them, it becomes a strength.

CHAPTER 14   CONFESSION #14: YOU CAN'T HOLD EVERYONE ACCOUNTABLE ALL THE TIME

And when accountability is recognized within those agreements, when people step up and deliver against a clear bar, it creates an opportunity to celebrate, not criticize. Because the real power of such contracts isn't just preventing conflict; it's making a foundation where recognition can thrive.

Recognizing Accountability Instead of Punishing It

Accountability is fragile. Handle it well, and it becomes a source of pride. Handle it poorly, and it turns into punishment. Across projects, I've seen the same mistake repeat: teams and individuals showed accountability, but instead of being recognized, they were micromanaged, blamed, or quietly ignored.

Take the migration project where two of us carried the bulk of the workload. We took charge because the deadline was too tight and the system was too fragile to distribute broadly. This was accountability in its truest form, stepping up when it was most needed. Instead of celebrating the effort, the rest of the team grew resentful. Accountability wasn't shared across the team, and this lack of recognition led to division instead of motivation.

The leadership team sought regular updates from developers to foster a sense of "ownership." While progress was made, developers sometimes felt their contributions were overlooked, as the focus was on individual value rather than team confidence.

The same dynamic emerged during retrospectives, where external stakeholders were heavily involved. People spoke up, raising issues in good faith. That was accountability: surfacing risks, admitting mistakes, and seeking improvement. The pursuit of honesty occasionally resulted in unintended consequences and feelings of being judged. Reflecting on past experiences did not yield actionable solutions; instead, they left

CHAPTER 14 CONFESSION #14: YOU CAN'T HOLD EVERYONE ACCOUNTABLE ALL THE TIME

lasting impressions. Had those moments been approached with gratitude and curiosity rather than criticism, the team might have fully embraced accountability, rather than pulling back from it.

I observed that developers were often designated as "owners" of modules, despite having limited authority. They showed a strong sense of responsibility while navigating constraints from analysts, testers, and upstream dependencies. When challenges arose, they often had to defend their work and take on criticism for issues beyond their control. Ownership without empowerment turns accountability into a burden, holding people responsible for outcomes without giving them the tools to succeed. Recognizing their effort, instead of placing undue blame, could have reframed ownership as leadership rather than a source of stress.

Even middle managers faced this tension. For months, they passed down pressure, which strained the team without solving the deeper problem of underperformance. But the moment they acted, making changes to address underperformance, despite pushback, it had the opposite effect. That recognition of team concerns, although late, rebuilt morale. It showed that accountability isn't only about meeting deadlines; it's also about listening and responding.

And when development teams were forced to absorb production support, accountability became less clear again. Developers showed resilience, handling two commitments in a single sprint. Yet instead of being recognized for stepping up, they faced frustration from all sides: leaders still expected features on time, and support still leaned on them for fixes. The accountability they displayed wasn't celebrated; it was taken for granted.

The same happened when teams argued over accountability in the absence of an explicit agreement. Raising those concerns should have been recognized as foresight. Instead, the warnings were lost in conflict, and only after delays did the teams realize the value of agreements. Recognition could have reinforced the voices that saw the cracks early.

In every one of these cases, accountability was present. The team was showing up, owning the work, and carrying responsibilities they didn't have to. What failed wasn't the people; it was the response. Instead of recognizing accountability, we overlooked or mishandled it. We treated it more like an obligation than a strength.

The lesson is clear: recognition multiplies accountability, while punishment diminishes it. Every time accountability was acknowledged, the middle layer made adjustments to address performance gaps, and the team absorbed extra responsibilities; the result was stronger morale. Every time it was punished, micromanaged, blamed, or taken for granted, the result was frustration.

Recognition doesn't mean ignoring failure; it means acknowledging the effort it takes to own responsibility, even when outcomes fall short. It means asking, "What enabled you to step up, and how can we support that?" instead of "Why did this slip, and who's at fault?"

Agile thrives when accountability is celebrated as a value, not used as a tool of control. And the way to scale that recognition is by aligning around shared goals while still empowering specific drivers to lead. That balance, collective ownership with individual clarity, is where accountability finds its true home.

Shared Goals, Specific Drivers

Recognition is only half the equation. The other half is alignment, ensuring accountability is shared where it should be, while still providing clarity to the individuals driving specific outcomes. Without this balance, accountability can either fragment into blame or concentrate into dependency. Both are dangerous. The healthier path lies in collective goals paired with empowered drivers.

CHAPTER 14 CONFESSION #14: YOU CAN'T HOLD EVERYONE ACCOUNTABLE ALL THE TIME

The migration project highlighted a problem: two of us carried most of the workload due to its complexity and tight deadline. While the team delivered, the uneven workload led to frustration among team members. If the migration had been viewed as a common goal for the team, with everyone contributing in smaller but essential ways, the reliance on one another would have been lessened. Specific drivers, who have the skills to handle tough challenges, could still lead the way toward our shared goal. The key difference is that accountability would be spread among everyone, rather than concentrated in one place.

We see a similar pattern in how we track progress. In the project where leaders requested hourly updates, accountability focused on demonstrating individual performance. Developers accounted for every hour, testers prepared additional reports, and architects fielded constant requests. A healthier alternative is team-based dashboards visible to all, reflecting collective progress. While specific team members can still share key metrics or help resolve issues, the entire team will take responsibility for the results.

Retrospectives offer another lesson. When discussions shift to blame, taking responsibility can seem risky, discouraging open dialogue. We should ask, "What did we learn as a team?" rather than "Who failed?" In that environment, individual drivers, such as those who flag recurring blockers, are recognized not for failing, but for enabling improvement. The focus shifts from who to what, and accountability strengthens as a shared discipline.

The module ownership problem underscored the same point. Developers were called "owners" but left without authority. When delivery slipped, they carried the weight alone. That wasn't genuine ownership; it felt more like deflection. The healthier model would have been collective accountability for the module across developers, analysts, and testers, with one empowered driver to coordinate and align. Shared goals prevent isolation, and specific drivers prevent diffusion. Both are necessary.

CHAPTER 14 CONFESSION #14: YOU CAN'T HOLD EVERYONE ACCOUNTABLE ALL THE TIME

Even the middle layer's intervention reflected this principle. For months, accountability tended to flow downward as pressure rather than as alignment. Making changes to address performance gaps, despite resistance, reinforced the shared goal of protecting the team. This action filled gaps and showed that accountability involves listening. The manager's leadership in this change improved team morale and rebuilt trust.

And when development absorbed production support, the cracks in shared goals became obvious. The support team operated under the assumption that all shared responsibility. To stabilize production, we need to clearly define roles: support should lead efforts, with development as a backup.

In these stories, one key idea stands out: accountability works best when everyone is involved, but leadership must be clear and focused. Teams need goals they own together, but within those goals, someone must have the authority to drive alignment, unblock dependencies, and coordinate. Without shared goals, accountability becomes fragmented and divisive. Without specific drivers, it becomes diluted and meaningless.

Agile succeeds when these two forces balance. The sprint goal is a shared commitment. The product owner, module lead, or architect may act as a driver, but they do so within the boundaries of collective ownership. Everyone succeeds or fails together, yet no one is left without guidance or leadership.

The danger of missing this balance is what I have come to think of as "Agile theater," a topic that deserves its own reflection. Because when accountability is neither recognized nor aligned, all that remains is ceremony without substance.

CHAPTER 14   CONFESSION #14: YOU CAN'T HOLD EVERYONE ACCOUNTABLE ALL THE TIME

Agile Without Accountability Is Just Theater

Agile ceremonies, such as daily stand-ups and bi-weekly retrospectives, are straightforward to set up, with progress visible on a dashboard. Yet without accountability, these practices lose much of their impact. True agility is achieved when teams take responsibility, support one another, and align on goals.

When we review projects where accountability was weak, a clear pattern emerges. Relying too heavily on high performers created fragility rather than resilience. Micromanagement, framed as ownership, ended up eroding trust and confidence. Retrospectives sometimes slipped into blame sessions when accountability was focused on individuals instead of the team. When developers were given ownership without being empowered, they often found themselves carrying blame without the authority to resolve issues. The middle layer of management sometimes passed along pressure rather than fostering alignment. Teams without boundaries blurred responsibility, which strained trust, and missing agreements sparked confusion instead of clarity. Accountability was overlooked or misinterpreted rather than celebrated. And goals lacked alignment when they weren't paired with specific drivers.

Each of these failures shared the same root: accountability was either misplaced, distorted, or ignored. Agile theater emerges when accountability is hollow. Teams show up, ceremonies happen, but the outcomes don't improve. Leadership wonders why Agile "isn't working," but the truth is more straightforward: without accountability, Agile loses its essence.

The shift comes when accountability is reframed: not as blame, not as surveillance, and not as an unfair weight carried by only a few, but as a collective discipline supported by trust, clarity, and recognition. With that in place, Agile ceases to be a mere theater and becomes what it was meant to be: a way of working that delivers value, fosters learning, and strengthens teams.

CHAPTER 14 CONFESSION #14: YOU CAN'T HOLD EVERYONE ACCOUNTABLE ALL THE TIME

Takeaway Confession I used to think Agile meetings were the key to success, but I've come across numerous stand-ups and retrospectives that ultimately turned out to be a waste of time, and I ended up feeling unproductive. Agile struggles without accountability; it risks becoming just a show. When there is accountability, that's when you actually start making real progress.

CHAPTER 15

Confession #15: When Teams Don't Play As One

> *Coming together is a beginning. Keeping together is a progress. Working together is a success.*
>
> —Henry Ford

Many people see alignment as essential for Agile delivery. However, teams often struggle to achieve it. Teams do not intend to work in isolation; silos develop slowly and almost unnoticed. This happens due to changing priorities, different incentives, and the desire to protect individual areas. As a result, each part of the team may be active, but the overall progress stalls.

I've seen it happen in many ways. For example, frontend teams focus on improving screens. At the same time, backend APIs evolve in a different direction, QA often receives code late in the cycle, uncovering defects that extend timelines, or support and development sometimes face delays in clarifying ownership of issues, which can impact users. Each scenario had one thing in common: groups optimizing for their own success while losing sight of the product's success.

CHAPTER 15   CONFESSION #15: WHEN TEAMS DON'T PLAY AS ONE

The danger is that this misalignment often hides behind the appearance of progress. Jira tickets close, metrics look healthy, stand-ups proceed on time, but the moment a demo begins or users interact with the system, the cracks appear. What was marked "done" isn't really done. What seemed aligned is actually fragmented. Trust can fade over time, and with it, momentum becomes harder to sustain.

This chapter isn't about blaming teams for silos. It's about recognizing how easily they emerge and how costly they can become. More importantly, it's about the moments when we broke free of those patterns, when empathy replaced ego, when language shifted from "yours" and "mine" to "ours," when metrics became unifying rather than dividing, and when the first meaningful cross-disciplinary demo reminded us what real progress looked like.

In the sections ahead, I'll share stories of standoffs, invisible territories, false signals, and the cultural turning points that reshaped the way we measured success. Because in Agile, success is never about individual wins. It's about shared wins, and learning that lesson was one of the most challenging and most valuable experiences of my journey.

The UI vs. Backend Standoff

The first signs of problems within the team often appear where different disciplines intersect. In our case, tension developed between the frontend and backend teams. Both groups performed their roles effectively: the frontend team created a smooth and user-friendly interface, while the backend team ensured the system could handle growth and maintain data security. Yet when these two pieces came together, they didn't fit.

The human side of the conflict quickly emerged. Meetings often became tense discussions, with developers from both sides debating how to handle integration issues. Frontend teams encountered unexpected API responses, while backend teams noted that UI expectations didn't

CHAPTER 15 CONFESSION #15: WHEN TEAMS DON'T PLAY AS ONE

fully match the documented contracts. Each group defended "their part" of the system with passion, but few stepped back to ask the more complex question: was the product as a whole working?

The breaking point came during the first integration demo. The application looked great on the screen. The interface loaded successfully, and everyone was excited to see it in action. When the backend data was needed, some screens failed to load, and others displayed incorrect or missing information. The room grew quiet, and it was clear the outcome wasn't what stakeholders had hoped for.

As the architect in that moment, I found myself mediating rather than building. The real challenge was to focus on the final product instead of just individual tasks. Rather than focusing solely on code defects or contract mismatches; we facilitated discussions between the teams to review the requirements, clarify expectations, and agree on how to integrate the work. My role shifted from technical problem-solver to translator, turning "your work" and "our work" into a shared conversation about "the product."

The fallout, however, was unavoidable. We lost time to rework, rebuilding parts of both the frontend and backend to meet in the middle. Stakeholders, already cautious about timelines, began to question whether delivery goals would be met. The technical issues were painful, but the gradual loss of trust proved even more challenging. Once confidence is shaken, every future milestone tends to be viewed with more caution.

The eventual resolution didn't come from better code alone but from a cultural adjustment. We agreed to integrate earlier, testing end-to-end functionality incrementally rather than waiting until a demo to discover failures. In stand-up meetings, we now focus on finding integration risks instead of just sharing updates. We emphasize using "we" to show that a feature is only complete when it works on both the frontend and backend.

The APIs and interfaces mattered, but what mattered more was whether the team could see themselves as part of one product rather than two separate pieces stitched together. The lesson was clear: alignment has to be built not only into systems but also into conversations. And when silos appear, they need to be addressed early, before they surface in a demo.

This tension between invisible boundaries sets the stage for a deeper issue: the friction of territories that aren't written down but are felt in every interaction.

Invisible Territories, Real Friction

Some conflicts arise silently in the background with no indication. Within my team, despite the Scrum team setup, the mindset often reflected functional boundaries. Designers, developers, and testers had their own arena. Over time, it created a friction that could have stalled delivery.

I first noticed it when the backend team delivered APIs without consulting the frontend. They finished their work and were confident that the interfaces were stable. However, when the UI team attempted to use the APIs, they ran into issues—certain fields weren't available and behaviors differed from expectations—leading to integration challenges. Both teams wanted to avoid issues, but by focusing on their own areas, they both contributed to the problem. The backend team felt they had met the requirements, while the frontend team felt blocked from moving forward. Ownership ended where the boundary began.

The same pattern repeated elsewhere. QA often began testing only after development declared code complete, which meant some defects surfaced later than they might have been caught earlier. Support teams sometimes viewed incidents differently when the root cause pointed back to development. Even in leadership, the split persisted, with product managers often emphasizing speed of delivery while architects highlighted technical sustainability. Each domain had its champions, but none of them carried the whole product.

I was caught in this web as well. More than once, I realized I was protecting my perspective rather than prioritizing collaboration. It wasn't just the teams, leaders, and me who were reinforcing the very silos we claimed to want to break down.

These invisible territories rarely caused immediate explosions. Instead, they created a slow burn, a background hum of inefficiency and reduced confidence. Tasks were neglected, and we uncovered dependencies too late. Frustration grew as individuals defended their own roles instead of collaborating in the challenging situations. As deadlines approached, this frustration escalated into open conflict, with groups pointing to one another as the source of delays.

The real breakthrough came when we made those invisible lines visible. Mapping dependencies and involving the support team in sprint reviews blurred role boundaries, transforming separate domains into a shared landscape.

The lesson was clear: friction arises when shared responsibility is unclear. Without someone to actively redraw the map, the project suffers.

But invisible territories don't only shape responsibilities, they also distort how we measure progress. In the next phase, the misleading sense of progress created by Jira tickets would give us the illusion of alignment while hiding deeper fractures.

The False Safety of Jira Tickets

If silos create friction, Jira can sometimes mask it from view. The board fills with green, tickets slide neatly to "done," and velocity charts climb upward. From a distance, everything looks orderly and under control. But inside the system, the reality may be very different: what appears complete on the board may not always translate into a working product.

CHAPTER 15   CONFESSION #15: WHEN TEAMS DON'T PLAY AS ONE

We faced a problem during a release that involved several integrations. Every team finished their assignments, and the dashboards were fine. However, after integration, the user interface was missing data from the backend. The APIs responded in formats that hadn't been fully validated against real workflows.

This gap was not only technical but also culturally rooted. Teams often equated story completion with fulfilling their responsibility for the larger project. When stakeholders raised issues about inconsistencies, team members sometimes pointed to completed stories as evidence of their progress.

The illusion was most dangerous when time pressure was present. During one deadline-driven sprint, the team focused on closing points quickly, which sometimes came at the expense of coherence. It gave everyone a sense of momentum until the demo exposed the truth. Stakeholders who had felt reassured by weekly reports were surprised when the system appeared fragmented in the demo. The trust diminished in that moment and required months to rebuild.

To change this trend, we modified how we utilized Jira by monitoring not only tickets but also the advancement of epics and significant milestones. Epics were monitored and used to assess the completeness of features. In our stand-ups, we changed our emphasis to "what's functioning in unison" instead of merely "what's finished." It was a slight linguistic shift, but it changed the dynamic: the board shifted from being viewed mainly as a scoreboard to serving as a conversation starter.

The real lesson was this: Jira can reflect progress, but it cannot create it. Tools don't deliver value; teams do. A green board loses meaning if the demo doesn't succeed.

And when metrics mislead, tension tends to rise, driven less by the work itself and more by how strongly people defend their perspectives. That's where the story turns next.

CHAPTER 15   CONFESSION #15: WHEN TEAMS DON'T PLAY AS ONE

When Ego Beats Empathy

Few things slow down delivery more than expertise defended without openness. I saw this repeatedly when teams, and sometimes myself, chose to defend their position rather than understand someone else's challenge. In Agile environments where collaboration is supposed to be second nature, ego can quietly undermine collaboration.

One project crystallized this pattern. Backend developers maintained that their APIs were accurate and well-documented, while the frontend team raised concerns that they did not fully meet user needs and requested changes. Disputes arose in meetings as both sides cited technical reasons, but the real issue was a lack of understanding, not a lack of intelligence.

Under the Nexus framework, multiple Scrum teams needed to integrate their efforts. When issues arose, rather than collaborating closely, teams often attributed the issues to one another. "Our stories are done; the issue must be theirs." Technical pride sometimes acted as a shield, preserving self-image while slowing shared progress. The framework didn't collapse because of a lack of skills; it faltered because empathy was absent.

I wasn't immune either. I sometimes held tightly to architectural principles even when the team needed functional progress. It took time and some difficult reflections to understand that empathy, recognizing the pressure on developers and the frustrations of testers, was just as important as technical accuracy.

The impact of ego was consistent: additional rework, reduced trust, and strained relationships. When empathy finally entered the room, when backend developers sat with UI teams to walk through real scenarios, when leaders invited support staff into discussions about live incidents, the tension eased. Friction didn't disappear, but it began to support problem-solving rather than block it.

CHAPTER 15   CONFESSION #15: WHEN TEAMS DON'T PLAY AS ONE

What I learned was simple but easy to forget: ego tends to close doors, while empathy helps open them. In Agile, bridges are built more easily with empathy than with ego. You need empathy to span the gaps.

And that shift, from individual defense to collective ownership, paved the way for the next turning point: introducing the concept of "we."

Introducing the Concept of "We"

The key to breaking down barriers was not a new tool or a significant process change. It was a simple change in how we talked about things. At some point, we shifted from talking about "you" and "me" to focusing on "we." This may seem small, but it significantly improved how we work together.

I first noticed it during a period of agitation when support and development were in disagreement. Both sides debated intensely about ownership of production issues. They clearly defined their own roles and limits in these matters. When both continued to struggle alone, their frustration gave way to a realization: neither could succeed on their own. The discussion smoothly transitioned from highlighting gaps or past handoffs to a collaborative approach focused on finding solutions together. That single word, we, diffused defensiveness and created room for joint ownership.

Another lesson came in smaller, almost accidental moments. A group chat thread between teams solved an issue in fifteen minutes that weeks of meetings could not resolve. Instead of setting clear boundaries, people focused on getting results. The way they expressed their request was noteworthy; it reflected a more collaborative spirit: "We would appreciate having this completed by tomorrow," rather than "your team hasn't completed this yet." This shift in phrasing had a positive impact on the overall tone of the conversation. It wasn't about avoiding blame; it was about claiming progress together.

Even in demos, the shift became visible. Earlier, a broken integration often led to back-and-forth over ownership. Once we began using the term "we," people approached demos differently. Teams collaborated across the entire process, focusing on the product's overall functionality rather than just individual roles. This mindset strengthened unity and underscored our shared purpose: delivering meaningful value to our users.

I realized that "we" is more than a word; it is a practice. It encourages everyone to acknowledge that accountability and credit are shared. At first, it feels uncomfortable, especially in cultures that value expertise and ownership. However, once people adopt it, the practice tends to spread quickly. As conversations occur, trust increases, and teams begin to view themselves as part of a larger group rather than separate units.

The power of "we" laid the foundation for trust. And that trust was tested most consistently in the stand-ups that followed.

Stand-ups That Build Trust, Not Just Status

The daily stand-up is a ceremony that highlights a team's culture by sharing updates, identifying challenges, and fostering alignment. It reveals how well the team collaborates versus operating in parallel. I've seen stand-ups at both extremes: some felt more like scripted recitals, while others were transformed into moments of genuine collaboration.

In the early days, our stand-ups leaned heavily toward the former. Developers would list what they had "done" yesterday and what they planned "today," but little meaningful discussion emerged. People didn't mention the blockers not because they didn't exist, but because they lacked trust and felt that admitting a problem might be seen negatively. The result was a routine of surface-level updates, with the real issues hidden until they surfaced elsewhere, often as late-night catch-up sessions or urgent bug fixes.

CHAPTER 15 CONFESSION #15: WHEN TEAMS DON'T PLAY AS ONE

The pressure of fixed deadlines only exacerbated the situation. People avoided speaking up in stand-ups, fearing that leadership would use their blockers as evidence of underperformance. The unfortunate irony was that the meeting intended to surface risks ended up burying them instead. The cost of silence showed itself in long evenings, broken builds, and growing frustration.

We changed the purpose of our stand-up meetings. Instead of asking about individual progress, we started asking, "What's stopping us from reaching our sprint goal?" This small change, from focusing on "me" to concentrating on "us," made a big difference in our discussions. Blockers became opportunities for teamwork, rather than individual struggles. When one developer said they were stuck, another quickly offered to work together to find a solution. QA identified testing challenges early, allowing developers to resolve issues before they escalated.

Effective stand-up meetings promote a culture of trust and open communication. During one such session, a developer noted challenges in completing a feature due to some ambiguities related to the API details. What might have become a last-minute effort was addressed and resolved amicably in just ten minutes. That was when I realized: stand-ups build trust only when people feel safe enough to share openly.

Looking back, stand-ups are less about reporting and more about relationships. They can either reinforce silos, with people focused on individual progress, or help dissolve them, with people offering their support. The choice isn't in the format; it's in the trust the team builds together.

When we establish trust, we open the door to something more profound: aligning not just on tasks, but also on how we measure success as a team.

CHAPTER 15 CONFESSION #15: WHEN TEAMS DON'T PLAY AS ONE

Shared Success Metrics

The numbers used to measure team behavior significantly shape it. Metrics often become the story teams use to describe their progress. But if those numbers reward siloed work, silos will flourish. I've seen firsthand how chasing the wrong metrics can reinforce division, and how redefining them can open the door to alignment.

In one project, velocity became the primary measure of success. Each team celebrated the number of story points they had completed by moving tickets across the board. Their progress looked impressive on paper. The situation was challenging: completed stories often did not become usable features, integration issues accumulated, and stakeholders were left waiting for results. Velocity alone is not a guarantee of success; it can sometimes become a distraction. It sometimes fosters competition between teams, with each one eager to "outscore" the others. This leads to activity without real progress.

The turning point came when we began tracking epics instead of just stories. Epic burn-down charts revealed something uncomfortable: despite all the ticket activity, progress on business-critical features lagged behind expectations. Stories were ending, but the bigger goals remained. This led to a necessary shift as teams focused on tasks that connected the frontend and backend, even if they weren't the most visible or glamorous tasks. Completing an epic became a collective win rather than just an individual achievement.

During a sprint, the backend team completed the APIs, while the frontend team finalized their screens; however, the project experienced delays because a key dependency had not been resolved. Reviewing the burn-down chart revealed the issue. Once the gap was identified, both teams collaborated on a solution, which improved the project and fostered greater trust.

The shift to shared success metrics helped reframe stakeholder conversations; instead of reporting ticket counts, we focused on the value delivered, including features launched, defects reduced, and customer workflows unblocked. Aligning our metrics with their success criteria helped rebuild team confidence.

The lesson was simple: what you measure often shapes what you motivate. Story points and velocity still had their place, but only as signals, not as end goals in themselves. The true measure of success became whether we delivered meaningful value together. Once the team shared the metrics, they also took on ownership.

That shift also changed how we viewed victories. Progress wasn't only about code anymore. Sometimes, the most significant wins came from alignment itself.

Team Wins That Weren't Code

Some of the most significant victories in Agile delivery come from collaboration and behavior changes, not only from commits, pull requests, or successful builds. These successes may not be reflected in Jira or velocity charts, but they can have a greater impact on a project than completing a single feature.

Inviting real users to our demos taught us valuable lessons. During user testing of our product, we uncovered valuable insights, unexpected workflows, and usability considerations. This experience highlighted the importance of feedback and the value of customer perspectives.

Developers, testers, and product analysts collaborated closely and resolved in a few hours an issue that had previously delayed progress for days. This positive change enhanced collaboration in future sprints, helping turn obstacles into opportunities for collective improvement.

CHAPTER 15   CONFESSION #15: WHEN TEAMS DON'T PLAY AS ONE

There were also quieter wins, moments when we improved the way we worked rather than what we built. Setting dedicated focus periods initially seemed minor, but it reduced late-night work and improved outcomes. Additionally, creating agreements between support and development teams helped clarify ongoing questions about responsibilities.

Features may come and go, and systems often evolve, but the practices of listening to users, collaborating across roles, and building trust create a lasting influence. They actively shape the culture and influence how future challenges are addressed.

And eventually, these cultural wins made their way into our demos. For the first time, we moved from showing separate pieces of work to presenting something cohesive; we were presenting something cohesive, built together.

The First Real Cross-Disciplinary Demo

Many Agile teams have experienced the disappointment of a demo that didn't go well. Features may seem complete on their own, but they can fail when put together. We've lived through these situations more than once, watching stakeholders' enthusiasm fade as polished screens froze or APIs returned unexpected results. Those failures left lasting lessons, but they also set the stage for one of the most pivotal wins in our journey: the first demo where everything finally worked together.

That success didn't arrive by accident. It came after weeks of frustration, when teams had grown weary of attributing issues to one another. Leadership created a shared testing environment to encourage early integration, rather than waiting until the end of the sprint. We also started holding daily stand-up meetings with all teams. These brief sessions allow developers, testers, and analysts to discuss and solve problems as they arise. Instead of waiting for sprint reviews to reveal surprises, we caught issues mid-sprint and resolved them before they snowballed.

CHAPTER 15   CONFESSION #15: WHEN TEAMS DON'T PLAY AS ONE

When demo day arrived, the difference was immediately visible. The frontend seamlessly integrated with backend services, QA scripts ran smoothly, and the workflows aligned with what stakeholders had been requesting since the beginning. For the first time, we delivered something cohesive rather than separate parts. You could feel the relief in the room, not only from leadership but also from the teams. This was more than just a technical success; it showed that working together can overcome the barriers that had slowed us down.

The atmosphere lingered long after the meeting ended, following that demo. Developers collaborated on integration tasks, while testers grew more assured that any issues would be addressed. Stakeholders changed their perspective from concentrating on "your deliverables" to adopting "our release," fostering a shared sense of achievement and reshaping the team's sense of identity.

What stood out to me most wasn't the applause from stakeholders, but the pride on the teams' faces. They had experienced what it felt like to succeed together. And once a team experiences that, it's difficult to return to old patterns.

The first real cross-disciplinary demo became a milestone, not only in delivery, but also in culture. It proved that the Agile team has shared values, not isolated victories.

And that realization brings us to the final confession of this chapter: Agile teams are sustained less by ceremonies or tools, and more by the power of shared wins.

Agile Teams Are Built on Shared Wins

Looking back, the misses follow the same thread. Each group could demonstrate progress, with nice screens, solid APIs, and tidy tickets, but the product didn't move as a cohesive unit. We had a demo where the first click just waited. Another sprint where tests passed, yet no real task

CHAPTER 15 CONFESSION #15: WHEN TEAMS DON'T PLAY AS ONE

could run end-to-end. The board suggested progress, but the room told a different story. Ultimately, only what worked in front of an audience mattered.

What actually helped wasn't a new diagram or dashboard. It was a small human choice. In an after-lunch stand-up, a developer, tired and a little embarrassed, said they were stuck. A teammate jumped in before I asked. Later that week, a tester waved down a backend engineer in the hallway to walk a bug, side by side, instead of filing it and forgetting it. Even the language from leaders shifted: less "your piece, my piece," more "let's get this over the line." None of it was dramatic, but the mood shifted nonetheless.

Shared wins create a different kind of impact. Once a team ships something real together, individual wins matter less on their own. Ego backs off. People listen more. Stakeholders notice too; they stop seeing stitched-together parts and start seeing product that felt alive and cohesive.

Takeaway Confession For years, I treated progress as a pile of parts, closed tickets, modules handed off, and code in production. I came to see that my view was incomplete. Those are only signals. If the thing doesn't work for a user, and if the team can't trust each other while making it, then we haven't truly progressed. The work that lasts is the work we finish together.

CHAPTER 16

Confession #16: Agile for Lean Tech Teams

Never doubt that a small group of thoughtful, committed citizens can change the world; indeed, it's the only thing that ever has.

—Margaret Mead

In the last chapter, I reflected on what happens when teams don't play as one, when handoffs, silos, and competing priorities can slow delivery. But not every challenge comes from teams being too divided. Sometimes, the opposite is true: the team is so small, so tightly knit, that division is far less likely. There are no silos to break down, because there aren't enough people to form them in the first place.

That was the reality I faced just before moving into service companies, at the edge of my product experience. I wasn't part of an extensive program with multiple Scrum teams. I was part of a small startup with fewer than 12 people, creating products that would normally be handled by larger teams. The drive to succeed often outweighed our resources, necessitating the assumption of various responsibilities and blurring the distinctions between roles.

CHAPTER 16 CONFESSION #16: AGILE FOR LEAN TECH TEAMS

This chapter is about those lean teams, their energy, their risks, and the lessons they offer. It's about how agility in its purest form often shows up when resources are scarce, not abundant. And it's about how the foundations of Agile at scale are laid not in big organizations with complex frameworks, but in the small teams that learn to move fast, stay disciplined, and carry heavy loads with astonishing resilience.

Small Team, Big Dreams

When I look back at the earliest days of my career, just before stepping into the world of service companies, nothing comes close to the raw ambition of being part of a fledgling product company. It was at the edge of my product experience, a time when everything still felt wide open. I was the very first employee: an architect in title, but in truth, one of many roles rolled into one. My colleagues were a diverse group, comprising a handful of freelancers, a couple of directors, and an abundance of ideas. The dream was enormous: to build a product that could serve a government client, the kind of scale typically handled by much larger teams with structured approval processes.

Initially, the team's small size was energizing. With only one developer, decisions were swift, iterations were rapid, and there was no need to navigate governance boards. A single developer could not carry the weight of an entire government-grade product. We expanded to what we called "a pizza team": small, self-contained units that could, in theory, design and deliver independently. Even then, the contrast was stark: we, fewer than a dozen people, took on work that usually spanned multiple departments and involved hundreds of staff.

The tension was constant. Each new feature felt like scaling a steep mountain with limited tools. Deadlines loomed, not because external authorities imposed them, but because we wanted to prove to ourselves and to the outside world that we could deliver. I remember how intense those early months were, leading up to the launch of our very first product. And when that launch finally succeeded, despite significant odds, it gave us both confidence and momentum. Only then did we take on the challenge of a second product. If we could deliver once, surely we could do it again. That conviction was both exhilarating and daunting.

In my role as architect, I often stood at the crossroads between ambition and pragmatism. Logic might have suggested tempering expectations, cutting features, or slowing down. But this was a startup. So, we leaned into ambition, encouraging the team to think big, to stretch themselves, and to find creative ways of delivering what larger teams might typically handle with greater manpower. Every decision became a balancing act: simplify the process, automate wherever possible, and focus only on the essentials.

What made the experience so powerful was how it forced everyone to gain end-to-end exposure. In larger organizations, people often work within well-defined roles; one person handles the database, another the testing scripts, and another the business requirements. In our lean setup, boundaries dissolved. Developers learned about deployment, architects reviewed business logic, and directors participated in design discussions. It was about survival and ownership. That raw exposure built a muscle memory I carried into every role afterward: the ability to see the whole system, not just a piece of it.

Of course, there were pitfalls. In the drive to execute, the process often became an afterthought. Documentation sometimes followed delivery, and testing occasionally competed with delivery speed. We achieved more in a short time than seemed possible, but not without a cost, long nights, heightened stress, and the ongoing risk of missing important details. What we lacked in structure, we compensated for with sheer energy, but energy alone is never sustainable. Small teams thrive on momentum, but if ambition isn't balanced with discipline, the very thing that makes them fast can eventually burn them out.

Looking back, those years taught me that small teams have a unique strength: they can achieve clarity and progress without the overhead that can slow down larger groups. They move faster because they must. They innovate because they have no choice. And they see the product end to end, which builds resilience and insight that no process guide can teach. The hunger to "make it big" can push people beyond sustainable limits.

The boundaries between roles matter far less than the collective willingness to take ownership of the outcome. That realization sets the stage for the next challenge we faced: what happens when everyone wears more than one hat, and the lines between responsibilities blur.

Wearing All the Hats

Small teams define themselves by their ambition and survive by wearing every possible hat. In the startup I joined, at the edge of my product experience, role definitions were flexible guidelines rather than rigid rules. Everyone did everything. Developers tested and wrote requirements. Architects designed, coded, and sometimes stepped in as product owners or even designers. Even directors sometimes rolled up their sleeves to test, analyze, and contribute to code, engaging directly with day-to-day delivery. It wasn't a strategy we carefully designed; it was a necessity, born from the sheer smallness of the team compared to the size of the dream.

At first, the blur was almost disorienting. A tester might point out a missing requirement, and the developer fixed it right away. A director might challenge a design decision, and they would open the IDE and show what they meant. The energy quickly spread through the team. We made a conscious effort to avoid saying, "That's not my job." We asked, "Who can help right now?"

One moment stands out. We were racing toward the first launch, pushing to make the product usable by real government users within a tight timeline. Despite having developers, testers, and even a part-time designer, gaps appeared every day. That's when the reality of "cross-skilling" took over. A developer would volunteer to test another's module. Although titled as an architect, I stepped in to design user flows and clarify requirements directly with stakeholders. Directors carried the burden of being product owners in one meeting, and then picked up bugs in another. Instead of slowing us down, the fluidity accelerated delivery. Every person grasped the entire system, allowing them to make decisions in minutes instead of weeks.

Everyone understood accountability without needing labels: if you touched something, you owned it and supported whoever was working nearby. Boundaries often blurred, but accountability remained clear. That distinction is crucial.

I found the list of hats to be endless. I was an architect by role, and I also served as a developer, tester, business analyst, designer, and even a stand-in product owner. Some days I reviewed code; other days I drew wireframes. At first, I wondered if this was a diluted expertise. But over time, I saw how much stronger it made me. It provided me with a comprehensive view of delivery, not just technically, but also organizationally. It taught me to respect each role, not as silos, but as perspectives needed to get a product out the door.

The lesson has stayed with me ever since. If you ever get the chance to work in a startup or a small, scrappy team, I would encourage you not to hesitate. You will gain exposure that is difficult to replicate in a larger organization. Nowhere else will you have the chance to be a tester in the morning, a designer at lunch, and a product owner by evening, all while still carrying out your original role. It's exhausting, yes. But it is also phenomenal.

If I were advising a lean team today, I'd tell them this: You are the only team that can make your target possible. No process document, external consultant, or formal role boundary can replace what your team achieves together. If a teammate is blocked, it doesn't matter if they are a developer, tester, or designer; give them a hand. Many of history's most significant

CHAPTER 16   CONFESSION #16: AGILE FOR LEAN TECH TEAMS

events began small, emerging in environments where boundaries blurred. People respected their roles, but they didn't allow those definitions to limit what they could achieve.

This culture of stepping outside formal lanes didn't just help us deliver; it set the foundation for how we thought about execution itself. It taught us that process was valuable only if it enabled output, never if it slowed us down. That realization leads naturally to the next challenge we faced: how to simplify without cutting corners.

Burnout in the Name of Velocity

In a startup, velocity doesn't come from charts, metrics, or dashboards. It comes from a shared hunger to prove the team's worth. We measured velocity by the features we shipped, the speed at which we turned ideas into working code, and the milestones that showed how a small team could take on responsibilities usually handled by much larger groups.

At first, that drive was exhilarating. As our first product approached launch, nights grew longer and weekends began to blur into workdays. Every extra hour felt like proof that we could compete with the giants. No one imposed that pace; it came from within, from pride in building something significant with so little.

But ambition has a way of turning into exhaustion. The signs appeared quietly. Code reviews became less detailed, feedback from testers was brief, and discussions in meetings dwindled as exhaustion took over the energy of debate. I experienced it as well, continuously transitioning between the roles of architect, developer, tester, and designer, all while striving to maintain team morale. Coffee became a substitute for meals, and weekends were just another chance to get back on track. We carried our fatigue almost like a badge of honor, convinced it demonstrated our dedication.

CHAPTER 16   CONFESSION #16: AGILE FOR LEAN TECH TEAMS

In service projects, burnout often arose from top-down overcommitment, limited recognition for achieved goals, and the expectation that the team could continually absorb more work. In the startup, things were different. No one pressured us; we motivated ourselves.

The slowdown arrived as a gradual dulling of our edge. Quality slipped. Creativity narrowed. We were still producing, but the spark was gone. What once felt like joyful improvisation turned into dragging ourselves across the finish line. That was the moment I understood: burnout doesn't care whether it comes from external pressure or from personal ambition; the outcome is the same. Ignore human limits, and both speed and quality will erode.

For me, the lesson was personal. My role as architect was to stretch the team, to prove that small could achieve outcomes typically associated with much larger teams. In reality, my responsibility should also have been to protect the team's sustainability. Ambition matters, but ambition without discipline is reckless. Sometimes the bravest act isn't pushing harder, it's slowing down just enough to endure.

If I were speaking to a lean team today, I'd tell them this: speed isn't proof of greatness. Sustainability is. A team that can deliver steadily, learn as it grows, and still have energy for the next release will always outlast the one that shines intensely but fades quickly. In a small team, losing even one person to exhaustion is like losing an entire department in a larger organization. Protecting energy isn't a luxury; it's a necessity.

Looking back, we realized that we made sure to learn from the experience of burnout. Retrospectives, work-in-progress limits, even short breaks, these aren't ceremonies for their own sake. And it was that realization that pushed us to rethink how to simplify our work without cutting corners that kept us safe.

CHAPTER 16   CONFESSION #16: AGILE FOR LEAN TECH TEAMS

Simplifying Without Cutting Corners

In a lean startup, embracing simplification was essential for survival. With a small team working on products intended to meet rigorous standards, there was no space for complex procedures or detailed documentation. Our daily stand-up meetings were brief and focused. We made decisions through direct conversations instead of escalating them through layers of committees.

And it worked, up to a point. I remember a night when a key feature was only partially completed, and rather than stopping for an official design review, we came together as a team and outlined the solution on a piece of paper. The developer immediately transitioned from the sketch to writing code. A tester who was nearby pointed out edge cases on the spot, and I made updates to the backlog as needed. Within hours, the feature was not only built but tested and ready to demonstrate. In larger organizations, that same feature might have required weeks of reviews, approvals, and handoffs. Our stripped-down approach gave us speed, and in that moment, it felt like proof that less really was more.

However, simplification has a shadow side as well. In one project, the development and support teams engaged in disagreements over where accountability should reside. Developers assumed their role ended with a working build, while support assumed they were inheriting a fully documented, production-ready system. Neither was entirely wrong, but without agreements in place, the blurred ownership caused delays and frustration. We had simplified by skipping what felt like bureaucracy, but in reality, we had overlooked an important safeguard.

The lesson came into sharper focus in my startup experience. Even in our stripped-down world, there were things we could not afford to oversimplify. Testing, for example. It was tempting to skip formal test cases because "everyone" was testing everything. Still, the first time an overlooked scenario made it into a release, we understood that some

CHAPTER 16 CONFESSION #16: AGILE FOR LEAN TECH TEAMS

guardrails are non-negotiable; similarly, though shortened, retrospectives remained essential. Without them, the fatigue from constant delivery cycles would have accumulated silently. By holding onto just enough discipline, we could move fast without eroding trust in what we delivered.

This balance, knowing what to cut and what to keep, is more complicated than it looks. Simplifying ceremonies, replacing hour-long meetings with quick syncs, or collapsing documentation into living notes are all examples of clever simplification. But removing accountability mechanisms, overlooking alignment agreements, or neglecting testing discipline can be examples of risky oversimplification. One protects energy; the other puts quality at risk.

Over time, I came to realize that the art of simplification is not about stripping everything away, but about stripping away the right things. It is the difference between pruning a tree so it grows stronger versus cutting back so far that growth is stunted. Lean teams thrive on directness and minimalism, but they must also identify which lines they should never cross.

Looking back, I see how both experiences, the startup and the service projects, taught the same lesson from opposite perspectives. In one, we encountered too much overhead; in the other, we faced too little discipline. The sweet spot was somewhere in between: ceremonies light enough to keep us moving, but strong enough to keep us accountable.

That balance also shaped how we communicated. Once you realize the value of simplifying structure, the next natural question becomes: how can we make communication itself simpler, faster, and more direct? And that brings us to the next reality of lean teams, the power of direct communication.

CHAPTER 16   CONFESSION #16: AGILE FOR LEAN TECH TEAMS

The Power of Direct Communication

If there is one thing that small teams teach you quickly, it is that communication cannot afford to be complicated. In a startup, you don't have layers of hierarchy or committees to pass messages through, and you can't afford meetings that don't move work forward. The only communication that matters is the kind that moves work forward.

I remember how naturally this unfolded in our early product days. A director who might, in another setting, remain distant from the details actively looks at a design concern, sits down next to the developer, and opens up the environment to illustrate a point. There were no formal escalation paths, and no emails were waiting in approval chains. A requirement clarification that could have taken days in a service organization was solved in five minutes because the architect, tester, and product owner roles were all represented at the same table, sometimes literally by the same person wearing different hats.

This directness wasn't just efficient, it was liberating. It allowed us to avoid the pitfalls of over-orchestration, where discussions sometimes stretched longer than the work itself. Instead of debating whether a backlog item was "ready for development" in a formal review, the person with the question asked the person with the answer. Teams solved decisions that usually required formal reviews, checkpoints, and reports through quick, human conversations. They fueled the pace of delivery not just with coding speed, but with seamless communication.

The contrast became clear later, in my service delivery experiences. There, communication often defaulted to ceremony. Teams usually spent a lot of time in meetings and updates that frequently felt more draining than productive. One particular instance stands out: a conversation in a Teams chat that connected different groups managed to solve a tricky problem in just a few hours, something that weeks of formal meetings had failed to achieve. That thread showed what I had already learned in the startup: sometimes all the team really needs is a direct line to each other, without the weight of the process slowing it down.

Of course, direct communication has its risks. In one project, a critical clarification was shared verbally but never documented. A few weeks later, when the new feature didn't work as the stakeholders had hoped, the lack of a written explanation created misunderstandings later. In our startup, we were able to launch new features quickly; however, sometimes the reasons behind our decisions weren't captured, and we had to revisit them later. The takeaway was clear: while being straightforward helps us deliver faster, not keeping a simple record of our decisions can lead to gaps in understanding later on.

In lean teams, speed is everything, and this speed often stems from direct communication among team members rather than relying on formal processes. However, in every environment, whether a startup or a service, the principle remains the same: communication exists to move work forward, not to weigh it down.

For me, this realization was transformative. It taught me that meetings are only helpful when they reduce confusion; otherwise, they risk becoming unproductive. It also taught me that agility doesn't come from how well we follow a framework; it comes from how directly we connect the people doing the work to the information they need.

Once we adopted this direct approach, we naturally began asking another question: if talking directly was faster than orchestrated meetings, could working asynchronously sometimes be even quicker than talking at all? That question led us to our subsequent discovery, the surprising power of asynchronous communication.

Async Over Orchestration

Many people think that being agile means everyone must always be connected and in sync. However, smaller teams often find that having excessive meetings and check-ins can sometimes slow progress. While meetings may seem like they are helping you make progress, if you're

CHAPTER 16 CONFESSION #16: AGILE FOR LEAN TECH TEAMS

part of a small group where everyone has several roles, unfocused discussions can consume valuable energy and time. This is why we turned to asynchronous communication, which allows us to work more independently and efficiently.

In the startup, async wasn't a formal strategy; it became a practical necessity. We didn't have time to gather in long sessions to debate requirements or review every decision. A quick note in the backlog, a comment in shared documents, or even a late-night message was enough to keep things moving. Everyone was close enough to the work to understand context, so updates didn't need to be wrapped in ceremony. A developer could jot down an assumption, and I could respond as an architect later; by the next morning, the team had already adjusted course. The work flowed without waiting for everyone to be in the same room at the same time.

In service delivery, orchestration often centered on daily syncs, weekly checkpoints, and monthly governance boards. It consumed significant time and energy that might otherwise have gone into delivery. I once suggested protecting focus time by moving updates to async channels. The idea was met with skepticism, as if being present in meetings was equated with working. But when we experimented, even briefly, the results were noticeable. The team delivered more, interruptions decreased, and updates continued to flow. It was a glimpse of what startups live every day: async isn't about avoiding work; it's about enabling efficiency.

Of course, async has its risks. We found our direct notes practical in the moment, but when a new developer joined, we found that new team members sometimes struggled to understand the reasons behind choices made months earlier. Async speeds delivery, but it can also scatter context if not anchored with lightweight documentation.

The lesson was clear: orchestration is not the same as coordination. Orchestration often involves bringing every team member into the decision-making process. In contrast, coordination does not need everyone. For lean teams, as long as people knew where to look for updates and trusted each other to follow through, the system worked.

Looking back, asynchronous communication is one of the quiet yet powerful superpowers of lean teams. It's not glamorous, and it doesn't show up on velocity charts, but it frees teams from the delay of waiting. And once you experience that freedom, you begin to see another truth: being lean is not about being careless. Async doesn't remove the need for discipline. In fact, the smaller the team, the greater the need for discipline in striking a balance between speed and quality.

That realization sets up the next lesson we learned: lean doesn't mean undisciplined.

Lean Doesn't Mean Undisciplined

One of the easiest mistakes to make about lean teams is to confuse simplicity with sloppiness. From the outside, it may appear that startups or small groups are improvising their way forward, cutting corners to move quickly. But I learned soon that lean doesn't mean careless. In fact, the smaller the team, the more discipline matters, because even small missed details or skipped safeguards can have a disproportionately large impact.

In our startup, we often blurred roles, held brief meetings, and made quick decisions. Yet, there were areas we couldn't compromise. Testing was one of them. Early on, we initially experimented with a more ad hoc approach to testing, assuming that since "everyone" was testing everything, we didn't need a structured approach. It worked until it didn't. The first time a missed scenario made it into a release, it was a wake-up call. From then on, we agreed that testing discipline, however lightweight, was non-negotiable. Even when a developer also acted as a tester, we maintained the principle that we couldn't sacrifice quality for speed.

I had already seen the darker side of neglecting discipline in larger service projects. In one team, gaps in coding discipline resulted in unstable builds and reactive fixes. Another time, overcommitment

CHAPTER 16   CONFESSION #16: AGILE FOR LEAN TECH TEAMS

without disciplined planning led to burnout, leaving people to manage unsustainable workloads. Those environments proved that skipping guardrails doesn't save time; it just defers the cost until later, when the fix is far more painful.

What I came to appreciate is that discipline doesn't have to mean ceremony. We didn't need mountains of documentation or hours of reviews. Instead, our discipline showed up in smaller, sharper habits. Code reviews, even brief ones, continued to occur. Retrospectives, even if brief, still provided us with an opportunity to learn and adapt. Automated scripts replaced manual repetition wherever possible. These were not just costs; they were protection against mistakes that could have seriously set back what we were trying to achieve.

Discipline also played a role in commitments. In lean teams, ambition often tempts you to take on more than you can realistically deliver. We encountered that challenge more than once. It was discipline, not enthusiasm, that forced us to ask, "What really matters this sprint? What will move the needle?" Without that restraint, we would have stretched ourselves too thin, trying to do everything but finishing nothing.

The irony is that in large organizations, discipline can sometimes be obscured under layers of process. It becomes a checklist activity, something people comply with rather than believe in. In a small team, you can't afford that luxury. There's no one else to absorb the extra work. If you skip testing, the issue will eventually surface for users. If you skip planning, your sprint will likely falter. If you skip reflection, mistakes are likely to repeat. The discipline is not in the framework; it's in the team's mindset.

Looking back, discipline was the difference between sustainable speed and reckless speed. It gave us the ability to move fast without falling apart. Lean didn't mean "do whatever you want." It meant "do what matters most, and do it well."

That commitment to shared discipline also shaped our development of resilience. In lean teams, you don't always get the luxury of deep benches or redundant specialists. This meant that the next lesson became critical: cross-training was essential for survival.

Cross-Training Wasn't Optional

In a lean startup, redundancy doesn't come from headcount; it comes from cross-training. With fewer than a dozen people building products that would typically require entire departments, we couldn't afford for knowledge to remain isolated. If one person was blocked or unavailable, the whole team slowed down. The only way to survive was to ensure that everyone had sufficient knowledge of everything to keep progress moving forward.

It wasn't a formal program of rotations or certifications. It was organic, driven by necessity. A developer who wrote backend code one day might step into testing the next. I, though officially the architect, often filled in as business analyst, tester, or designer. Directors wrote requirements, ran test cases, and sometimes even built features. Each role became a shared responsibility rather than an exclusive specialty.

The payoff was immediate. I remember one sprint where a critical bug appeared late in testing. Our only dedicated tester was already overwhelmed, and waiting for them to clear their queue would have delayed the release. Instead, two developers switched gears, validated the fix themselves, and worked with me to document the outcome. What could have stalled the sprint instead became a non-event, because the team had already built the muscle of stepping outside their comfort zones.

I had seen the opposite dynamic in service projects, where teams worked in strict silos. Developers coded, testers tested, analysts wrote requirements. The boundaries between them were rigid, and crossing them was not common. The result was predictable: frustration when something fell between the cracks. In one case, the absence of cross-training even led to arguments about who was accountable. Development assumed support would own production readiness, while support assumed development would hand over complete documentation. No one had the breadth to step in, so the gap eventually created tension.

That experience only reinforced what the startup had already taught me: cross-training isn't optional; it's vital for lean teams. It's the difference between resilience and fragility. A small team without cross-training can stall quickly if even one person is absent. A large team without it often struggles with bottlenecks and accountability gaps. However, when knowledge is shared, a team can adapt, cover for one another, and keep moving forward even when surprises arise.

Cross-training also had another benefit: it built empathy. When a developer spends time testing, and an architect steps into a product owner role, we will begin to appreciate each other. These experiences not only hone skills but also strengthen the team's bond. We were learning to see the product from every angle.

Looking back, I realize that cross-training was the foundation of our resilience. It wasn't about everyone being an expert at everything. It was about ensuring that no single person was a bottleneck and that knowledge was never concentrated in a way that created control risks. Cross-training meant freedom, the freedom to deliver without concern that one absence, one block, or one silo could significantly slow progress.

And it gave us the courage to do something that lean teams often struggle with: saying "no." When you build resilience within the team, you begin to recognize that the real danger lies not in what's lacking internally but in what continuously emerges from the outside.

CHAPTER 16   CONFESSION #16: AGILE FOR LEAN TECH TEAMS

The Value of Saying No

If there's one skill lean teams struggle with more than any other, it's saying "No." Ambition drives startups forward, but it also tempts them to accept every opportunity, every feature request, and every deadline as if refusal might be seen as a sign of failure. In our small product company, that temptation was constant. Having built one successful launch, we felt the pressure to take on the next big thing without hesitation. Every new idea felt like an obligation to prove that our first success wasn't a fluke.

For a while, we said "Yes" to almost everything. When customers suggested new features, we often accepted them without fully weighing the costs. When directors envisioned extensions to the roadmap, team members were convinced that we could stretch just a little further. The word "No" felt dangerous, in a team already small, with blurred roles and a culture of cross-training, it felt like refusing a request might risk the trust we had worked so hard to build.

However, ambition has its limits, and the cracks eventually began to show. I have noticed that in the second product release, every team member was stretched well beyond their capacity, yet new requests kept piling up. The fatigue began to affect the quality of the output, which only compounded the workload. By saying "Yes" to everything, we were unintentionally saying "No" to sustainability.

In service projects, the option of saying "No" was rarely part of the vocabulary. Stakeholders made the commitments; only information will be passed on to the team. Teams often still delivered by whatever means they could, but at the cost of fatigue, frustration, and a decline in quality. I still remember the sting of finishing a massive sprint only to see credit for the work disappear. It was a stark reminder that overcommitment doesn't always guarantee recognition; sometimes it leads to invisibility.

The contrast between the two contexts, startup versus service, taught me a valuable lesson. In service delivery, the inability to push back stemmed from external pressure, such as leadership or clients dictating

CHAPTER 16   CONFESSION #16: AGILE FOR LEAN TECH TEAMS

the terms. In the startup, the hesitation to push back came from within: our pride and hunger to prove ourselves. Both led to the similar outcome: exhaustion and compromised delivery.

Over time, I learned that "No" is not a rejection but a boundary. It protects the team's energy, preserves the quality of what's already committed, and forces clarity on priorities. Saying "No" to one request often means saying "Yes" to finishing something that truly matters. I began encouraging the team to pause before committing: Can business live without it? How are they operating today? What could be offloaded if the new feature is business critical?

Looking back, I realize that some of the most important decisions we made weren't about what to build, but about what not to build. Every product, every team, regardless of size, faces a flood of requests and ideas. The discipline to decline, to defer, or to redirect is what separates a team that survives from one that burns out.

And that discipline connects directly to scaling. Because the truth is, the ability to say "No" rarely gets easier with size; it often becomes harder. Which is why the final lesson of lean teams is so essential: Agile at scale begins with Agile when small.

Agile at Scale Begins When It's Small

I learned more about Agile in a startup setting than from any training or framework; it emerged from a small team with big dreams. Every principle we now discuss at scale, focus on outcomes, collaboration across roles, prioritization, and adaptability, was something we lived by daily because we had little choice.

We took on many different roles because the work needed to be done. We learned that prioritizing self-care is as important as ambition. Clear communication and good record-keeping help prevent misunderstandings. We adopted flexible hours, prioritized organization, and supported each other by sharing skills. We learned the importance of saying "No" to protect what truly matters to us.

In larger organizations, these lessons often get obscured by scale. Processes multiply, silos reappear, and the temptation grows to think that Agile is about rituals rather than results. But scaling doesn't create agility; it magnifies whatever habits a team already has. If the foundation is weak, scale tends to amplify existing challenges. If the foundation is strong, the scale extends its reach.

The truth I carry from those days is simple: agility begins small. Providing tangible benefits while remaining focused, organized, and flexible is a skill that can be developed with limited resources and unclear roles, especially when facing larger goals. An organization's DNA embodies agility, and this DNA directly influences whether the scaled organization thrives or struggles.

Takeaway Confession Agility isn't something you discover when the team gets big; it's something you either live when the team is small or risk losing along the way. The lessons of lean teams, shared ownership, disciplined execution, and the courage to say "No" are not survival hacks. They are the essence of Agile itself.

CHAPTER 17

Confession #17: Execution vs. Process, The XP Influence

> *Ceremonies don't deliver values; working software does.*
>
> —Unknown

In the previous chapter, we discovered that when our team is small and we have limited resources, we need to simplify our roles and focus on completing tasks efficiently. This experience demonstrated that being agile and quick to adapt means prioritizing action over adhering to strict rules and procedures.

The same lesson applies to larger companies as well; rituals may create the impression of health, but underlying challenges can still emerge. Adopting Agile processes is shown positively in the report, but the results tell a different story.

CHAPTER 17   CONFESSION #17: EXECUTION VS. PROCESS, THE XP INFLUENCE

That's when Extreme Programming, or XP, began to resurface in my thinking. For many, XP is a relic, one of Agile's earliest cousins, with its own strict set of practices. But the deeper I looked, the more I saw that XP emphasized execution over rules. Pair programming, refactoring, testing early, continuous integration, and shared code ownership weren't theoretical exercises. They were habits that shifted Agile from theory into action.

We didn't formally adopt XP; it has been integrated into our work to help us stay effective under pressure. This chapter reflects on those moments, revealing that genuine execution, not just rituals, is the true essence of Agile.

The XP Developer Who Changed Everything

The turning point for us didn't come from a new tool or an Agile coach; it came from pairing people who had never worked side by side before.

I still remember the first time I asked a senior developer to sit with a junior for an entire story. On paper, it looked inefficient. The senior had years of expertise, the junior was still finding their footing, and pairing them seemed like it might reduce velocity. But what unfolded surprised everyone.

The senior developer brought deep technical instincts, shortcuts born from experience, a keen sense for pitfalls, and patterns that juniors had not yet encountered. The junior, on the other hand, wasn't weighed down by "the way we've always done it." They asked naive but essential questions, challenged assumptions, and even suggested unconventional approaches that the senior would have dismissed outright if working alone.

Instead of slowing us down, the pairing sparked new energy. The code quality went up, but so did creativity. Seniors began to appreciate the freshness of new ideas, and juniors felt valued for more than just routine tasks. That subtle shift changed the team's behavior: people weren't just coding; they were learning in real time.

CHAPTER 17   CONFESSION #17: EXECUTION VS. PROCESS, THE XP INFLUENCE

In hindsight, that was our first taste of XP in action. We didn't call it Extreme Programming, and we weren't following a set of rules or a playbook. But by introducing deliberate pairing, I accidentally created the conditions for execution to flourish. The team discovered that the fastest way to deliver wasn't to isolate expertise, but to combine it, putting two minds on one problem and letting the sparks fly.

That was the moment I realized XP wasn't just a historical footnote in Agile's story. It was alive, and it had just walked into our team.

What began as a simple test quickly evolved into something more significant. The excitement from our first collaboration made us wonder if this approach could benefit more team members. This curiosity led us to incorporate pair programming as a regular part of our work together.

Pair Programming That Actually Worked

Once the first senior-junior pairing clicked, the obvious next question was: Could this actually work beyond one experiment?

We tried it again. And then again. Before long, pairing wasn't just a survival tactic or an experiment; it was part of how we got work done.

The most surprising thing wasn't the quality of the code, though that improved noticeably. It was the shift in team dynamics. The juniors who had once been hesitant to speak up during refinement sessions were suddenly bringing bold suggestions. They had tasted what it was like to test an idea in real time with someone more seasoned, and that confidence carried over into group conversations.

The seniors also began to change. Many of them admitted later that they were relying on familiar patterns, approaches they trusted, but hadn't always stopped to ask whether those patterns still applied. As they worked alongside juniors, they had to explain why they coded in a certain way, and this process of explanation often revealed habits worth challenging.

CHAPTER 17 CONFESSION #17: EXECUTION VS. PROCESS, THE XP INFLUENCE

Sometimes, when a junior team member asks what seems like an "obvious" question, it can lead to important insights. It can help simplify a design or uncover a solution that is more complex than necessary.

Of course, not every pairing was smooth. There were awkward mismatches, moments of frustration, and days when personalities clashed more than ideas. But even those rough edges carried value. The act of pairing made invisible tensions visible. It exposed assumptions early, instead of letting them sit buried until the integration phase or, worse, production.

One sprint retrospective summed it up best. A developer who had once groaned about "hand-holding juniors" admitted: "I realized I'm learning as much as I'm teaching." That confession mattered more than any chart or metric. It showed that pair programming was about execution, delivering value faster because people were actually thinking together, rather than in parallel silos.

Looking back, pairing worked because it addressed the challenges we were facing: knowledge gaps, uneven code quality, and a lack of shared understanding. XP didn't arrive in our team as dogma. It came through execution, one partnership at a time.

As we paired more, our conversations wandered beyond the new code. We revisited older modules, uncovering long-unasked questions. What once seemed "just the way things are" now appeared different through two perspectives. This sparked a culture of refactoring.

Refactoring As a Lifestyle

Pair programming didn't just improve the way we wrote new code; it changed how we saw old code.

When a senior and a junior sat together, one of the first things they often did was scroll through existing modules. What had been "just the way things are" suddenly looked different under two sets of eyes. Juniors, with their curiosity, asked why a method was so long or why the same logic appeared in three places. Seniors, who had worked around these issues for years, found themselves answering out loud and realizing they didn't like the answers.

That's when refactoring stopped being a task reserved for "someday." It became part of the conversation. Instead of waiting for a dedicated refactoring sprint that always seemed out of reach, developers began making minor improvements in the moment: renaming a variable, splitting a method, cleaning up duplication. At first, it felt insignificant, but over time, it built a culture of constant improvement.

I recall a specific pairing session where a junior identified a chunk of repeated logic scattered across different services. The senior shrugged, "Yeah, that's technical debt we've been carrying." But the junior pushed: "Why don't we just extract it now?" They did. What would have been another forgotten sticky note in the backlog turned into a 15-minute fix that saved hours of debugging later.

The beauty of refactoring as a lifestyle was that it didn't slow execution; it fueled it. Code became easier to understand, easier to change, and less fragile under pressure. When the team needed to add a critical feature, they could move faster because the cleanup from the previous day had paved the way.

Not everyone loved it. Some stakeholders questioned the value of spending time improving existing code instead of building new features. But the results spoke for themselves: fewer defects, faster merges, and smoother demos. Over time, even skeptics admitted that the team delivered more consistently when refactoring was part of the daily routine, rather than an optional extra.

They unlocked not just the sharing of knowledge but also the sense of accountability. Once people saw the mess together, it became harder to overlook. Cleaning as you go became a team habit, not an afterthought. Refactoring wasn't just a practice. It was a mindset, a lifestyle woven into execution.

As we improved our code, we recognized that confidently making changes required more than clear organization; we needed a safety net for mistakes. We realized testing should be integrated into the development process from the start, rather than just occurring after coding.

Testing That Guided, Not Just Validated

Before our team adopted XP practices, testing often came later in the process. We wrote the code first and then tested it. If a defect arose, we relied heavily on QA to identify it. The unspoken assumption held that testing aimed to prove whether something worked, rather than to influence how it was built.

Pair programming and the habit of refactoring began to change that. When two people stared at the same problem, especially a senior and a junior, the question often came up: "How will we know this actually works?" That question naturally prompted developers to write tests earlier, sometimes even before they wrote the first line of code.

It wasn't always structured Test-Driven Development, but it was pretty close. Developers started creating tests to enhance their understanding of a story. Writing the test beforehand compelled them to specify behavior clearly, rather than vaguely. Initial tests sometimes revealed gaps in the requirements before the team wrote any production code.

A junior developer attempted to create a unit test for an edge-case scenario, though some were initially skeptical; however, the test failed and revealed an error in the logic. This highlighted the importance of better code coverage, ensuring that even edge cases outside the test plan were included.

Gradually, testing transitioned from being a safety net to a tool for design and development. We began to notice trends: fewer last-minute surprises, quicker debugging, and increased confidence in refactoring because the tests were there to support us. Demos became less stressful since stakeholders were witnessing not just something that "appeared to work," they were seeing functionality supported by a reliable framework of green checkmarks.

The team began to appreciate that tests weren't a tax on execution; they were an accelerator. They gave clarity before code, direction during coding, and confidence after coding. Instead of testing trailing execution, testing was now guiding it.

The confession here is simple: we once treated testing as validation, but XP taught us it could be navigation. It turned our work from reactive fixes to proactive design. And once we felt that difference, there was no going back.

As testing began guiding our work, another truth became clear: the simpler the design, the easier it was to test, maintain, and evolve. Complex solutions slowed us down, while simple ones kept feedback fast and reliable. That realization pushed us toward our next lesson, treating simplicity not as an afterthought, but as a survival strategy.

Simplicity As a Survival Strategy

The more XP practices crept into our day-to-day work, the more apparent one truth became: complexity often worked against us.

Early in my career, I was guilty of over-engineering. As an architect, I wanted every solution to be future-proof, flexible, and "elegant." It looked good on diagrams, but the team often bore the cost: longer development cycles, and fragile releases. When deadlines loomed, that complexity became unbearable.

Pair programming started to break that cycle. With a junior sitting beside a senior, there was little appetite for building castles in the air. Juniors asked straightforward questions that seniors sometimes overlooked: "Why do we need all this abstraction?" "Isn't there a simpler way to do this?" Refactoring reinforced the same lesson. Every unnecessary

CHAPTER 17 CONFESSION #17: EXECUTION VS. PROCESS, THE XP INFLUENCE

layer became one more obstacle to clean code. Tests quickly revealed the challenges of ornate solutions; the more complex the design, the harder it was to cover with meaningful test cases.

That's when we began to live by a quiet motto: the simplest thing that could work. It wasn't about cutting corners. It was about resisting the temptation to solve problems we didn't yet have.

I recall a particular backlog item where a developer suggested creating a comprehensive rules engine for what was, at that moment, merely a few configurable parameters. The proposal seemed logical in principle; it would adapt well if we eventually required a multitude of rules. However, a junior team member interjected: "At the moment, we only need three rules. Why not just implement those three straightforwardly and enhance them in the future?"

That decision saved us weeks. More importantly, it taught us to invest effort where it mattered: in execution, not in speculative architecture. You can implement the rules engine later, if needed. In practice, it never was.

Simplicity turned out to be our lifeline. Under pressure, it was the thing that let us move faster. It made the code less painful to maintain and kept us from getting stuck in endless debates. We still cared about design, of course, but not so much that it hindered us. XP taught me an important lesson: the "best" design isn't the one that looks the most sophisticated, it's the one that lets you ship something today and still change it tomorrow.

I have to admit, I was often the one pushing for overbuilding. That instinct came from me as much as from anyone else. What changed me wasn't theory, but the team itself. Pairing, testing, and constant refactoring pulled me back toward simplicity. In the end, that's what carried us through.

Simplicity shaped how we built features, but it also demanded discipline in how we integrated them. Clean, lightweight designs only delivered value if they played well together in the larger system. That's when continuous integration stopped being just a practice and became part of our team's rhythm, almost like muscle memory.

CHAPTER 17   CONFESSION #17: EXECUTION VS. PROCESS, THE XP INFLUENCE

Continuous Integration As Muscle Memory

If there was one habit that changed the rhythm of our team more than any other, it was continuous integration.

Back in Confession #3, I described how broken builds placed significant strain on the team. Hours, sometimes days, were lost chasing integration issues. Developers dreaded merges because every merge felt uncertain; any dependency, configuration, or overlooked change could cause issues.

XP's answer was straightforward: integrate early, integrate often. At first, it sounded like extra work. Why keep merging small changes constantly when you could batch them up and "be efficient"? But the more we practiced, the more we realized that CI was insurance.

The initial weeks were challenging. We established automated pipelines to execute builds and tests with each commit. All at once, red failure notifications appeared frequently. It was a sobering realization of how delicate our system truly was. However, rather than allowing those failures to accumulate, we started addressing them as a fire alarm: pause other activity until the issue was resolved, ensuring no progress continued on a broken build.

That discipline slowly rewired us. Merges became smaller. Tests became sharper. Developers began thinking twice before committing unfinished or risky changes. CI stopped being a rule to follow and became a part of muscle memory.

I remember a moment when one developer, late in the day, hesitated to push a half-baked fix. In the past, they might have checked it in and hoped for the best. But this time they said, "I'll wait, I don't want to be the one who breaks the build tonight." That hesitation wasn't fear; it was accountability. The team had internalized that execution wasn't just about writing code quickly; it was about keeping the product in a consistently releasable state.

The biggest surprise was how CI changed our relationship with stakeholders. Demos no longer carried the suspense of "Will it crash today?" We demonstrated progress with calm assurance, as the code presented was the same code that had withstood numerous automated integrations. This dependability fostered trust more quickly than any presentation or sprint summary could.

Continuous integration transformed our work into a consistent rhythm. Successful execution relies on small, steady steps that are tested and integrated. Once it became muscle memory, we couldn't imagine working any other way.

As we improved our integration process, our team dynamics evolved. Daily meetings shifted from routine updates to focused discussions, helping us stay on track and achieve our goals effectively.

Stand-ups Became Tactical, Not Theatrical

Stand-ups had always been part of our rhythm, but for a long time, they sometimes felt more like a routine than a genuine team collaboration. Each person took a turn, gave their update, and the Scrum Master (me included) nodded along. It was safe, predictable, but not very impactful.

The change came when execution began to drive everything else. Pairing, refactoring, and continuous integration had made progress more visible, and the old format of "Yesterday I did X, today I'll do Y" no longer worked. People started bringing live problems to the stand-up instead of polished updates.

One morning, instead of reporting, a developer said, "Our test suite is running slow, and it's blocking merges. Can someone pair with me right after this?" That brief comment reshaped the priorities for the day. Another time, a junior admitted during stand-up: "I don't fully understand the logic in this module. Can someone walk me through it before I commit?" That openness saved us from hours of rework later.

CHAPTER 17   CONFESSION #17: EXECUTION VS. PROCESS, THE XP INFLUENCE

Stand-ups became less about performance and more about planning the next move. The questions shifted subtly: not just "What did you do? But what's blocking you? Who can help? What should we swarm on today?" Instead of walking away with a mental checklist of individual progress, the team left with a tactical execution plan.

It wasn't always smooth. Some days still slipped into rote status reporting. But when stand-ups worked, they felt like a quick tactical huddle: fast, focused, and grounded in reality. The goal wasn't to prove we were busy. It was to make sure the next 24 hours actually delivered value.

That was the XP influence bleeding into the ceremony. We didn't abandon the ritual; we reshaped it to serve execution. The team reshaped daily stand-ups into tactical briefings, focusing on execution.

As our team meetings shifted to focus on specific tasks, we recognized that our success depended on a shared responsibility. Everyone needed to contribute to keep things running smoothly, leading to a key idea: sharing ownership of our work.

Shared Code Ownership in Action

One of the quietest yet most powerful shifts XP brought to our team was the concept of shared code ownership.

Before that, our codebase was a patchwork of personal territories. Everyone had "their" modules, and working on someone else's code often felt uncomfortable. If a bug cropped up in a part of the system and the "owner" was out, the team would stall. We didn't call it that at the time, but we faced the risk of the bus factor.

Pair programming began to chip away at that wall. Seniors sitting with juniors naturally walked them through the code they had written months earlier. Questions like "Why is it designed this way?" and "What happens if we change this?" facilitated real-time knowledge transfer. Suddenly, code that was once tribal knowledge became team knowledge.

Continuous integration reinforced the same lesson. Since merges were happening daily, everyone had to take care of the entire system, not just their own slice. If you broke the build, it wasn't "your" code anymore; it was the team's problem. Accountability extended beyond personal boundaries.

The day a bug appeared in a module typically managed by a senior specialist, the shift became obvious. Instead of waiting for him to be free, two other developers, neither of whom had initially written that part, paired up and fixed it within hours. What would once have sat idle for days was resolved before the customer even noticed.

Not every developer loved it. Shared ownership meant no one carried the whole burden alone. It also meant ideas flowed more freely: one person's clever refactor became another's teaching moment.

The confession here is that I once believed ownership meant responsibility, the pride of guarding a personal piece of the system. XP flipped that on its head. Ownership wasn't about protecting territory. It was about spreading responsibility so wide that no part of the system depended solely on a single person.

When shared ownership took root, the team became faster, safer, and more resilient. The code no longer belonged to individuals. It belonged to everyone.

As the team shared task ownership, it became clear that quick feedback was essential. Collaborative activities like testing ideas and integrating solutions highlighted the importance of timely responses to ensure progress.

The Power of Tight Feedback Loops

If there's one thread running through every XP practice we adopted, it's feedback. Pair programming gave instant peer feedback. Tests gave immediate technical feedback.

CHAPTER 17   CONFESSION #17: EXECUTION VS. PROCESS, THE XP INFLUENCE

Continuous integration gave system-level feedback. Shared ownership meant that feedback wasn't filtered or delayed: it was direct, constant, and impossible to ignore.

Before this shift, feedback was often slow and delayed. A bug might only surface weeks later in QA. Design flaws would linger until integration. Stakeholders' reactions came at the end of a sprint review, by which time we had already sunk weeks into the wrong path. By the time feedback arrived, it was too late to act efficiently.

XP shortened all of that. The loops got tighter. The cost of change dropped.

I recall a sprint during which we tested a new workflow feature. We would have postponed showcasing our progress until demo day. However, by collaborating, writing tests from the start, and making daily small commits, we managed to create something functional within a few days. We brought a stakeholder into a brief call during the sprint and guided them through our work. Their response was direct: "This isn't quite what we intended."

In the old model, that feedback would have arrived two weeks later, accompanied by far more rework. Instead, it came on the third day. We pivoted immediately and shipped the correct version by the end of the sprint review. What could have been a failure turned into a success story, simply because the feedback loop was short enough to matter.

Not every piece of feedback was easy to accept. Occasionally, junior members identified weaknesses in the designs of their senior counterparts during pair programming. There were also times when automated tests uncovered assumptions that had gone unnoticed. Initially, those instances were uncomfortable. However, over time, the team came to understand that experiencing discomfort early on was better than facing a major issue later.

XP taught us that feedback wasn't a side effect of process; it was the heart of execution. The faster we learned what was wrong, the faster we could make it right. And once the team became accustomed to working within those tight loops, waiting weeks for answers began to feel impractical.

I once viewed feedback as something external, something that occurred "after" the work was done. XP taught me that feedback is an integral part of the work itself. Execution without feedback isn't accurate execution; it risks becoming guesswork.

All these insights: pairing, refactoring, early testing, frequent integration, shared ownership, and quick feedback, led us to a key realization: the true power of XP lies not in adding rituals, but in the understanding that execution unites everything.

Execution Over Ritual—The Confession

Looking back at this chapter, I can trace a clear pattern: every XP practice we adopted, including pairing, refactoring, testing early, continuous integration, shared ownership, and feedback loops, brought us back to the same truth. Execution mattered more than ritual.

We didn't abandon Scrum ceremonies. We still held planning sessions, stand-ups, and retrospectives. But XP reminded us that those ceremonies were never the point. They were scaffolding, not the structure itself. The real structure was execution: writing clean code, delivering working features, and learning fast through feedback.

There were plenty of times when our rituals got in the way. Long refinement sessions that added no clarity. Stand-ups that slipped into routine status updates. Retros that sometimes revisit the same challenges without resolution. In those moments, the process felt heavy. XP cut through that weight by focusing us on doing the work rather than talking about it.

CHAPTER 17 CONFESSION #17: EXECUTION VS. PROCESS, THE XP INFLUENCE

The confession is uncomfortable but straightforward: for a long time, I relied on rituals because they gave me a sense of stability. They made me feel like the team was "doing Agile the right way." However, those rituals didn't carry us through when builds broke, deadlines loomed, or customer expectations shifted overnight. Execution did.

And yet, it wasn't reckless execution. XP taught us discipline, to refactor constantly, to test early, to integrate often, to share ownership, to seek feedback at every step. That discipline gave execution its power. It wasn't a process for its own sake; it was a process in the service of results.

When teams forget that, Agile becomes a mere formality. When they remember it, Agile becomes unstoppable.

Takeaway Confession Agile isn't about ceremonies, charts, or frameworks. It's about execution, shaped and strengthened by discipline. XP gave us that discipline. It reminded us that value is delivered not through ritual, but through doing the work, collaboratively and continuously.

CHAPTER 18

Confession #18: When Agile Rules Bend (and Break)

Adapt what is useful, reject what is useless, and add what is specifically your own.

—Bruce Lee

Agile was supposed to make everything simple. That's what I thought when I first stepped into environments where Scrum, Nexus, or other frameworks were in play. Follow the ceremonies, respect the rules, and agility would emerge. At least, that was the promise.

But in practice, I saw something very different. Teams that closely followed the process but struggled to deliver meaningful outcomes. Competently run meetings that did not achieve their intended outcomes. Charts that showed progress but did not always reflect meaningful forward movement. Agile, in those moments, risked feeling more like routine performance than a mindset.

And yet, the opposite was true, too. Under pressure, the teams often found their stride as they bent or even broke the rules. Pausing a sprint because QA demanded it, creating technical stories as placeholders when the backlog wasn't ready, or abandoning ceremonies altogether to push through a critical delivery, these didn't look like Agile on paper, but they produced outcomes that mattered.

This chapter examines a contradiction in focusing too much on rules and frameworks, sometimes losing sight of their true purpose. It shows that genuine agility is not delicate; skipping a meeting or changing guidelines doesn't weaken it. The challenge often lies in an overly rigid commitment to processes, which can divert us from achieving our broader objectives.

The Day We Skipped a Retrospective

Retrospectives are supposed to be the heartbeat of continuous improvement. They are the one ceremony where a team has space to step away from the delivery treadmill, reflect, and ask: How can we improve? At least, that's the intent.

The team asked me to improve our retrospectives, as they had not been effective. From the very beginning, I noticed a lack of energy during these meetings. Although everyone attended, the atmosphere remained subdued and engagement was limited. It was clear the team needed more engaging discussions and stronger collaboration.

Leadership recognized the problem as deadlines loomed, teams rushed through retrospectives, prioritizing delivery over reflection. The focus shifted toward meeting productivity targets, with less emphasis on deeper challenges or continuous improvement.

The team followed that cue. To the team, retros were just another recurring meeting. Something to attend, acknowledge briefly, and move past without much engagement. They didn't resist them, but they didn't embrace them either. It was a box to tick, not a space to learn.

CHAPTER 18 CONFESSION #18: WHEN AGILE RULES BEND (AND BREAK)

Then came the sprint, during which we skipped a retrospective altogether. The release date was looming, backlog pressure was high, and no one raised an argument for holding the retro. The invite was on the calendar, but we ignored it. The team continued working, pushed the code, and closed the sprint.

At the time, I convinced myself it was the right decision. The team hadn't been sharing much during retrospectives anyway, and leadership treated their input as a lower priority compared to delivery. I believed that spending the time writing or testing code was better than sitting through an hour of silence.

But later, the moment lingered with me. Skipping the retrospective wasn't just about losing one meeting. It symbolized what retros had become for this team: a ritual that had lost its value for the team. We could discard it without immediate impact, because little meaningful change was happening within it.

Looking back, I realize the danger wasn't in skipping that retro. It was in having retros that no one cared about. A healthy team would have fought for that space, even against a deadline, because they would have believed it mattered. This team didn't. Leadership didn't. And eventually, I stopped too.

That day taught me something important: retrospectives don't fail when you skip them; they fail when you run them without a clear intention. Agile ceremonies only matter when they serve a purpose. Without that, they aren't improving. They become more like performance than improvement.

It wasn't just retros that risked becoming routine. The same thing showed up in how we defined "done." On paper it looked clear, but in practice, deadlines bent the meaning until "done" often meant something less than finished.

CHAPTER 18   CONFESSION #18: WHEN AGILE RULES BEND (AND BREAK)

Definition of Done…ish

One of the most challenging aspects of collaborating with a disengaged team wasn't just the ceremonies; it was coming to a consensus on what "done" actually entailed. Although we had a Definition of Done that outlined clarity, acceptance criteria, and business approval on paper, that distinction often became unclear when deadlines clashed with reality.

During one sprint, the team really needed to deliver a vital feature fast, but the backlog was incomplete and disorganized. They hadn't finished the business stories, and the acceptance criteria were still unclear. Rather than remain inactive, the team created technical placeholders, interim stories intended to keep visible progress moving while waiting for the actual business stories to be completed.

Everyone knew these placeholders weren't truly finished. The vague acceptance criteria meant being "done" was more about having a framework than delivering a working product. By the end of the sprint, the board showed progress, and we closed the stories; the team also acknowledged in chats that further rework would be needed.

Surprisingly, that rework didn't derail us. Anticipating the situation, the team left room for refinement and adjustment. The placeholders provided them with a technical foundation and an understanding of the problem space. When the proper user stories finally arrived, the groundwork was already in place. Instead of causing chaos, the rework fit into the flow.

Leadership and stakeholders saw these "done-ish" stories in sprint reviews. Their reaction was measured. They weren't excited because the stories weren't final, but they were relieved to see the team moving forward instead of reporting "blocked." For leadership, visible momentum was more important than perfect clarity.

It turned into a juggling act for me. From an architect's perspective, I was uneasy. I firmly believe that setting clear standards for delivery is crucial because it eliminates any room for misinterpretation. It's vital to acknowledge that marking something as "finished" when it's only a temporary step can slow overall progress.

CHAPTER 18 CONFESSION #18: WHEN AGILE RULES BEND (AND BREAK)

I remember sitting in one review and thinking, "This isn't the right way to do it, but it's evolving according to the situation." It may not apply to every team, but I know many in the world who fall into the same scenario. Strict definitions could have slowed us down significantly. Flexibility kept us alive.

It wasn't perfect, and it definitely wasn't spotless. But in that situation, "done" just meant "good enough to move on." I stopped saying it with certainty. Instead, I began phrasing it more cautiously: this is done... kind of.

It was another reminder that definitions and estimates can look tidy on the board while reality tells a different story. The same tension showed up again in how we sized work. What looked like a simple three-point story often carried the weight of a thirty-point feature.

The 3-Point Story That Became 30

Estimation helps teams find predictability. In this delivery, it became more of a cover than an accurate measure.

We weren't working on stories at all. We were working on features that were large, complex, and critical to the business, which needed to be delivered under an impossible two-month timeline. In the planning stage, the team broke them down into user stories. Some even received a low size estimate of three points, resembling neat, well-shaped units of work. But that was more of a formality. Everyone knew the reality: these "stories" were features in disguise.

The whole delivery carried that pattern. We completed an entire release in two months, pushing through a mountain of functionality that would have usually taken far longer. Estimates didn't reflect complexity; they were just placeholders. The team labeled items "three" or "five" not because they reflected reality, but because the board required estimates to track.

CHAPTER 18   CONFESSION #18: WHEN AGILE RULES BEND (AND BREAK)

The work itself told a different story; extended work often spilled into evenings and weekends. We measured progress not by points burned down but by features that we integrated, tested, and signed off on under pressure. It was demanding. But it was also necessary. Business leaders had made it clear: this release was too critical to delay.

Unlike some situations where stakeholders questioned why small stories ballooned, there was no surprise here. Everyone, from leadership to the developers themselves, knew the sizing didn't reflect the true effort involved. The appreciation came not from tidy burndown charts, but from the sheer hard work and commitment the team poured in.

For me, it was a dual-hat moment. The architect in me saw the cracks: technical debt piling up, the Definition of Done stretched thin, and features presented as stories. However, I knew the alternative, slowing down to argue about estimation accuracy, wasn't realistic under the circumstances. The only thing that mattered was delivery.

Looking back, that entire release was less about precise Agile estimation and more about meeting survival-level delivery needs. The numbers on the cards were misleading, masking the reality that the team was hauling thirty-point loads while claiming only "three." It wasn't organized or smart, but it got the job done.

That experience taught me how numbers can craft a narrative, despite the challenges behind them. Soon after, our leaders assigned us a task that transformed how we managed multiple tasks simultaneously.

The Leadership Request That Broke WIP Limits

The moment came in an offline conversation. Leadership communicated it directly, without process language or negotiation. The message was clear: both were priorities. We needed to incorporate shipping features

CHAPTER 18   CONFESSION #18: WHEN AGILE RULES BEND (AND BREAK)

for a critical release and address urgent production issues. There was no trade-off, no sequencing, no room for delay. It was an instruction, not a discussion.

The team's reaction was almost immediate and almost silent. Nobody pushed back. No one asked which should come first. Everyone just nodded and got to work. The pressure was clear enough: features and fixes, parallel priorities, no excuses. Instead of picking one, we split our attention and tried to do both.

The effects were evident on the board. At first, the "in-progress" lane appears normal, but complexity lay beneath: a mix of stories, urgent issues, and technical placeholders. The team had everything marked as "in progress," which created the impression that we were moving forward, but actually, it slowed us down.

Stand-ups became the daily reminder of the fracture. Instead of a crisp, focused update, each person rattled off three or four threads: "yesterday I touched X, today I'll push Y, and I'll also review Z." It became an activity without clear completion, a motion without real momentum. Progress spread so thin that it never felt substantial.

QA felt the burden first. New changes continued to arrive while yesterday's tests were still incomplete. Defects weren't appearing dramatically; they accumulated gradually, making the release more fragile over time. QA eventually raised a clear warning: unless we paused, testing would fall behind and release quality would suffer.

As an architect, I felt the squeeze from both sides. I understood the trade-offs. I even tried to explain to them that chasing both stability and delivery without limits would hurt both. But in that moment, the pressure from customers left no space for prioritization. Both sides demanded results, and was not able to convince anyone to make a choice.

CHAPTER 18   CONFESSION #18: WHEN AGILE RULES BEND (AND BREAK)

Looking back, the lesson was a sharp one. Leadership pushed hard, and the team also struggled to renegotiate focus. We treated everything as equal priority and tracked it all under a single "in-progress" lane. When customers struggle to prioritize, the burden shifts onto the team. If everything is a priority, then nothing truly is.

The issues we faced extended beyond project reports and spilled into our daily meetings. What should have been quick check-ins turned into struggles with scattered information and confusion, leading to awkward pauses and a lack of direction.

When Stand-ups Go Silent

Stand-ups are meant to be quick moments of alignment, a way to keep the team in rhythm without breaking the flow of delivery. But with the disengaged squad, I was asked to "fix," and they often felt like the opposite.

I vividly remember those early weeks. The team stood in a circle, and the energy was low. Updates felt monotonous: "I did this yesterday, and today I'm going to do that." Conversations often ended in silence, and during slower progress, the pauses became longer. My instinct was to step in with a few questions: What's causing the delay? Have you considered this option? What's going on with that system integration?

The effect was immediate, and not in a good way. Blank stares. Awkward silence. Team members shifting in place, unsure how to respond. They weren't used to being challenged that directly in stand-ups. What should have been a space for collaboration sometimes felt more like questioning than discussion. The silence was more than uncomfortable; it signaled that the team had not yet engaged fully with the process or with me as their Scrum Master.

CHAPTER 18   CONFESSION #18: WHEN AGILE RULES BEND (AND BREAK)

The technical perspective brought to our team contributed positively to our dynamics. We addressed the technical challenges at the end, and interested participants were allowed to stay. The meeting was then transformed into working sessions to solve their problems.

The leadership stance was clear: address the team's challenges, deliver outcomes, and ensure results. Their focus wasn't on whether the ceremony was smooth, but on whether progress was being made. The team largely treated the stand-up as another recurring meeting. Participation felt mechanical, and ownership did not increase.

As our team has grown, the need for streamlined communication has become essential. Our discussions have changed from dynamic exchanges to lengthy updates, resulting in less engagement and weaker team dynamics. Increased visibility from leadership has led to reduced open conversations, making meetings feel more like coordination checkpoints than collaborative problem-solving.

To enhance team cohesion and our operational framework, it became clear that meaningful discussions fostering open communication were needed. The lengthy stand-up meetings revealed issues beyond declining participation; they emphasized the importance of transparency and honesty among all members to avoid turning them into mere formalities or off-topic conversations.

I've encountered challenges such as disengaged participants and lengthy meetings, which have been crucial to my growth as an architect. These experiences highlight the importance of aligning our discussions with the core objectives of each meeting.

Those silent or drawn-out stand-ups showed me the limits of ceremonies when intent was missing. We could run them perfectly by the book and still leave with no absolute alignment. That realization set the stage for one of the clearest lessons I carried forward, sometimes following the process isn't what drives delivery at all.

CHAPTER 18   CONFESSION #18: WHEN AGILE RULES BEND (AND BREAK)

Process Adherence vs. Product Delivery

One of the clearest lessons I carried forward came from a two-month delivery where I was working as an architect, not a Scrum Master. The business had committed to a critical release under a compressed timeline, and every hour mattered.

By the book, we should have been running a complete Scrum process: sprint planning, backlog refinement, reviews, retrospectives, and daily stand-ups. In reality, none of that fit the situation, so the team set aside most ceremonies. In their place, we ran intense workshops and worked directly with stakeholders. Conversations were fast, focused, and practical. We operated more like a product company, moving from discussion to delivery without ceremony in between.

Leadership supported this shift completely. They didn't ask for velocity charts or sprint reports. Their stance was clear: deliver the release, regardless of the specific process followed. For once, there was no pressure to demonstrate process compliance. The only success criteria were working features, delivered on time.

The team responded with relief. With fewer ceremonies filling the calendar, they could dedicate more time to building. The workshops felt purposeful because they were tied directly to immediate outcomes. Instead of process driving behavior, urgency and ownership took over. Ironically, by ignoring the framework, the team experienced agility in a very direct form: tight feedback, rapid adaptation, and continuous delivery.

For me, as an architect, this experience was both validating and instructive. I had seen this kind of agility before in product companies, where iteration and execution took precedence over rituals. However, for this team, it was the first time they had truly experienced agility. They discovered that Agile was not about simply following framework steps; it was about focusing energy on delivery.

CHAPTER 18 CONFESSION #18: WHEN AGILE RULES BEND (AND BREAK)

Balancing structure and effective outcomes enables teams to work more efficiently and fosters collaboration. Being flexible and adapting to changes is often essential for achieving success.

The experience revealed a key truth: the framework was just a tool and sometimes a hindrance. What truly mattered was the team's mindset, adaptability, and the quality of their delivery. This became evident when comparing situations where the framework was used without the right mindset.

Agile Framework ≠ Agile Thinking

One of the most common traps I've seen in Agile is confusing the framework with the mindset. Scrum, Nexus, SAFe; they all provide structure. But structure alone doesn't make a team agile. I learned this lesson the hard way, both in small teams and scaled programs.

With the disengaged team, the framework was followed on paper. Stand-ups, reviews, retrospectives, all the ceremonies took place. But delivery didn't follow. The team went through the motions, but ownership is missing. They were "doing Scrum," but they weren't being Agile. The framework was present; the mindset was absent.

At scale, the gap became even more apparent. In one Nexus setup, a key meeting intended to align teams on future business features was redirected. Instead of identifying dependencies for the upcoming value, the focus shifted to daily production issues. Even the Product Owner became focused on firefighting. Over time, the meeting lost its original purpose entirely. It appeared to be a Nexus event on the surface, but the intent was lost. If the goal was to solve short-term problems, leadership could have just created a new series. Instead, they repurposed a critical meeting, and the framework became more about form than purpose.

CHAPTER 18   CONFESSION #18: WHEN AGILE RULES BEND (AND BREAK)

What struck me was that leadership didn't equate "doing Scrum" or "doing Nexus" with being Agile. They started with excitement. However, as time passed, they shifted their focus toward short-term goals, losing sight of the bigger picture. The framework didn't fail on its own. It failed because the underlying thinking eroded.

The contrast was sharp when I looked at the critical deliveries I'd been part of. In one case, a release was delivered within two months with very few formal ceremonies. We worked through workshops, stakeholder conversations, and direct execution. The system wasn't perfect, but it enabled the team to work efficiently. They communicated well and adjusted quickly to changes. When tasks were unfinished, they found temporary solutions rather than halting all progress. This flexibility showed that it is more effective to keep moving and improving rather than waiting for complete certainty.

The teams noticed a shift in their work approach. Operating as product-oriented groups energized them and allowed them to move quickly, keeping them closer to their goals and reducing procedural delays. However, they acknowledged that this fast-paced method might not be sustainable in the long term without risking burnout.

On the other hand, when they relied on structured frameworks, they found some guidance. If teams focus too much on strict rules, they can lose their enthusiasm and creativity.

I have come to realize that frameworks like Scrum or Nexus are fundamentally tools for teams, rather than complete solutions. One team might follow the rules exactly and still feel stuck, while another team might bend some guidelines and become more agile. The key is not the rituals themselves but the mindset of the people involved. Agile practices should be flexible, encouraging everyone to focus on achieving their goals instead of just following the motions of the process.

The distinction between framework and mindset became clear when the team questioned established rules. It wasn't the leadership or processes driving change, it was the QA team. Their demands forced us to recognize that ensuring quality sometimes requires interrupting our usual workflow.

Breaking the Sprint to Fix the Problem

Scrum tells us that a sprint is sacred. Once committed, the scope should hold steady until the sprint ends. In theory, it provides stability and predictability. In practice, I learned that sometimes stability is the very thing that keeps you from fixing the real problem.

One of the clearest examples came not from leadership or product, but from the QA team. Mid-sprint, they raised a red flag: defects were increasing, and the pace of new development was exceeding the team's testing capacity. It wasn't a slight adjustment; they were asking for a complete pause. The message was clear: stop building temporarily, or the foundation would become unstable.

The request directly challenged Scrum discipline. Cancelling a sprint isn't supposed to be routine. However, the logic was unavoidable in this case. What good was delivering half-built features if quality was deteriorating behind them? After difficult conversations, we chose to break the sprint. Development slowed, QA caught up, and stability returned.

The experience was unsettling. As an architect, I felt the potential for technical debt increasing; as someone responsible for delivery, I felt the weight of breaking cadence. But it also revealed a truth: sometimes the team itself, not leadership, knows when the process is getting in the way of the product. Listening to QA in that moment helped us avoid larger problems later.

CHAPTER 18 CONFESSION #18: WHEN AGILE RULES BEND (AND BREAK)

Breaking from traditional sprint methodology can have its advantages. We moved away from regular ceremonies and adopted a workshop approach, allowing the teams more space to focus on construction.

In general, taking such breaks does not denote failure; instead, it reveals the underlying problems. The adaptation is a signal of the team's courage to stop, align, and move on, which ultimately will save the delivery.

That moment taught me that breaking cadence isn't weakness, it's awareness. But it also sharpened another realization: when teams follow process without intent, even the most "stable" sprint or ceremony can hide fragility. Pausing for QA made sense because it served the product. Yet I had seen too many other cases where process continued for its own sake, long after its purpose was gone.

Process Without Purpose Is Just Theater

Agile ceremonies were never intended to be a performance. However, in practice, I often found myself watching rituals unfold in a scripted manner. The motions were correct, the checklists ticked, but the purpose was unclear or diminished.

The clearest example came in retrospectives. The team sat together, but no one said a word. The ritual took place with everyone present, the format followed, yet no insights emerged. The meeting ended the way it had begun: in silence. We had a retro on the calendar, but no reflection, no change. It was theater, not improvement.

Leadership sometimes reinforced the same illusion. Even when business deliverables were missing, they applauded compliance. Burndown charts, point totals, and velocity graphs became proof of progress. It didn't matter that the progress was hollow. The team had "burned points," and the charts looked good, so the process was praised. In those moments, Agile risked becoming performance art, appearing controlled without driving accurate delivery.

CHAPTER 18   CONFESSION #18: WHEN AGILE RULES BEND (AND BREAK)

At scale, I saw it again. Nexus events, intended to align multiple teams, drifted into reporting rituals. Production issues consumed the agenda. Teams recited updates, leadership nodded, and everyone left. The framework was intact, but the intent had evaporated. Instead of looking forward to business features, the system shifted to focus on daily firefighting. It was a clear example of process without purpose.

The contrast became sharper when I compared those moments with the two-month critical delivery: workshops and direct conversations with stakeholders replaced ceremonies. In the midst of production chaos, few guidebooks offered relevant guidance. The fixes, workarounds, and on-the-fly decisions weren't in Agile literature, but they kept the business running.

That's when it became clear to me: process is only ever a means to an end; without a purpose, it becomes empty. A retro without reflection, a chart without value, a meeting without an outcome; they risk becoming theater. When the process loses its purpose, the motions may continue, but the outcomes are already lost.

The empty periods, silent reflections and purposeless Nexus events, highlighted the fragility of processes lacking significance. Yet, these experiences helped me see their resilience. While Agile methodologies seemed vulnerable without purpose, they proved robust when their guidelines were applied flexibly.

Agile Isn't Fragile, It's Flexible

For years, I carried the belief that Agile was fragile, that if we skipped a ceremony, bent a rule, or deviated from the framework, the whole thing would collapse. What I've learned instead is that Agile's strength comes from its flexibility. The rules can be bent, even broken, yet the mindset remains.

CHAPTER 18   CONFESSION #18: WHEN AGILE RULES BEND (AND BREAK)

I saw the fragile version of Agile in the disengaged team. They followed the ceremonies mechanically. The structure was there, but it produced limited value. When retrospectives were silent or stand-ups were lifeless, it highlighted that a process without purpose struggles to sustain agility.

I saw it at scale as well. Nexus events drifted into the theater when consumed by firefighting. The intent to align on business features was lost, replaced by daily distractions. On paper, the framework looked intact, but in practice, it proved brittle. Even a small shift in focus weakened the purpose.

But I also saw Agile at its most flexible. During the two-month critical delivery, we abandoned ceremonies and focused on workshops, conversations, and execution. It wasn't sustainable, but it delivered value when it mattered most. In another case, the team built technical stories to keep moving forward when the backlog wasn't ready. These weren't by-the-book practices, yet they reflected agility more effectively than rituals alone.

And when QA raised their voice to demand a pause, breaking the sprint to restore quality, it showed another dimension of flexibility. That choice didn't undo Agile. It was strengthened. The team adapted, corrected course, and delivered better.

Each of these moments reinforced the same lesson: Agile isn't about protecting the framework at all costs. It's about protecting outcomes. The framework is a tool; the mindset is the anchor. When people cling to the tool without the mindset, Agile feels fragile. But when teams stay focused on value, adaptation, and collaboration, Agile proves itself to be remarkably flexible.

CHAPTER 18 CONFESSION #18: WHEN AGILE RULES BEND (AND BREAK)

Takeaway Confession   For a long time, I confused protecting the framework with protecting agility. I clung to ceremonies, compliance, and process because I thought that was my role. However, the truth is that Agile never broke when we bent the rules; it broke when we lost sight of our purpose. My confession is that it took struggling stand-ups, diverted Nexus meetings, silent retros, and even a sprint paused by QA for me to see it clearly: Agile wasn't fragile, it was my own perspective that was. Once I let go of my obsession with process and trusted the mindset instead, I finally understood what agility really means.

CHAPTER 19

Confession #19: The Frameworks Are Coming, Don't Panic

> *It is not the strongest of the species that survive, nor the most intelligent, but the one most responsive to change.*
>
> —Charles Darwin

It started with an email. Another framework rollout was on its way, this time with a name and a promise: SAFe, Nexus, scaled Scrum, pick your acronym. At first, I was curious. Could this be the change that solves the problems we've been circling? Or was it just another cycle of process-heavy Agile?

Over time, I learned that frameworks arrive with the weight of expectation. Leadership loves them because they promise order. Teams sometimes embrace them because they offer clarity. Coaches swear by them because they come with roadmaps. But the truth I saw on the ground was more complicated. Frameworks were helpful in some places, but in others, they added a layer of complexity.

CHAPTER 19 CONFESSION #19: THE FRAMEWORKS ARE COMING, DON'T PANIC

I sat in ceremonies that consumed significant time but offered limited delivery progress. I saw Scrum of Scrums that often felt more like reporting sessions than coordination forums. I watched Jira dashboards were highlighted even when business outcomes did not fully align. And I endured coaching efforts that motivated teams but had limited influence on decision-makers.

Yet, I also saw moments where a framework worked. SAFe PI Planning created real energy, with teams aligning around multiple sprints in a single day. In a two-month release, skipping ceremonies and focusing on workshops helped the team deliver results without burning out.

This chapter explores both sides. The following stories illustrate the outcomes of treating frameworks as templates versus tailoring them to fit specific situations. The main point is straightforward: it's never about the framework itself; it's about the context in which you apply it.

The Email That Launched a Thousand Trainings

When I joined the consulting engagement, the team was already running on SAFe. The framework was already in place, embedded in how the team worked. Program Increment (PI) planning was part of their rhythm.

My first reaction was curiosity. It wasn't theater; it felt like a fundamental shift. What stood out right away was how they planned a couple of sprints. In regular Agile, backlog preparation is usually for the next sprint or two, but here the anchor stretched further. That approach made the work feel more deliberate.

The PI planning was a single-day, big-room event. The entire team participated in the half-day session, which the organizers structured with breakout rooms. During those sessions, the excitement was evident. The energy came naturally from the teams themselves, rather than being externally prompted.

CHAPTER 19   CONFESSION #19: THE FRAMEWORKS ARE COMING, DON'T PANIC

I was in observation mode as an architect. My role wasn't to run the event but to see how it worked. There was no conflict between architecture and SAFe's approach to handling dependencies; the planning process flowed smoothly without friction.

The team organized training sessions, introduced supporting activities, and adjusted project management tools, leading to smoother ways of working. Team members readily adopted these adjustments, which streamlined tasks without introducing unnecessary steps.

Looking back on that first week, this might actually work. The thought process was more advanced than what I was used to. Where I might suggest preparing a backlog for sprint N+2, they were already looking at iterations that spanned across multiple sprints. It wasn't about just reacting; it was about preparing.

Still, one thing was missing. Even with SAFe's discipline in planning, the equivalent of Nexus-style syncs wasn't happening. It wasn't a major issue, though I felt additional cross-team meetings could have further supported dependency resolution.

That first week left me with two impressions: SAFe represented a significant shift, and my curiosity was the right lens to view it through. It helped me see both the structure that worked and the gaps that remained.

SAFe showed me how structure could create energy, but sustaining that alignment day to day was another matter. Beyond PI planning, the focus shifted to coordination meetings, especially the Scrum of Scrums, which promised connection but often brought its own challenges.

Scrum of Scrums or Just More Meetings

The Scrum of Scrums happened every day, and it often stretched to nearly an hour. Attendance fluctuated. Attendance was inconsistent, and the meeting often lacked clear facilitation. There was no real time-box, and the format was left loose. It wasn't in my control, so all I could do was participate and observe.

CHAPTER 19 CONFESSION #19: THE FRAMEWORKS ARE COMING, DON'T PANIC

The Scrum of Scrums was initially designed for Scrum Masters to discuss inter-team dependencies and obstacles. Over time, leadership voices tended to guide discussions, sometimes centering heavily on one team's challenges while others waited.

Preparation was minimal. Teams often attended without structured preparation. Dependencies, when raised, weren't solved. The team captured them in a PowerPoint deck that received incremental updates day after day, but concrete follow-through was limited.

There was an ongoing expectation to demonstrate progress. Each team had to display charts and points burned. Dependencies were also present, but were only listed as a line item on each slide and discussed briefly before proceeding.

I raised my concern more than once. I suggested reducing the frequency, tightening the agenda, and limiting participation to Scrum Masters only so the discussion would stay focused. I even suggested better facilitation to bring structure back. But nothing changed. The meeting continued in the same way, day after day.

The behaviors in the room told their own story. Engagement varied, with some multitasking or keeping cameras off. A few only paid attention when their team's turn came. Leadership voices were the most prominent, while engagement from others was less consistent.

What frustrated me most was that the original intent of the Scrum of Scrums was missing. It should have been about dependencies and blockers, but it became more of a routine status update for leadership than a forum for addressing dependencies.

That was the reality: a meeting that kept happening every day, but without the purpose it was meant to serve.

The challenges of daily coordination revealed a pattern in work tracking. Meetings guided conversations, while tools influenced visibility. Although Jira aimed to clarify team progress, its usage sometimes obscured delivery. The focus shifts from calendar ceremonies to the complexities of boards and dashboards.

CHAPTER 19   CONFESSION #19: THE FRAMEWORKS ARE COMING, DON'T PANIC

Jira As a Jungle

For a couple of releases, one team maintained only stories without epics. That approach made it difficult to forecast delivery across a larger scope. Since the team wasn't part of SAFe, they didn't participate in PI planning; however, even within their own sprints, the lack of epics created a gap. Teams were tracking stories, but they couldn't see the bigger picture.

Dependencies posed another challenge. Each team managed its backlog separately, and they didn't maintain links across Jira boards. On one occasion, two teams duplicated work due to a missed dependency link. Although Jira had the capability, teams didn't use it consistently.

Leadership focused heavily on burndown charts. In meetings, charts often looked good, points were burning, lines were trending down, even when alignment with business deliverables was uncertain. The emphasis stayed on execution speed rather than outcomes. I challenged this more than once, but the reliance on charts didn't change.

Teams resorted to offline slides and spreadsheets for reporting because they didn't fully trust Jira as a comprehensive solution. Team leads and Scrum Masters prepared them for leadership reviews. Jira was maintained "for the record," but the more detailed discussions often happened through manual trackers. Using dashboards as the sole reference point could have avoided this overhead.

I have observed that the team uses offline reporting instead of utilizing JIRA dashboards and reports, which introduced extra processes that did not consistently achieve their objectives.

Jira showed gaps in tools and outcomes; coaching revealed gaps in people and expectations. Tools could be tweaked, but real change depended on how teams and leaders adapted. This shift set the stage for lessons about people, not systems.

CHAPTER 19   CONFESSION #19: THE FRAMEWORKS ARE COMING, DON'T PANIC

The Coach Conundrum

In my projects, we worked with both external and internal Agile coaches. It was always one coach at a time, usually only during the first few weeks, rarely more than two months. Their focus was on helping teams start with energy and confidence, and then moving on.

The teams were motivated by the coaches. They felt empowered and supported in their work. At the same time, stakeholders maintained close oversight of delivery. This created a conflict: coaches tried to give teams freedom, while stakeholders pushed for predictability and control.

The conflict never came from the teams. Coaches were always thinking of what benefited the team, and the teams responded positively. The tension often arose between coaches and stakeholders, who were approaching delivery from different priorities.

The coaches spent most of their time with the teams on the ground. That was useful, but it left a gap. Leadership was seldom included in coaching efforts. I felt this imbalance clearly: teams learned new ways of working, but leaders didn't adjust their expectations. If both had been coached equally, the benefits would have been more substantial.

As an architect, I found coaches supportive. They understood the importance of my role and treated me as part of the system. They were also clear and articulate; I never had to reframe their advice before the teams could take action.

Still, the limits of their role were visible. Coaches could inspire people, but they didn't have the authority to change the system. The first weeks were exciting, but once they left, the momentum collapsed. Without adjustments in leadership practices, earlier patterns resurfaced, and the initial team energy diminished.

CHAPTER 19   CONFESSION #19: THE FRAMEWORKS ARE COMING, DON'T PANIC

If I could design coaching differently, I would make it a two-sided approach. Teams should be empowered, but leadership also needs to be coached to understand and support the framework. In my experience, only the teams received attention. That was the most significant gap: coaching started strong, but without leadership involvement, its impact was limited.

Coaching revealed how momentum faded without leadership support. From there, another challenge emerged: ceremonies that grew heavier than the value they provided.

Ceremony Creep

Agile promised focus, but sometimes the weight of ceremonies tipped the balance the other way. I observed this most clearly when teams running two-week sprints had to follow the same timeline of ceremonies designed for three or four-week sprints. They crammed everything, sprint planning, reviews, retrospectives, refinements, and PI planning, into the same rhythm. For a short sprint cycle, this approach often felt excessive.

The outcome was clear: in the first days of a sprint, the calendar filled up with meetings. The idea was that the following days would be lighter, but in practice, it rarely worked that way. By the time you counted Scrum meetings, refinements, and syncs, the week was already meeting-heavy.

Teams experienced pressure as meeting durations sometimes stretched to four to six hours, reducing time for focused work. This shift from the Agile goal of 1 to 1.5 hours of meetings reduced productivity and frustrated developers and testers. This challenge presents us with an excellent opportunity to enhance our collaboration and foster greater creativity and teamwork.

Leadership, however, maintained the stance that "this is the process." Even when delivery slowed, they continued to enforce the ceremonies. The teams continued to hold meetings as a way to tick the box, providing evidence that they were following the framework, even if the practical benefits were limited.

CHAPTER 19   CONFESSION #19: THE FRAMEWORKS ARE COMING, DON'T PANIC

I tried to intervene. From my architect's perspective, I advocated for reducing, consolidating, or shortening meetings. The reception was reserved, and no adjustments were made. I eventually attended only the sessions where I could make a meaningful contribution. This sometimes left me as the outlier, struggling to reconcile the framework's requirements with the team's practical needs.

The most challenging example of ceremony creep I observed was in sprint planning. Some teams would arrive at planning without grooming at all, or with partially prepared stories. Grooming occurred during the planning session itself, prolonging meetings for hours. The team pulled stories that weren't ready into the sprint. Unsurprisingly, many of them rolled over, sprint after sprint, often carried over unfinished.

When planning our meetings, we must consider their purpose to ensure they provide real benefits rather than take up time. Our goal should be to establish a meeting routine that aligns seamlessly with our team's workflow.

This situation can lead to "ceremony creep," where a good idea for organizing things turns into a rigid schedule that can end up consuming more energy than it provides.

Ceremonies showed how structure can slip into rigidity. The next question was how to keep the value of frameworks without letting them become constraints, a balance between structure and flexibility.

Framework vs. Flexibility

Frameworks were never the problem. The real problem arose when they experienced additional layers of traditional reporting placed on top of them. Leadership wanted Agile ceremonies, but they also wanted the comfort of conventional reporting packs. That combination added significant overhead. And behind it sat an even bigger assumption: a single framework could apply to all situations.

CHAPTER 19   CONFESSION #19: THE FRAMEWORKS ARE COMING, DON'T PANIC

It's essential to follow best practices, and being flexible, especially as deadlines approach, can make a significant difference. Leaders might feel a bit wary about changing meeting formats or shifting tasks around, but being open to these adjustments can foster trust and lead to excellent outcomes.

Teams initially complied quietly in rigid moments, but eventually grew quieter, indicating the need for timely support. Introducing flexibility quickly boosted morale, allowing people to focus on meaningful work rather than spending disproportionate time on process and documentation.

As an architect, there was never really a struggle between theory and practice. Practical experience always outweighed book knowledge. Delivery was the anchor. If the teams and leadership relied on me to ensure outcomes, then adaptation wasn't optional; it became the clear path forward. Coaches sometimes questioned whether that was "Agile enough," but most understood that when the textbook didn't work, creative adjustments had to take its place.

The clearest example of flexibility saving the day came during a two-month release cycle. Instead of layering sprint ceremonies on top of long release planning, we skipped all the usual ceremonies: no daily stand-ups, no retrospectives, and no extended refinement sessions. We conducted focused workshops whenever we needed alignment. The team stayed concentrated on delivery, and the workshops created just enough space for coordination. It wasn't by the book, but it worked, and the release landed on time without burning out the team.

The clearest example of rigid adherence backfiring was the Scrum of Scrums. The framework required daily meetings, but instead of resolving dependencies, they devolved into status-style meetings. Conversations focused on leadership, teams stayed passive, and few significant issues were resolved. They continued the ritual simply because it was in the book, while overall delivery effectiveness declined.

CHAPTER 19 CONFESSION #19: THE FRAMEWORKS ARE COMING, DON'T PANIC

Frameworks matter, but they're only as good as the flexibility around them. The lesson was simple: don't throw away the structure, but don't let it trap you either. Agility without adaptability isn't truly agile.

Flexibility kept frameworks useful, but culture shaped whether they truly worked. That's the deeper lesson: frameworks guide, but only culture makes them real.

Frameworks Don't Fix Culture

Frameworks can create structure, but they cannot fix culture. I saw it more than once: teams hit their velocity targets, burned more points than committed, showed charts trending in the right direction, and still struggled to deliver meaningful value to the business. It looked like success on paper, but customers saw through it. In one project, even with an Agile coach driving the process, stakeholders stated directly that it wasn't meeting their expectations. They didn't care about the velocity or the process; they wanted outcomes.

The gap came down to culture. You can adopt Scrum, SAFe, or Nexus, but if people don't change the way they work together, the framework risked becoming more of a formality. Silos persisted. Developers, testers, architects, and Scrum Masters each spoke the correct Agile language, but when the meeting ended, they reverted to old habits.

Sometimes, they used softened language in ceremonies to appear collaborative, while avoiding the real issues at hand. What you saw in the meeting room wasn't what was happening in practice.

Leadership behaviors sometimes contributed to the issue. In retrospectives and reviews, leaders often softened or avoided difficult conversations to maintain a subtle approach. They praised reports for conveying information to management, even when discrepancies existed between the reports and actual outcomes. They often reinforced compliance over open candor.

CHAPTER 19   CONFESSION #19: THE FRAMEWORKS ARE COMING, DON'T PANIC

For me, this was the most challenging aspect of balancing roles. As an architect and Scrum Master, I often knew the root issue was cultural, not procedural. However, there was pressure to participate in process-driven routines. Many times, I usually had to set aside these issues, recognizing the environment was unlikely to change quickly unless we were lucky enough to work with stakeholders who truly wanted sustainable, organic success. Those leaders existed, but they were uncommon; when present, they made a significant impact.

Coming from product companies, I learned to be straightforward and precise. When I spotted cultural cracks, I called them out directly. I identified missed outcomes, disengaged teams, and silos that gave the appearance of collaboration. It wasn't always well-received, but for me, hiding these issues would have been worse.

Looking back, the single most significant cultural shift that could have made frameworks effective was cross-team ownership. If people took responsibility beyond their narrow lane, many barriers would have been broken down. Without that, every framework still fell back into silos and reporting games.

There were small wins. I remember one case where UX and Development broke their silo. As soon as they started working together, they quickly resolved the issue. That moment showed that culture change mattered more than the framework itself.

Culture proved frameworks aren't enough on their own. Yet in the right moments, structure applied well could genuinely help.

When the Framework Helped

Not every framework moment felt superficial. Sometimes, when applied well, the structure actually made things better. The clearest example I saw came from SAFe PI Planning.

CHAPTER 19 CONFESSION #19: THE FRAMEWORKS ARE COMING, DON'T PANIC

The event ran as a single-day, big-room session. Everyone was there, the whole team together, and the format gave it a different kind of energy. Rather than scattering discussions across weeks of smaller meetings, it was one structured half-day with breakout sessions, allowing focused and concise discussions. Instead of carrying questions over sprint after sprint, people resolved them right there in the room.

What struck me most was the planning mindset. In a typical Scrum cadence, backlog thinking often ends with the next sprint. However, the planning extended further in this regard. Teams weren't just looking at the next two weeks; they were already working in terms of N+2 sprints, connecting work across a couple of iterations.

The energy came naturally from the teams themselves, rather than being externally prompted. In the breakout sessions, participants were engaged, discussing openly, mapping dependencies, and suggesting more effective ways to sequence work. You could sense that they owned the process, rather than just attending it.

From my seat as an architect, I was mainly in observation mode. However, even then, it was clear that the framework was helpful. The team identified and discussed dependencies that would usually linger until a Scrum of Scrums. They answered technical questions that might have required separate sessions on the spot. The planning structure gave space for alignment that ad hoc meetings never managed to achieve.

It wasn't perfect, but it worked. When I compared it to some of the painful experiences elsewhere, such as the less effective Scrum of Scrums sessions, the overloaded ceremonies, and the reporting layers, this felt different. In this case, the framework functioned as a supportive tool rather than an overhead.

The biggest lesson I took away was that frameworks help when they create alignment and clarity in one shot, rather than dispersing it across numerous meetings. That's what SAFe PI Planning did: it concentrated energy, gave teams a clear horizon, and left them with a shared understanding of what lay ahead. In this instance, the framework lived up to its promise.

When frameworks worked, it was because they were tailored, not copied. That contrast led me to the next lesson: tailoring over templating.

Tailoring Over Templating

There's a common issue with Agile practices: the assumption that a single standard approach could fit all teams. Many leaders prefer uniformity in meeting formats, reports, and the pace of work. Although this may seem organized, it often falls short in practice.

Strict adherence to methodology sometimes led to significant challenges, such as daily Scrum of Scrums sessions that often became leadership-driven status discussions and consumed time without resolving dependencies. Additionally, organizations added waterfall-style reporting layers to Agile practices, which shifted the team's focus toward preparing slides and compliance metrics rather than delivery.

In contrast, customizing frameworks was effective. For a project with a two-month release cycle, we eliminated all Agile ceremonies and opted for targeted workshops for alignment. This approach kept the team focused, fostered effective collaboration, and ensured the successful completion of the release.

The same was true in SAFe PI Planning. The event succeeded not because it adhered to the book, but because the organizers tailored it: they held a single-day, big-room session with breakout discussions that provided teams the space to plan across multiple sprints. Rather than spreading dependencies and conversations across multiple weeks, the format concentrated them into a focused alignment session. That tailoring turned a heavy framework into a practical tool.

CHAPTER 19 CONFESSION #19: THE FRAMEWORKS ARE COMING, DON'T PANIC

The difference was clear. Relying strictly on templates reduced energy and engagement. Tailoring improved the situation. When teams encountered a structure that did not make sense, they initially followed the rules but soon became frustrated. However, when they adjusted their practices to fit their needs, they became fully engaged. Morale improved, delivery strengthened, and even initially skeptical leaders began to recognize the difference.

I learned a simple lesson: tailor frameworks instead of templating them. Context decides whether a ceremony adds value or wastes time. The teams that thrived were those who shaped the framework to fit their context, rather than applying it verbatim.

The Only Framework That Matters: Context

After examining all the frameworks I've seen rolled out, Scrum, SAFe, Nexus, and hybrids with reporting stacked on top, one truth stands out: context matters more than the framework itself.

I've seen teams follow every ceremony by the book, track every story point, even exceed their velocity commitments, and still struggle to deliver meaningful business outcomes. I've seen leadership enforce daily Scrum of Scrums, sprint after sprint, with few dependencies meaningfully resolved. And I've seen organizations cling to waterfall reporting layered on top of Agile practices, focusing on dashboards that looked impressive to executives but did not always reflect real outcomes.

On the other hand, I've also seen frameworks help when they were tailored to fit the situation. In the two-month release, skipping ceremonies and relying on focused workshops gave the team space to deliver without getting lost in overhead. In SAFe PI Planning, a single, big-room session with breakout discussions created alignment across teams more effectively than smaller, scattered meetings.

CHAPTER 19 CONFESSION #19: THE FRAMEWORKS ARE COMING, DON'T PANIC

The difference was rarely the framework itself; it was usually whether people applied it as a template or adapted it to their context.

Culture, leadership behavior, team dynamics, and release timelines all shape whether a framework succeeds or fails. If those factors are ignored, even the most mature framework can risk becoming more of a formality than a value-adding practice. If they're respected, even a heavy framework can become a lightweight tool.

Takeaway Confession I stopped asking, "Which framework should we use?" and started asking, "What does this team, in this moment, actually need?" That question has led to more consistent success than relying strictly on prescribed playbooks. Ultimately, the only framework that genuinely matters is context.

CHAPTER 20

Confession #20: Is Agile Forgetting Its Roots? Learning from Toyota

> *The most dangerous kind of waste is the waste we do not recognize.*
>
> —Shigeo Shingo

Agile is sometimes treated more as a corporate label, tied to certifications and dashboards, than as a working philosophy. The promise sounds appealing: faster delivery, teams that can pivot quickly, and absolute value delivered to customers in manageable pieces.

The real issue?

Many organizations risk losing sight of what Agile was meant to be from the start. Teams rush around looking busy, sprint velocity charts glow green, yet stakeholders often raise the question: "Where is the business value in what we deliver?"

CHAPTER 20   CONFESSION #20: IS AGILE FORGETTING ITS ROOTS? LEARNING FROM TOYOTA

Most people overlook this key point: Agile didn't originate in a corporate boardroom with consultants sketching diagrams. It traces back to Toyota's production line, where people approached work with an entirely different philosophy. They valued mutual respect, embedded quality into every process step, maintained smooth workflow, and pursued constant improvement. Toyota never stressed about keeping every worker busy 100% of the time. Their focus was on ensuring valuable work flowed seamlessly through their system without bottlenecks. They didn't add quality as an afterthought; they wove it into each step. Improvement wasn't a "spare time" activity. It happened every single day.

In this chapter, I'm returning to those foundational ideas. Not through academic theory, but by examining actual projects where these core principles were overlooked, and others where remembering them transformed everything. I've witnessed customers question our deliverables. I've observed teams caught up in activity that appeared essential but didn't translate into tangible outcomes. I've watched managers emphasize dashboards and metrics, sometimes at the expense of real outcomes. Losing your direction can happen easily when you're deeply immersed in work. Yet I've also experienced those pivotal moments, when someone pauses the work to suggest "this approach may not be effective" when teams finally document their actual workflow, or when leaders leave their offices to observe what really happens day-to-day.

What follows won't be an academic discussion of Toyota's history or a detailed lecture on Lean methodology. I didn't prioritize metrics over outcomes; instead, I let them happen naturally. The same applies to retrospectives, of which I have been a participant. I accepted progress that didn't always align directly with business value. After years of experience, I've concluded that we don't need additional frameworks or complicated procedures. We need to rediscover Agile's original purpose and return to the principles Toyota mastered years ago.

The best way to test whether we'd lost our way was to return to the very beginning, to the words that started it all: the Agile Manifesto.

CHAPTER 20   CONFESSION #20: IS AGILE FORGETTING ITS ROOTS? LEARNING FROM TOYOTA

The Manifesto Rediscovered

I discovered the Agile Manifesto years into my career, not at the beginning. When I finally encountered it in the service industry, I was struck by how straightforward it seemed: twelve principles and four value statements, written so clearly that I wondered why we built entire training programs and complex frameworks around them.

But reality buried that simplicity under layers of process. We often worked with layers of frameworks, certifications, and dashboards that created the appearance of progress but didn't always translate into real business value. Our ceremonies sometimes felt more like routine performances than genuine tools for collaboration. Daily stand-ups occasionally drifted into status updates and micromanagement. Retrospectives lost energy over time, making it harder to surface and address real problems. Nexus updates sometimes focused on smaller contributions, while the bigger picture was overlooked. Somewhere along the way, Agile's core message got lost in all the noise.

I watched this play out clearly in one project where everything looked perfect on paper. The burndown chart was flawless. Sprint after sprint showed steady progress, velocity climbed higher, and leadership smiled at every update. We looked like textbook examples of agile success. But I could feel the team's growing unease. We all had the same nagging question: where's the actual business value?

Eventually, our customer voiced what we'd all been thinking: "This looks nice, but where is the business value?" I wasn't surprised. They said out loud what had been eating at me for weeks. The team scrambled to explain how an upcoming story would complete the business flow, but we realized it wasn't a convincing explanation.

That wake-up call changed everything for us. We stepped away from relying on polished charts and recurring meetings, and refocused on what we were actually building. So, we pulled our chairs together and dug into what we were actually building. We spread out our epics, sketched some

353

workflows, and started asking the uncomfortable questions: Does any of this stuff connect to what the business wants? It wasn't about chasing some trendy methodology or fancy tool. We had to confront what we'd been dodging: creating software that real people would find helpful and worthwhile.

Reflecting on it now, I see how I'd stumbled into my own version of this trap. When I was an architect, I sometimes treated technical standards and established practices as unbreakable rules. Shifting into the Scrum Master world, I sometimes swapped those instincts for strict adherence to process, believing it might protect us from failure. Those old patterns resurface from time to time. When they do, the team shoots me a knowing glance, and I have to remind myself to step back.

The customer's direct question wasn't just a challenge to our work; it highlighted a gap between what we delivered and the value they expected. Agile isn't about performing the ceremonies perfectly or showing beautiful velocity charts. It's about ensuring our backlog priorities align with business outcomes and that we're not deceiving ourselves with impressive numbers.

That's what I rediscovered: the Manifesto isn't complex, and no framework was hiding it from us. It was sitting right there in front of us the whole time, in the principle we'd forgotten: working software that actually delivers value.

That rediscovery set the stage for a sharper contrast, one that became clearer when I compared our delivery pipeline to a factory line.

A Tale of Two Factories

On the surface, our team appeared to be a well-oiled factory line. Story points moved from "to do" to "done," velocity charts ticked up, and stakeholders smiled when the dashboards turned green. From a distance, it had all the appearances of efficiency.

CHAPTER 20   CONFESSION #20: IS AGILE FORGETTING ITS ROOTS? LEARNING FROM TOYOTA

However, anyone looking more closely would have noticed a different reality. Once work crossed into the business section of the delivery line, nothing came out. We were burning effort, consuming hours, filling reports, and yet delivering little that the business could use. The motion was there, but the value was missing.

That's when the comparison to Toyota came into my mind. In one discussion, I recalled Toyota's approach: "At Toyota, they stop the line when something is wrong. Could we apply that here? It wasn't a casual metaphor. I meant it literally. If nothing is coming out of the business end of the delivery assembly line, then something is broken. The right move is to stop, not push forward.

But that wasn't how our system worked. Halting delivery was often viewed as risky or undesirable. Leadership placed strong emphasis on whether the team met its velocity. That was the scoreboard. If the charts showed we hit the number, the review moved on. The team had no mechanism in place to track whether business delivery percentage improved. It didn't appear in the reports, so it never came up in the conversation.

The contrast with Toyota was clear. Toyota prioritizes quality and flow, encouraging workers to stop the line and fix defects immediately, showing respect for both the product and its people. Stopping is seen as maturity. In our Agile "factory," however, the focus is on continuous production, even if it yields no value.

And here's the more profound irony. Agile aimed initially to align with Toyota's values. Flow over resource utilization. Working results over impressive charts. Collaboration and respect for people. Continuous improvement is a way of life. The Agile Manifesto and the Toyota Production System resonate and connect in ways that people often overlook. Yet, in our implementation, we sometimes drifted toward a "process factory" model rather than a value-focused one.

CHAPTER 20 CONFESSION #20: IS AGILE FORGETTING ITS ROOTS? LEARNING FROM TOYOTA

We prioritized speed over quality, feeling pressured to maintain velocity, sometimes at the cost of moving forward with work that wasn't fully ready. While metrics created a sense of satisfaction for leadership, the team realized that no genuine product was reaching the customer.

The frustrating part was its visibility to everyone. Stand-ups sometimes drifted into micromanaged calls, retrospectives lost energy, and Nexus updates tended to highlight smaller contributions, while larger flow issues received less attention. We were stuck in a cycle of hard work, reporting progress, and dashboard improvements, yet business value remained stalled.

The Toyota comparison stayed with me because it wasn't theoretical; I had lived the opposite. If we had been following Toyota's discipline, we would have stopped the line. We would have fixed the broken flow before letting more work pile in. But instead, we found ourselves optimizing for the appearance of productivity rather than genuine outcomes.

That's why I see this as more than just a project anecdote; agile drifts when people forget its roots. Toyota's system thrives on respect for people, built-in quality, and continuous improvement. Our system, at least in that moment, relied heavily on velocity charts, creating an impression of progress. One produced cars that customers could drive. The other produced numbers executives could admire.

The difference matters. Because at the end of the day, customers don't engage with velocity charts; they use the product. And when nothing comes out of the line, green dashboards couldn't disguise the absence of outcomes.

Looking at flow was one side of the lesson, but Toyota also reminded me that flow is meaningless without respect for the people keeping it moving.

CHAPTER 20   CONFESSION #20: IS AGILE FORGETTING ITS ROOTS? LEARNING FROM TOYOTA

Respect for People

In many projects, "respect for people" felt more like a slogan on a poster than a lived practice. The prevailing mindset often leaned toward "just get it done." Deadlines mattered, numbers mattered, charts mattered, but people came second.

I clearly saw developers and testers raising concerns. Warnings about defects, timelines, or missing components were sometimes overlooked. I would add my voice, but it didn't make much of a difference. Leaders who ignored those warnings later admitted, "We should have listened to you." By then, challenges had already emerged.

Sprints followed one after another with no pause for recovery. There was little room to recover, and limited acknowledgment of the pressure people were under. Velocity and delivery were all that counted. Unsurprisingly, health concerns began surfacing, and a few key associates eventually chose to leave. Others raised concerns, though not everything reached leadership's ears. When they mentioned sustainability, it was sometimes viewed as an excuse.

Collaboration faced this issue as well. Agile aimed to eliminate silos, yet I noticed they still persisted. The teamwork between the development and quality assurance teams was a challenge, especially when multiple vendors were involved. The organizational division and specific goals impacted the true spirit of collaboration. Stakeholders can shatter those barriers by adopting a single delivery mindset.

Frequently, the leaders placed stronger emphasis on metrics. The team did not prioritize empathy, including an understanding of their frustrations, because they focused on delivery instead. That said, there were gems, rare leaders who walked the floor, asked questions directly, and treated people as partners rather than only as resources. They stood out precisely because they were exceptions.

CHAPTER 20   CONFESSION #20: IS AGILE FORGETTING ITS ROOTS? LEARNING FROM TOYOTA

My admission is essential: I never pushed the team to risk themselves for metrics. I was happy to support my colleagues by alleviating some of their pressures and preparing documents for management. Although I aimed to help, I now realize that this provides only a short-term solution, and we still have the exciting opportunity to tackle the larger cultural challenges ahead.

And that's where Toyota's principle of Respect for People rings loudest. It isn't about slogans or posters. Toyota recognized that true quality stems from valuing and empowering people. Agile was supposed to carry that same DNA. But in our projects, respect too often remained at the level of words rather than actions.

Respect matters, but respect also means giving teams the courage and authority to act, especially when the only honest option is to stop.

Stop the Line

There came a point where the defects piled up so heavily that the sprint itself was in jeopardy. QA raised concerns early, but instead of creating space to fix the issues, work continued as planned. Testing continued as if nothing was wrong, and defects stacked on top of each other. It was the very opposite of what Toyota preached: when the line is broken, stop the line.

I argued for a pause. Halting a sprint is better than jeopardizing the release. Initially, leadership was hesitant to stop, emphasizing completing story points rather than pausing for flow issues.

As days passed, the reality became undeniable. Defects multiplied, and frustration hit the team hard. They spent day and night clearing blockers, only to face a new set the next morning. After a few days of this cycle, they had exhausted their resources. That was the moment when it became clear: the line needed to be fixed before we could rerun it.

CHAPTER 20   CONFESSION #20: IS AGILE FORGETTING ITS ROOTS? LEARNING FROM TOYOTA

Eventually, leadership came around. After a couple of days, as the situation became clearer, leadership agreed that a pause was necessary. It wasn't an easy call. With the customer watching and delivery timelines hanging in the balance, it felt like a risk. However, the truth was that continuing without fixing it would have been worse.

Toyota's discipline creates a stark contrast in this situation. Their principle of Jidoka, which stops the line to fix quality at the source, is a form of respect. It demonstrates trust in the team to act responsibly, and it prevents waste by addressing problems before they escalate. In Toyota's world, stopping is maturity. In our environment, stopping often felt risky or difficult until it became unavoidable.

The impact of overlooking the principle was visible in the team's expressions. Frustration turned into resignation as their effort yielded little progress. Trust with stakeholders was strained. But what mattered in the end was how we recovered: by finally stopping, addressing the defects, and resetting the line. Only then did real value start to flow again.

That is the confession here. Agile, like Toyota, was never meant to reward motion for its own sake. The courage to stop the line, even when it feels uncomfortable, is what keeps delivery honest. I learned this lesson not from the charts or ceremonies, but from the frustration in the eyes of a team that understood better than anyone that they could not push forward a broken flow.

Stopping the line is only part of the discipline; the deeper challenge is ensuring quality is never passed forward in the first place.

Quality at the Source

Quality was never supposed to get bolted on at the end. Toyota called it built-in quality: every step of the process should prevent defects, not pass them forward. Agile inherited that idea, but in practice, I watched how easily it slipped away.

CHAPTER 20 CONFESSION #20: IS AGILE FORGETTING ITS ROOTS? LEARNING FROM TOYOTA

Automation, for example, often started late. In some cases, it wasn't integrated into the build pipeline. That meant defects surfaced only when someone manually ran smoke tests and published results. Instead of catching problems at the source, we let them pile up until the end of the sprint.

In the rush of initial releases, the pattern was always the same. Code reviews were sometimes skipped. Automated test suites sat unfinished. Unit tests were occasionally left aside. Teams met functional requirements, but we ignored everything else. On paper, progress looked good. In reality, it meant more focus was needed after delivery, because the underlying quality gaps came back to bite us.

Extreme Programming was supposed to help here with TDD, pair programming, and continuous integration; however, adoption was inconsistent. Some projects made it easier to apply those practices, while others required extra effort or different approaches. More often than not, teams tend to postpone them until prompted, and even then, coverage remains minimal. And the reasoning was usually the same: "We don't have time."

That line became a shield. Leaders wanted the sprint goals hit. Teams wanted to show progress. Quality at the source started to feel optional. Instead of pausing, we watched spikes appear. Acceptance criteria from unfinished stories were sometimes shifted into spike stories. It became a workaround, allowing the sprint to be shown as "delivered" even when the definition of done wasn't fully met. As Scrum Master, I let it happen. Because in the moment, progress (any progress) seemed better than a complete halt.

The cost wasn't abstract. I recall defects that slipped through every layer, including BA, DEV, QA, and UAT, and ultimately ended up in production. When that happened, the development team was often held primarily responsible, even though other roles also contributed. Some business scenarios were overlooked, leading to rework, escalations, and strained trust.

But the reverse was just as true. On the rare occasions when automated checks were in place, problems surfaced early. Those moments were almost invisible, ironically. When teams build quality in, failure were far less likely. The benefits weren't always fully appreciated until teams experienced the difference without those safeguards. Only then do they see what the automation had been protecting them from all along.

Looking back, here's my confession: I never forced the team to sacrifice quality for velocity. I gave the team the runway to address defects rather than push them to the end. My architectural background never left me; I still believe that quality at the source matters. But even then, I sometimes allowed the system to bend around it. Spikes and shortcuts kept the sprint moving, but at a cost.

Toyota's principle remains simple: prevent defects rather than fix them later. Agile, at its best, should mirror that. In our projects, the urgency to make progress often overshadowed the importance of quality. The honest confession isn't that I ignored quality; instead, it's that I sometimes accepted a level of quality that fell short of what was needed. At those moments, it felt easier to keep moving forward than to stop and address the issues.

Building quality into every step only works if improvement itself becomes part of the rhythm, not an occasional event.

Continuous Improvement, Really Continuous

Agile promises inspect and adapt. Toyota called it Kaizen: continuous improvement as a way of life, not an event. But in practice, I saw how easily "continuous" turned into "occasional."

Take retrospectives. On paper, they were supposed to be the heartbeat of improvement. In reality, I remember sitting through retros where nobody spoke up. The silence was thick. The team nodded politely, agreed

CHAPTER 20   CONFESSION #20: IS AGILE FORGETTING ITS ROOTS? LEARNING FROM TOYOTA

to whatever was suggested, and quickly wrapped up their meeting. It felt less like improvement and more like diplomacy. It seemed they were accepting everything to avoid conflict rather than opening up fully. I walked away thinking, "We're going through the motions, but nothing is changing."

The same problem appeared with backlog grooming. The team once suggested grooming ahead of sprints, but leadership placed lower priority on it. Instead, most grooming was rushed right before meetings. Stories often arrived partially shaped, with some questions unanswered. We were planning with incomplete information, and the pain showed later in delivery. Improvement ideas were available, but they were set aside because delivery took priority.

Recurring issues exposed the cost of skipping actual improvement. I saw defects reopened repeatedly because teams only fixed the immediate area of the bug. Under pressure to close defects quickly, broader impacts weren't always checked. The result? A new scenario would break days later, and the cycle would repeat. I encouraged testers and developers to consider broader coverage. Test broadly, code with ripple effects in mind, before reporting or fixing. It was simple advice, but it took multiple painful repeats before it stuck.

Most of the themes I've described throughout this book (silos, unfinished grooming, and ignoring business value) originated as my suggestions. I raised them early, but they were often sidelined. Only after more trouble piled up did leadership come back to me, asking for the very ideas I had proposed before. Improvement usually became reactive rather than proactive. Instead of integrating Kaizen into the rhythm, we treated it more like an emergency measure, using it only when problems grew too large.

And yet, I did see glimpses of actual continuous improvement. In one project, the team struggled to visualize how stories would actually be developed and tested. Grooming alone wasn't enough. So, I added a mandatory task to every story: a 30-minute connect where a developer and tester brainstorm together. They mapped out both the technical and business aspects before developers wrote any code or testers drafted test cases. Initially, the team resisted, viewing it as added overhead. But over time, it changed the dynamic. Questions that used to appear late in sprints surfaced early. Developers understood test scenarios better; testers saw the technical constraints sooner. A small change, a half-hour habit that led to smoother delivery. That was Kaizen at work.

Toyota's philosophy doesn't wait for quarterly reviews or crisis moments. Their improvement is daily, relentless, baked into the work. Agile was designed to echo that. However, in many of my projects, retrospectives often became quiet, grooming felt rushed, fixes were repeated, and improvements were postponed. We called it continuous improvement, but in practice it was far from consistent.

My confession is this: I didn't always push hard enough when I saw retros failing or improvement ideas sidelined. Sometimes, I led the ceremonies with a sense that little would change. Sometimes, I settled for surface fixes instead of pushing for structural ones. And that's the cost of drifting from Kaizen. Improvement goes beyond ceremonies; it depends on persistence, discipline, and courage. Without that, Agile risks falling into repeated patterns of the same mistakes.

Improvement also depends on leadership, leaders who choose to see the work up close rather than through the filter of reports.

Leadership Walks the Floor

Toyota leaders made a habit of visiting the gemba, the actual place where people worked. They believed that to understand problems, you don't sit with reports; you walk the floor, listen, and see reality firsthand. Agile promised a similar spirit of servant leadership, where managers remove obstacles instead of demanding numbers.

CHAPTER 20 CONFESSION #20: IS AGILE FORGETTING ITS ROOTS? LEARNING FROM TOYOTA

But in most of my projects, leadership rarely came close to the floor. They stayed in the dashboards. I still remember one engagement where leadership placed less emphasis on the team's concerns about business value. Leadership didn't want to hear about incomplete flows or customer readiness; they focused primarily on the velocity report. Every review boiled down to the same questions: "Did the team meet its velocity target? What do the numbers say?" It wasn't about value delivered; it was about metrics consumed.

That pattern repeated. Leaders often relied on me to provide "the numbers" rather than speaking directly with the team. It became a duplicate effort, reporting information already available in JIRA, but presented in a different format to match leadership's preferences. In frustration, I once asked: "Why not look directly at the JIRA dashboard?" But the request for numbers never went away. Leadership firmly fixed its lens on charts rather than conversations.

And then there were the exceptions, the rare gems. I once worked with a leader who genuinely walked the floor. I was serving as an architect at the time, and this person did what few others had ever done: patiently listened to every conversation, understood the ground reality, and addressed the team's concerns one by one. When customer-side issues arose, they handled the politics themselves, so the team didn't have to. They shielded the team, enabling them to focus solely on construction, the work they wanted to do. For once, the team's energy went into building rather than fighting. That experience stayed with me as an example of what leadership could look like when it aligned with Toyota's principle of respect.

Often, I found myself caught in between. The team wanted to discuss blockers, quality, and business readiness. Leadership wanted numbers and velocity. I became the buffer, not by choice but by necessity. It was exhausting, at times frustrating, and it often felt like I was managing two separate realities: the lived experience of the team and the sanitized metrics for leadership.

CHAPTER 20   CONFESSION #20: IS AGILE FORGETTING ITS ROOTS? LEARNING FROM TOYOTA

Looking back, I wish I had pushed harder for leaders to walk the floor themselves. But I also know that styles differ. Some leaders want to be enablers, others prefer to dictate. Unless they choose to step closer, it's difficult to compel that shift. Toyota built a culture where leaders saw the floor as their responsibility. Agile aspires to the same, but in many of my projects, leaders often remained focused on dashboards while underlying issues persisted within the teams.

When leaders focus on what truly matters, the next shift is natural: measuring flow instead of fixating on how busy people look.

Flow Over Resource Utilization

You know how Toyota cracked this code that now feels super obvious, but was totally mind-blowing back then? They realized that work needs to flow smoothly from start to finish. They discovered that keeping everyone looking busy doesn't magically create value. I mean, when the production line isn't cranking out cars, it doesn't matter if people are running around like crazy, if nothing helpful is coming out the other end, something's broken. What they cared about was cutting out waste, not putting on some big performance of being busy. In my Agile world, I witnessed the exact opposite happening. Managers placed heavy emphasis on keeping teams "100% busy" regardless of the actual workload. Velocity metrics were often celebrated, even when business value was less visible. Sure, the dashboards looked pretty. Utilization charts hit their targets; teams stayed fully loaded, but customers? They walked away empty-handed.

It really hit me when I became a Scrum Master and started tracking how our epics actually moved through the business pipeline. Suddenly, I could see what value really made it to customers, and I could spot all the gaps we'd been missing. Talk about a wake-up call!

CHAPTER 20 CONFESSION #20: IS AGILE FORGETTING ITS ROOTS? LEARNING FROM TOYOTA

We kept shipping user stories, but complete features? They never showed up. At times, our process felt like an assembly line producing isolated parts rather than complete features. Leadership had never bothered to keep track of this kind of thing before. When I showed them the data, they couldn't argue with the massive holes in our process. Instead of rolling this insight out to other teams, though, mine just became some experiment, totally disconnected from how everyone else operated.

Meanwhile, our ceremonies were a means for everyone to pretend we were making progress. Daily stand-ups often drifted into micromanagement rather than collaboration. Retrospectives sometimes fell flat, with little active participation because nobody wanted to tackle the real problems. And don't get me started on Sprint Reviews, stakeholders often redirected those meetings toward detailed status updates and turned them into the most boring status reports about tiny little contributions. The system made everyone look super-productive with numbers that moved in the right direction, but the actual flow? Significantly misaligned with value delivery. Toyota's approach would have highlighted this as a systemic issue: "If nothing's rolling off the production line, we've got a serious problem." But in our company? That conveyor belt just kept chugging along, empty or not.

As a Scrum Master, this gap really bugged me. So, I switched my team's focus from utilization metrics to actual value flow. But here's the thing: when you're working in a large organization where leadership still judges every other team solely by velocity, it gets confusing really quickly. My squad began to question whether they were even on the right path. I never flat-out told them to ignore the numbers, but stakeholders lived and breathed velocity charts, so any different perspective felt totally weird to them.

That's where I got to be honest. Sometimes I caved and reported utilization and velocity numbers just to fit in with the bigger system, even though I recognized it didn't fully reflect business value. I didn't want my team to get singled out for appearing "off track." But privately, I kept reminding both myself and them that those numbers were worthless if real value wasn't flowing to our customers.

Look, Toyota figured this stuff out decades ago. When utilization doesn't create actual flow, it risks becoming waste disguised as productivity. Agile, when it works right, follows the same logic. But the minute companies start measuring how busy people look instead of what's actually getting delivered? They lose sight of the underlying purpose. We don't need teams running at 100% capacity; we need value that actually reaches customers. Until flow becomes the thing we actually measure and care about, Agile will continue to evolve into a busy factory focused on activity rather than meaningful outcomes.

Chasing flow over busyness also reshaped how I thought about learning, it wasn't about manuals, it was about people who modeled the practice.

Learning from Masters, Not Manuals

Back in the day, Toyota figured out something innovative: if you want to learn, you've got to get your hands dirty. Not through lecture halls, but by pairing newcomers with experienced practitioners to tackle real problems together.

When Agile showed up, it clicked for me. This approach suggested, "learn by working with mentors, jump into real situations, get hands-on experience." I've seen this approach falter many times in practice.

I've met Scrum Masters with multiple certifications who still struggled when faced with real-world challenges. I remember one who couldn't answer when a client asked about business value. At times, the emphasis on processes overshadowed the realities of organizational dynamics, revealing a gap between what they learn and what actually happens.

CHAPTER 20 CONFESSION #20: IS AGILE FORGETTING ITS ROOTS? LEARNING FROM TOYOTA

Every team I worked with treated these methodologies as fixed rules, reluctant to adapt even when things were falling apart. One project in particular stands out; we strictly followed Agile practices, even though our client didn't fully understand the principles of Agile. We spent weeks on processes that looked polished but didn't fit the project's context. Ironically, by strictly following Agile rules, we undermined the very agility we were aiming for.

Over the years, I dove into Agile on various projects with some great mentors. Although some of the training was unclear, we managed to make it work by being up-front with each other. That honesty really built trust on our team. We focused on working together and actually caring about relationships. The results blew me away. It felt amazing to see what we could accomplish when we clicked as a team.

I started to question everything when changes were needed. If a book told me to go left, but the project needed me to go right, I would break the rules. Agile is about providing value, even if it means bending the rules. Coming from software development, I'd push the devs and testers to experiment with different approaches. Often, these unconventional ideas worked better than just following the playbook.

I relied less on methodology books and more on hands-on experience. I learned everything working at companies that were doing this stuff way before "Agile" was even a thing. Real learning happens through building products and solving problems.

Toyota truly leads the way by encouraging experimentation and learning from mistakes. By adopting this approach, we'll gain a much deeper and clearer understanding.

All these lessons circled back to the same conclusion: the only way forward is to return to the roots that made Agile meaningful in the first place.

CHAPTER 20   CONFESSION #20: IS AGILE FORGETTING ITS ROOTS? LEARNING FROM TOYOTA

Back to the Roots to Move Forward

Reflecting on these projects, the key takeaway is that we neglected the fundamentals. Customers questioned our value, and despite busy teams and positive charts, we reached a standstill. Problems accumulated as we pushed forward without reassessing, and discussions became stagnant. Leaders often focused on numbers and engaged less directly with the team.

These weren't failures of process knowledge. Everyone had read the same books, attended the same training sessions, and earned the same certifications. The gap was in practice, Agile is not about appearing busy, but about delivering value.

The standout moments included returning to our roots and mapping epics to business flow, which highlighted what mattered most. Prioritizing quality over speed during development was crucial for a successful launch. Brief discussions between developers and testers fostered collaboration and continuous improvement.

Toyota emphasized that building quality is essential, that flow is more critical than utilization, that leaders need to witness reality firsthand, and that improvement is a daily necessity, not an option. Agile originated from these same principles. Throughout my career, I've observed the consequences of ignoring these foundational concepts and the positive outcomes that arise when we re-embrace them.

At times, I could have pushed harder, let metrics take precedence over meaning, or stayed quiet when retrospectives went nowhere. But I also learned to shift, focusing on flow over velocity, value over busyness, and practice over manuals. Those lessons didn't come from certification slides; they came from the friction of real projects and the resilience of real teams.

Moving forward, Agile can only survive by going back to its roots. Back to its origins in practice, not theater. Back to the principles that Toyota proved decades ago. Back to the heart of the Manifesto, where working software and collaboration matter more than processes and tools.

CHAPTER 20 CONFESSION #20: IS AGILE FORGETTING ITS ROOTS? LEARNING FROM TOYOTA

New frameworks will continue to emerge, and metrics will remain tempting. But if we lose sight of the roots, none of it matters. The way forward is not new; it's remembering where we started and having the courage to live it every day.

Takeaway Confession   We need to get back to basics rather than relying on frameworks or certifications for the success of Agile. It's easy to become distracted by numbers or rituals, but we need to focus on stripping away everything and returning to basics.

Index

A, B

Accountability
   agile theater, 262
   agreements, 255–257
   drivers, 259–261
   empowerment, 244
   high performer, 244–246
   leadership, 251–253
   micromanagement, 243, 246–248
   ownership, 250, 251
   punishment, 257–259
   retrospectives, 248, 249
   team loss boundaries, 253–255

Agile rules
   charts, 317
   done, 320, 321
   flexible, 332
   fragile, 331
   framework, 327–329
   leadership request, 322–324
   process, 330, 331
   process adherence *vs.* product delivery, 326
   retrospectives, 318, 319
   sprint, 329
   stand-ups, 324, 325
   stories, 321, 322

C

Conway's Law, 128, 129
Cookie-cutter planning, 89
Cross-functional teams, 117
Cross-team communication, 128
Cross-team refinement, 119
Cultural challenges
   burnout, 239, 240
   costs, 224
   debt, 230, 231
   exit interview, 229, 230
   informal escalations, 232, 233
   leadership, 223
   leadership without awareness, leadership without trust, 237, 238
   microaggressions, 226, 227
   the 1-on-1 that changed role, 235, 236
   retrospectives, 233–235
   star performer, 224–226
   structure, 240, 241

Customer feedback, IT
  build feedback loops, 162, 163
  defensiveness, 161
  feature, 157
  innovation, 165–167
  integrating real voices, 159, 160
  leadership, 154
  product strategy, 164
  proxy, 155, 156
  stakeholders, 166
  support call, 158, 159
  users, 153

D

Deadlines, agile
  alignment, 113
  board meeting, 95
  emotional weight of time, 101, 102
  integrity, replanning, 110–112
  negotiation, 107, 108
  product owner, 105, 106
  retrospectives, 109, 110
  reverse engineering, 98, 99
  scope/quality, 100, 101
  Sprint planning, 97
  stakeholder theater, 103–105

E

Execution *vs.* process, The XP
  Agile processes, 301
  continuous integration as music memory, 309, 310
  feedback loops, 312–314
  pair programming, 303, 304
  refactoring lifestyle, 304, 306
  ritual, 314
  shared code ownership, 311, 312
  simplicity as survival strategy, 307, 308
  stand-ups, 310, 311
  testing, 306, 307
  XP developer, 302

F, G, H

Framework
  ceremonies, 341, 342
  coaches, 340
  culture, 344, 345, 349
  vs. flexibility, 342, 343
  Jira boards, 339
  leadership, 335
  SAFe PI Planning, 336, 337
  Scrum of Scrums, 337, 338
  templates, 347, 348

I

Integration testing, 175
Internal conflict, architect *vs.* Scrum Master
  anti-pattern, 21–23
  architect, 18, 19
  blueprint to feedback loop, 25, 26
  designing systems, 17
  high stakes, 29, 30

INDEX

meticulous planning, 20
minimum viable
    architecture, 27, 28
Nexus meetings, 20
situational approach, 32
stakeholders, 23, 24
testing, 31, 32

J, K

JIRA, 127
"Just enough" planning, 90

L

Leadership, 36, 131
Lean methodology, 352
Lean teams
    async over orchestration, 291–293
    cross-training, 295, 296
    direct communication, 290, 291
    discipline, 293, 294
    hats, 284, 285
    saying no, 297, 299
    service companies, 281
    simplification, 288, 289
    small team, big dreams, 282–284
    velocity, 286, 287

M

Meetings
    alignment, 211, 212
    asynchronous communication, 214, 215
    calendars, 216, 217
    decisions, 218–220
    leaders, 213
    management and clients, 220
    planning sessions, 221
    sessions, 206
    Sprint Planning, 209, 210
    stand-up, 208, 209, 222
    working sessions, 206, 207

N, O

Nexus, 115, 116, 118, 131–134, 317, 335, 344, 348
Nexus Integration Team (NIT), 118
NIT, *see* Nexus Integration Team (NIT)

P, Q

Pair programming, 307, 311
Program Increment (PI) planning, 336

R

Requirements
    agile compass, 91, 92
    agile, no requirements, 74, 75
    assumptions, 80–82
    building application, 73
    business process, 77, 78
    clarity, 93
    designs, 76

373

Requirements (*cont.*)
    discovery sprints, 82–84
    planning, 89, 90
    short-termism, 86–88
    sprint, 78, 79
    stakeholders, 84, 85
Return on Investment (ROI), 57
ROI, *see* Return on Investment (ROI)

S

SAFe, 335, 344, 348
SAFe PI Planning, 336, 345, 346
Scaled Scrum, 335
Scrum Master, 128
    Agile, 1, 2, 9–11
    architect to scrum master transition, 8, 9
    complex project, 13, 14
    leadership, 15
    manage code, 6, 7
    team in trouble, 4, 5
    trust, 11, 12
    unexpected transition, 2, 3
Scrum of Scrums, 134
Siloed approach
    design, 169
    development and QA, 185
    development and testing, 173
    dev *vs.* QA, 171–173
    integration problems, 170, 171
    meetings, 179, 180, 182–184
    misalignment, 177, 178
    from siloes to swarms, 180, 181
    team efficient, 186
    UX and developers, 175–177
Skills
    buddy system, 199
    coaching, commanding, 194, 195
    codebases, 202, 203
    communication, 191, 192
    developer, 188–190
    efficiency, 192, 193
    innovation, 200, 201
    leadership, 188
    retrospectives, 197, 198
    scaling processes, 203, 204
    sprint, 195, 196
SME, *see* Subject Matter Expert (SME)
Split-personality product owner, 124–126
Sprint disruption, 122, 123
Sprint planning, 120–122, 209
Stakeholders
    agile sales pitch *vs.* reality, 56, 57
    agile theater, 61–63
    alignment, 68, 69
    assumptions, 65, 66
    cultural layer, 70
    ownership and effort, 60, 61
    playing long game, 63, 64
    problems, 58, 59
    setting boundaries, agile misuse, 66, 67

sprint ceremonies, 71, 72
transparency, 55
Subject Matter Expert (SME), 4

T, U

Teams
    backend APIs, 265
    cross-disciplinary demo, 277, 278
    done, 266
    ego, 271
    invisible territories, real friction, 268, 269
    Jira, 269, 270
    metrics, 275, 276
    share wins, 279
    stand-ups, 273, 274
    UI *vs.* backend standoff, 266, 267
    victories, 276, 277
    "we", 272, 273
Technical debt, 35, 36
    business language, 45–47
    developers, 40
    emotional payoff, 52, 53
    legacy trap/inheritors, 49
    long-term fitness, 50, 51
    redefining done/changing habits, 47, 48
    retrospectives, 41, 44, 45
    Scrum Master, 41–43
    sysyem, 38, 39

Toyota
    Agile Manifesto, 353, 354
    continuous improvement, 361–363
    dashboards and metrics, 352
    factories, 355, 356
    leadership, 363–365
    moments, 369
    quality source, 360, 361
    resource utilization, 365–367
    respect for people, 357, 358
    retrospectives, 369
    Scrum Masters, 367, 368
    stakeholders, 351
    stop the line, 358, 359

V

Velocity
    culture, 147, 148
    delivery, 150, 151
    epic-level readiness, 145, 146
    fragmentation hidden cost, 141, 142
    metrics, 146, 147, 149
    progress, 139, 140
    quality, 139
    sprint reviews, 138, 144
    stakeholders, 138, 152
    stakeholders, team, 143, 144

W, X, Y, Z

Waterfall model, 70

GPSR Compliance

The European Union's (EU) General Product Safety Regulation (GPSR) is a set of rules that requires consumer products to be safe and our obligations to ensure this.

If you have any concerns about our products, you can contact us on ProductSafety@springernature.com

In case Publisher is established outside the EU, the EU authorized representative is:

Springer Nature Customer Service Center GmbH
Europaplatz 3
69115 Heidelberg, Germany

Batch number: 09467209

Printed by Printforce, the Netherlands